The Joy of Football

Edited by
Brian Glanville

Hodder & Stoughton
LONDON SYDNEY AUCKLAND TORONTO

Illustrations by David Napp

British Library Cataloguing in Publication Data
The Joy of football.
    1. Soccer——Anecdotes, facetiae, satire, etc
    I. Glanville, Brian
    796.334   GV943.2

    ISBN 0-340-39439-0

Contents

Contents

Contents

Introduction

It is well over twenty years since I edited *The Footballer's Companion*, a collection of writing on the game which, as I said at the time, seemed to me utterly to contradict the conventional wisdom that football had produced no writing worthy of being preserved. Comparisons are both odious and irrelevant, but much that passes for literature in the lauded realm of cricket now often seems whimsical or over-written. An ingrained snobbery towards football in Britain, where the upper classes first originated the game, then abandoned it for so many years, has led to a curious, conditioned disdain for writing about the sport, quite unknown in Europe and Latin America, where everybody follows it. In the last twenty years or so, a number of excellent writers have emerged in Britain, liberated by the consequences of our bloodless 'social revolution', the rise from the working classes of actors, writers, and academics who love football, and comprise a new audience. Journalists such as Hugh McIlvanney, David Lacey, and Hunter Davies, who spent and recorded such a memorable year with the Spurs, have enriched the football press. Eamon Dunphy's *Only A Game?*, a disillusioned diary, has provided a professional footballer's insight of rare percipience and value. John Moynihan, especially in *The Soccer Syndrome*, has at his best provided a gloriously antic, idiosyncratic, evocative view of the game, at every level.

It has always seemed to me that there are two quite valid ways of writing about spectator-sports, football among them; from the inside or the outside. In a sense, the latter may even at times be more valid. To examine these sports too closely may simply be to destroy them. The appearance may itself be the essence. What we see and know on the field is, like a theatrical performance, perhaps the reality. What goes on off stage, or off the field, is almost secondary; marginalia.

That is why I especially prize *jeux d'esprit* such as those of John Moynihan; in themselves no less 'real' than the revelations of Eamon Dunphy or Hunter Davies. A novel such as Bernard Malamud's *The Natural*, with its underpinning of Arthurian legend, its flights of verbal fancy, or a fantasy such as Robert Coover's *The*

Universal Baseball Association, makes statements about baseball, and spectator-sport at large, as valid as any documentary exegesis.

In *The Footballer's Companion*, I tried to give some picture of the growth of the game, 'in depth and detail'. Literary criteria were thus sometimes relaxed in favour of historical relevance. That job done, and the sheer quantity of subsequent good writing being now what it is, I have had to be more exigent.

The Joy of Football is more compact than the earlier collection. Strict choices have had to be made, and when it came to players, I looked for the new, the more recent, rather than the old. Since 1963 there has been no English book such as Maurice Edelston and Terence Delaney's splendid *Masters of Soccer*, combining as it did elegance of style with close observation. But the era it dealt with is remote now, and I felt it time to ring the changes. Besides, if we no longer have a portrait of the incomparable Stanley Matthews *per se*, there is a fine evocation of him and his magic skills in Paul Gardner's memory of the 1953 'Matthews Final', as seen by a fan.

In the section 'Peaks and Valleys', Arthur Hopcraft – a gifted writer who sadly, prematurely and irreplaceably left the press box – tells of the downfall and despair of Tony Kay; a footballer who might well have appeared among The Stars, had he only completed his aborted career.

There are still, quite clearly, gaps, but an anthologist must cull what he can. To pay or persuade a writer to sit down to produce what one wants isn't 'allowed'. How splendid it would have been to have had, say, McIlvanney on Cruyff, or Geoffrey Green on Beckenbauer; but the pieces don't exist.

Once again, you will find in these pages Camus, the ex-goalkeeper, who tells how much football has taught him of morality; Bennett, Priestley, Pinter, De Montherlant, Giraudoux; and now Nabokov, too. (The translations incidentally are my own.)

It was De Montherlant who once wrote that, when he was on his death bed, he would think about a pass given him one day by a team-mate, with all the faith in him that it implied; he certainly wouldn't wonder why no poets had been produced by the Midi.

With such literary credentials and endorsement, football hardly needs to adopt a defensive stance. The world's most popular game has often been properly and memorably celebrated.

February 1986   BRIAN GLANVILLE

Part One

THE FASCINATION OF FOOTBALL

Football in Palermo

PAUL GARDNER

The question is, does soccer generate more passion than other sports? I think it does. Partly because it is so much closer to the lives of its followers than other sports, partly because of its worldwide appeal that makes it a vehicle for nationalistic fervour, and partly because of the nature of the sport itself. It is, after all, a sport in which low scoring is the rule. During a game there is a constant building up and letting down of emotions — expectations are frustrated far more often than they are rewarded. The scoring of a goal, the one goal that could decide the game, means the joyful, explosive release of dammed-up hopes for one group of fans, utter despair for the other.

I have been trying to define soccer, but it remains teasingly beyond definition, as elusive as the soccer ball itself. Yes, yes, there is the flavour of the ingredients: a free-flowing ball game, a dance, a sport of the people, the passions, the frustration, the grace, the power, the humour . . . but the final mixture, the final proportions, that is something that each must create for himself.

For me, when I want to reduce soccer to a single occasion, I think not of the Matthews Cup Final,* or indeed of any big game, or even of the lads of Stafford Rangers. I think of a hot, sultry summer's day in Sicily some ten years ago. I had spent the afternoon among the glories of the cathedral at Monreale, but my mood of satisfaction and enchantment was broken by the bus ride back to Palermo. The heat, the noise, the crowds, the fumes — as we entered the city, I knew I was going to faint. I brusquely pushed my way to the door, lurched off the bus and stood for a moment or two watching it roar off in a cloud of grey dust. I had no idea where I was, but I was going to walk for a while until I felt better, then catch another bus.

I remember very little of the street. There were buildings, I suppose, some stores, and then, after a few hundred yards, a gap that led to an open space where I could hear and see boys playing soccer. I walked over and sat down against the wall of a little hut, the only shade around. The boys seemed to be about twelve years

* See page 44.

13

old and there were, I eventually worked out, sixteen of them – they were difficult to count for the movement was constant. A whirl of sixteen little bodies chasing a battered lop-sided ball would rush past me in one direction, then come roaring back in the other, giving off shouts and dust in about equal proportions. The goals, I remember, were marked by little piles of rocks, except that one of the piles had an upright stick wedged into it, a stick that would periodically topple to the ground, at which the game had to be stopped while it was resurrected. The other important thing about the game was the far touchline, which ran along the top of a railway cutting. Anyone kicking the ball over that not only had to go down and get it, but had to sit out of the game for five minutes. This I discovered from a boy so banished who came and sat next to me.

'American?'

'No, English.'

'Ah . . . you know Bobby Charlton?'

The international language, the names of soccer's stars; we talked about the sport for a couple of minutes, when he jumped up and rushed back into the game, convincing everyone his five minutes were up, turning to me for support, because *l'inglese* had a wristwatch.

His name was Salvatore, and he was the undisputed star of the game; his skinny little legs with their incongruously large black shoes were everywhere, and he was a source of mixed wonderment and amusement to his friends. A hefty swing of his leg sent the ball spinning wildly off the edge of his foot, straight up in the air; never stopping for a moment, he ran around in a tight little circle looking for the ball until it dropped, like a padded thunderbolt, right on top of his head. One of the other boys who had been watching this brief scene suddenly spun around and I could see his face, pulled tightly closed, his eyes wrinkled up, his mouth stretched and compressed into a thin grinning line, his hands dropped helplessly at his sides. He made not a sound, but I have never seen such a wonderful portrait of pure joy.

I stayed on to watch that marvellous little game until the shadows grew bigger than the players and it was time for everyone to go home. I was walked to the bus stop and put safely aboard amid promises to return, cries of Bobby Charlton, and predictions that Italy would win the World Cup. And that was it. Italy did not win the World Cup, and I never did return to that dusty patch of waste ground on the outskirts of Palermo. Or perhaps I did, for I have relived that evening many times, a golden evening spent under the spell of soccer.

from THE SIMPLEST GAME *1976*

Never Walk Alone

ROY HATTERSLEY

There well may be, scattered somewhere between Newcastle United and Exeter City, a few thousand purists who see football as an art and watch it to enjoy the objective beauty of rhythm and form. The rest of us want to see *our* team win. We will follow it right on to the end of the road. We are the tribe and the team are our warriors. They will never walk alone.

Of course, the songs of love and loyalty ring out with especial fervour on days of victory. On the day that Nottingham Forest won the Football League, their highly disciplined red and white regiments stood in well-ordered rows on the terraces and gesticulated with ferocious composure in the direction of the vanquished Coventry counterparts. This year, at Liverpool, the fourth championship in five years was greeted with songs of praise sung with a practised precision of which the Huddersfield Choral Society would have been proud. Last Saturday at Hillsborough, where Sheffield Wednesday are less accustomed to triumph, escape from the Third Division was simply celebrated by a good-natured riot. Long before the final whistle blew, the spectators began to come over the fence that divides pitch from people, like a mass escape from Colditz. Using the wire mesh as ladders, they rolled across the top and down the other side as if commando training were an entrance requirement for the Owls Supporters' Club. For a while, the police stemmed the tide, waiting until they were poised for the descent and pushing at their exposed point of balance. The first few toppled over backwards like Aunt Sallies at Wadsley Fair. But when the referee signalled quietus by spreading his arms like a man embracing martyrdom the frenzy really began. Suddenly the police at the palisades were outnumbered by a hundred to one. It was Rourke's Drift with the Zulus showing mercy. The thin blue line was overrun and the pitch occupied. A constable's helmet curved through the air, following a route taken a few moments earlier by a long, low goal kick.

The team vanished, totally submerged in their ardent admirers. In the apparent safety of their box the Directors sweated at the sight of life being squeezed out of their investments. From time to time a shirtless player reappeared, bobbing uncertainly on the shoulders of jubilant fans whose determination to pay their respects transcended all concern about whether or not their idols would survive the idolatry. Gradually, the strikers, the midfield men and the back four struggled and squeezed their way into the dressing-room, rashly to reappear in the front row of the reserved seats.

It was then that the fans invaded the Directors' box, mountaineering up the north face of the stand, roped together with blue and white scarves. Long after the evacuation and occupation, when the hands had been shaken and the champagne opened downstairs, I climbed back to the scene of Sheffield Wednesday's triumph and their Directors' rout. A giant snake of teenage celebrators was zigzagging across the pitch in an endless conga. What grass remained had been trampled a damp brown. The low spring sun cast fluttering shadows across half of the pitch, images of the flags that have fluttered over the ground since the glory days of the World Cup.

The fans had been waiting for fourteen years for something to celebrate. Some of them had barely been alive that long, but the folk memory stretched back to Wembley in 1966 and they had inherited their fathers' frustration with the failures that followed. The match itself was wholly uneventful, a goalless draw with few shots, no spectacular saves, and most of the players huddled together in the centre circle for the largest part of the proceedings. But the single point had confirmed Sheffield Wednesday's position – third in the Third Division table. We were promoted. We were up. We had overcome.

It had been a long campaign since relegation from the First Division in 1970. For me the high point had come in Oxford in March. We won 2–0, and I stood with the real fans behind the home team goal. I admit at once that my original intention had been to sit in the luxurious ease of the stand. But all seats being sold, I queued for standing room on the bank of Bunker's Hill, or whatever Spion Kop is called at Oxford. The terrace of my initial choice turned out to be enemy territory so I set out, complete with kid gloves and blue Burberry, to find the homeland of rosettes and rattles at the other end of the ground.

The last obstacle of my escape-route was an iron gate manned by a commissionaire with three rows of medal ribbons and no respect for travelling Northern fans. The contempt in his voice was more for me than for the band of dancing dervishes who were intoning a ritual imprecation within their cage. The imprecation concerned the victims of 'the Boxing Day massacre' (Sheffield Wednesday 4: Sheffield United 0). The contempt concerned my ignorance of the fate that would befall me inside. 'You can't go in there,' he said, 'that's for them.' In a South Yorkshire accent, thickened by emotion, I told him: 'I *am* one of them.' The gate clanked shut behind me.

I spent most of the afternoon next to a young man in a sleeveless cricket sweater, which, at fight sight, proclaimed either membership of the Free Foresters or I Zingari. The impression of gentleman cricketer was, however, undermined by the absence of a shirt. But the pink exposed arms and the parts of the neck and chest visible beneath the long, lank hair proclaimed an enthusiasm for games that Raffles himself would have admired. There were owls tattooed on both biceps and the message – 'We are Jack Charlton's army' – running from wrist to elbow.

At the end of the long embrace with which we celebrated Wednesday's second goal, he asked me with deep suspicion whether or not I was Roy Hattersley. I admitted it. Had I, as he believed, appeared in 1977 on a local radio programme and proclaimed my undying affection for 'the Wednesday'? I pleaded guilty again. Without an iota of irony he held out his huge right hand, displaying the word 'hate' etched on the knuckles. 'Shake it,' he said. 'In those days it took a real man to say he followed Wednesday.'

Last Saturday it was easy, for success was there to be shared by anyone who wore the blue and white. So we waved our banners and threw our caps in the air with an enthusiasm that almost excelled the joy in victory over Germany in 1966. Third in the Third Division is not one of football's great achievements. But it provided a taste of supremacy for 30,000 fans to whom life had provided few opportunities for exultation. For most supporters, football offers them the one chance to become acquainted with glory. As long as they are there cheering on the terraces, they never walk alone.

from POLITICS APART *1982*

School

JOHN MOYNIHAN

I went to a Rugby school and hated the game. Buried in a steaming scrum, with my ears almost severed by the weighty hips of two second-row forwards, I stared at the grass below and, as a heel lashed into my nose, dreamt of the fruits of the outside world beyond the school gates.

In particular, the main apple was Association Football, an unmentionable code at our institution which burned with minor snobbery.

Three or four of us would take the *round* ball out on Sunday afternoon and boot it about hopefully between a pair of rugby posts and inevitably the master in charge of school rugby would appear with his walking stick and 1st XV scarf on the edge of the touch line, his retriever licking lovingly at his cavalry-twill trousers.

I remember the look of hatred he used to give us, although there was nothing he could do about it, except glare, as we were allowed in theory to kick a soccer ball about on Sundays. His moustache full of the cold cream he used to rub on to keep away a selection of nameless spots which grew up in the week during his classics classes, would spread over his cheeks as he pushed out his ample lips in agony and frustration. But we felt we were Frank Swift and Tommy Lawton and Stanley Mortensen and we took no notice of him.

Because soccer was not a polite word, we pressed on, educating ourselves from the outside with such 'Red Cross' gifts as the *Football Association Book for Boys*. During this era there was a figure in a soccer educational series we took to in these volumes named Mr Wrinkle – 'the old school coach' – a father figure if ever there was one.

Mr Wrinkle was a warm-hearted, inoffensive sort of man with a cap, a scarf, a long droopy moustache and a pipe which drooped out of the corners of his mouth. He had, like so many men similar, a repressed homosexual tendency which amounted to asking young admirers back to tea and letting them snuggle against his knee-caps by the fireside.

Mr Wrinkle grew more and more indispensable to us, and when in later years I met the artist, Robert Hunt, who created his image, I was amazed by Hunt's lack of concern about the great game. Hunt, a good illustrator with long sideboards and a tendency to shout at parties, showed very little interest apart from saying he had gone to the Valley as a boy. The creator of Mr Wrinkle turned out not to be a fanatic of the terraces but a bustling Bohemian with a love for straight Scotch rather than Mr Wrinkle's constant recipe for a growing soccer player: lemonade.

But Mr Hunt appeared much later in my life than Mr Wrinkle, who was at one stage deeply necessary to me. Mr Wrinkle's sole love was a small blond boy with freckles called Dan. Dan sometimes seemed slightly frivolous and lacking in gratitude to all Mr Wrinkle's intrinsic instructions.

He was a fickle hero of his school team and Mr Wrinkle, wrapped up warmly against the cold of a northern winter, would plod out to watch his games. Mr Wrinkle had something of a reputation as a footballer during the reign of Queen Victoria, when he had played good class amateur football. We had seen drawings of him during this era wearing long flapping shirts done up at the point of the swollen adam's apple by a button, a huge club badge on his left nipple, a long pair of black shorts below his knees, a pair of boots which would have winded an elephant, and outside his socks a pair of shin pads the size of Norman shields.

He was full of memories and, after watching Dan play, standing the other side of the opposition's upright so he could view every flicker of Dan's perpetual industry, he would ask the young blond back to tea with some of his friends for advice.

Dan always came with alacrity because he was a perfectionist. At our rugby school we noted everything Mr Wrinkle had to say, envying the way Dan was able to snuggle up against Mr Wrinkle's knees for advice.

Mr Wrinkle lived in a cosy, little Victorian house, in an inoffensive part of town and his hearthrug was one of the nicest places you could find at five thirty p.m. on a Saturday afternoon, with the cold mist coming down outside and the street lamps throwing out dingy, yellow beams.

Mr Wrinkle would sit back and puff at his pipe while Dan and his friends lounged round the fireside drinking tea, eating endless cakes and looking at Mr Wrinkle's scrap books.

One afternoon Dan came across a rather titanic photograph of a player in one of Mr Wrinkle's albums, with a long black drooping moustache, and black convict's hair cut.

'Who is this chap with the moustache,' he asked Mr Wrinkle who was leaning back in his chair idly scratching his still muscular thighs. Mr Wrinkle sucked at his pipe which lolled from his mouth and stared in silence for a moment towards the crackling fire. The boys looked up at him in wonder and waited for him to speak, but for a moment the great man was struck dumb with ecstasy.

Then he rose to his feet and the boys, out of politeness, followed suit allowing him to stand with his backside facing the hearth. Mr Wrinkle then spoke in a mixture of North-country and Grammar School English. He said that the man with the moustache 'was Wotherspoon', his trusted right-winger, 'with a burst of speed as good as Meredith and a body swerve which Tom Finney would find it hard to equal now'.

'Wotherspoon once took a corner I'll never forget,' said Mr Wrinkle. He stood against the fire, his pipe still drooping out of a corner of his mouth, a trace of tea hanging from his moustache and demonstrated how Wotherspoon had done it.

'I well remember how he looked for a point six to ten in front of the goal-post! – and the way he glued his eyes on the ball as he kicked it.' Mr Wrinkle curled his right foot over an imaginary football and stared down hard at the carpet. 'And how his body leant back in the art of kicking.'

Dan crouched down at Mr Wrinkle's feet and stared up at him licking his lips at the story. His friends stood round in respectful silence holding their hands clenched together. Mr Wrinkle was getting more and more excited.

'The ball was placed in front of the goal-mouth, dropping just in front of myself . . .' There was a pause as he took a sip of tea and looked at the boys so as to give them time to absorb the story. He continued: 'Myself, who was playing centre-forward, saw an opening.' Mr Wrinkle leaned forward aggressively and hit out towards the opposite wall with his left foot. 'It was an easy goal. But it was really Wotherspoon's kick which scored it.'

On these occasions Mr Wrinkle was full of anecdotes which usually culminated in his hitting the ball into the net, although he modestly always illustrated with a touch of genius by a colleague.

The freckly Dan was not always able to do things as easily as Mr Wrinkle by the fireside. He had certain neurotic tendencies, a certain raggedness when it came to approach, sloppiness near the goal. His whole playing outlook was fraught with problems and he leaned heavily on the father figure, Mr Wrinkle, as an analyst after his bad game. Mr Wrinkle gave him his fireside as couch and we young readers were allowed to observe the sessions. They usually had happy endings.

Dan sometimes went into a school game with deep forebodings. The school hero would lose his confidence early on and his colleagues, who relied on him to score last minute goals to win vital matches, would hang their heads and mutter at his sloppiness. There was nothing of the superman about Dan. His vulnerability shone out in pathetic streaks on the school playing fields. Mr Wrinkle would stand on the touch line running a pair of sad, almost senile eyes over his favourite and trying to discover what was wrong.

Dan never got a scolding from Mr Wrinkle, which is why we admired the old man so much. There were no Stanley Cullis roastings at the end of a bad performance. Only a warm, affectionate squeeze which Mr Wrinkle deposited round Dan's muddy thighs with his hand.

In one disastrous game Dan's team were drawing 2–2 and the

time was ripe for Dan to score the hero's goal. His left-winger got away, out past the clumsy lunge of the opposing right-back and pulled back a perfect centre for Dan. The boy rose high in the air as if pulled by a kite but something behind the goal, possibly the sight of Mr Wrinkle sticking out his chin in suspense, caused Dan coyly to shut his eyes and he missed the centre altogether. The other team broke away and scored the winning goal.

Dan was a picture of misery after the game and nobody would speak to him. He shuffled out of the school gates into the street and there hidden behind a lamp-post breathing deeply was Mr Wrinkle wrapped up in winter woollens, his cap pulled down over his ears so that the piece of hair jutting out at one side looked absurd. He took Dan's arm and gave it a gentle squeeze: 'Come and have some tea, Dan.'

The boy accepted with alacrity, sensing that only his analyst or adviser, or rather Mr Wrinkle could help him. He settled down in Mr Wrinkle's narrow little chair the old man usually reserved for himself, while Mr Wrinkle willingly took the hard backed chair opposite. Dan's blue and white blazer stood out in the cheerful room decorated with portraits of Mr Wrinkle as a player, and his hands shook slightly as he held his teacup.

Mr Wrinkle was less affectionate than usual. He took his pipe out of his mouth and waved it earnestly towards Dan: 'I saw it,' he said. Dan looked sad knowing that what Mr Wrinkle had seen was horrible. 'Keep your eyes on the ball, son. Practise on your own,' said Mr Wrinkle dribbling slightly at the mouth.

They sat there for a long while eating crumpets and staring into the red embers of the fire and talking about the art of heading, until Mr Wrinkle gave Dan a warm squeeze of the hand and said he would have to go home because he had to go out to get the classified football results edition.

Dan went away and that night began to practise by lamplight in the back alleys of the semi-detached area where he lived. Other boys, who watched him thudding the ball with tons of neck muscle power against the wall and sending back the rebounds with his forehead as if he hated the sight of the ball, roared with laughter.

As we looked at Dan being laughed at we sympathised with him because we were used to being laughed at ourselves when we kicked a football. Dan's problems became our own.

Dan went on heading the ball against targets or walls all that next week and took no notice of the scorn thrown at him. Mr Wrinkle's advice had become an obsession with him. At nights he dreamed of Mr Wrinkle looming over him and telling him to head to the ball.

Dan used to wake up soaked in sweat thrusting his head backwards and forwards. Unlike many other boys of his age group, he still had no masturbatory tendencies.

Came the big match the following week and Dan gleaming in his striped strip ran out onto the field full of confidence and anxious to do well. It went well for him. During the game he remembered Mr Wrinkle's advice as the ball came over from a corner – 'Watch the ball until it hits.'

Dan got up high and kept his eyes open despite Mr Wrinkle's presence again behind the goal. He no longer felt coy or shy and he headed the ball into the top left-hand corner of the net like a rocket. There was a great roar from his school supporters and his colleagues hugged him.

After the game Mr Wrinkle intercepted Dan, who with childish enthusiasm for the moment and with the lack of gratefulness natural to the young, had almost cut the old man dead. Mr Wrinkle had to throw out an arm and stop the lad from rushing past him. Dan stood there panting with pleasure, his freckles moving up and down in the red glow of evening. 'With practice, you can flick the ball wherever you want,' said Mr Wrinkle.

Dan gave a brief nod and turned away to the dressing room. Mr Wrinkle went home to tea, alone. He did not ask Dan back again until the lad had another bad game because he found him less bumptious on those occasions. But he was very fond of the lad in general. He would have to sort him out about being a big head. It was part of his training.

But Dan didn't go back to Mr Wrinkle's after that because the story was dropped. We presumed Dan didn't need the old man's advice any more because he had learnt all the basic fundamentals. Or Mr Wrinkle had died.

from THE SOCCER SYNDROME *1966*

Stamford Bridge

JOHN MOYNIHAN

I got up at dawn, dressed and tiptoed out of the house. The red streaks of early morning sky hung over the bombed site on the other side of the road like a gigantic mural in a dark museum.

Suddenly the sound of steps, tap tap tap, men moving forward down the Fulham Road, heads bent, sleepy eyed. We fell into a group but silence reigned apart from the sound of our shoes on the pavement, down past the Forum, past a dairy and the clink of milk bottles in the interior.

A cold early spring morning in March 1950, going down the Fulham Road to buy a ticket for the Arsenal–Chelsea Cup semi-final at White Hart Lane the following week. Up at dawn for a ticket which would be sold later that morning. Up at dawn, because this was a game that we were counting the hours to see, biting our nails and fearing the enemy from Finsbury Park. Up at dawn to buy our passes for a supreme contest.

As we passed the Redcliffe Arms, the crowd became denser. It could have been the afternoon of an ordinary match day, a special solemn intensity building up, the pace quickening over Stamford Bridge and, then, the queue.

The queue stretched from the turnstiles, coiling round into the Fulham Road and on towards Walham Green station. It stretched on and on and I began to wonder and fear if I would get a ticket. I found the tail and it grew quickly behind me.

Phosphorous-coloured, dawn faces in the queue became more familiar as daylight gathered strength. The ones up front, the real fanatics, had been camping out all night, but while they were picking and scratching at spots on their faces and aches in their crutches, we at least had come from our beds. A police horse passed nudging us against the railings, so close we could have shaken the beast's white tail. The policeman looked down at us without compassion.

About eight o'clock a man in front of me started to talk. He was a tall, dull-faced man with a jaw so narrow that it fell away like a precipice round the edges of his blue lips. He had already rolled a cigarette and the smoke puffed up into the air with his breath, coiling away through the railings of the hospital on our left. Tobacco was spread on his greasy mackintosh. He looked like a hundred others in the queue, with that brown trilby.

23

'If Chelsea lose next week, I'll put my head in a gas oven,' he suddenly said. It was an ideal way to start the morning, something to remind us of the agonies and tensions of the game ahead.

I imagined this man on his knees pressing that chinless jaw on the grill, turning on the taps, saying: 'You bastards, Arsenal, you bastards.' I could sniff the gas there in the early morning as the man went on talking to a charge of youthful supporters around him.

'Chelsea can't lose. Look what they did to Manchester United. They'll slaughter 'em,' said one of the youths.

'They'll win all right,' said the gas man. 'I've been watching them since 1920 and this is their best. Gallacher, Wilson, Mills, you can have 'em, Bentley's the bloke. Now look at it this way, his speed and shot, he's got it. Leslie Compton won't see him. But I'm still telling you that if Chelsea lose I'll put my head in a gas oven.' His companions laughed.

Visions again of him on his knees offering a solemn last speech to the turkey stains in the oven about his hatred and humiliation at the hands of Swindin, Scott, Barnes; Forbes, Compton, L., Mercer (captain); Cox, Logie, Goring, Lewis, Compton, D. Turning on the taps and saying through his nose: 'I hate the fucking lot of you.' Death in Wandsworth at 5.33 a.m.

Chelsea had announced they would start selling the tickets at ten, so we still had a long wait. Some of us read the Sunday newspapers and picked up the comments about Chelsea. There was a long piece by a writer in the *Sunday Dispatch*, 'What has happened to turn this famed team of brilliant individuals and great inconsistency into a side which are now being talked about instead of being merely laughed at. The answer is simply that Chelsea are now a team.'

The gas man picked on this. 'He's right. This is the best Chelsea side. Now look at those wing halves. Armstrong's a worker and he's got class, Mitchell's a beauty. Look at the way they nailed Manchester, bloody nailed them.'

'What a goal,' said a youth offering us the grandeur of that moment.

We all knew about the goal, Bentley's shot from the edge of the Manchester United penalty box from Billy Gray's back heel which roared up into the roof of Crompton's net with John Carey looking up speechless with horror. A youth behind me bit me in the neck after that goal to celebrate Chelsea's march in the semi-final. It was accidental but half meant, my neck having bounced into his jibbering mouth as the stadium erupted and men fainted away. It was my first love bite and there was blood on my blue and white scarf after the game.

'That goal, well bloody hell it was the best goal ever,' said the gas man. 'In like a bloody rocket. Crompton got a good smell of burning bleeding leather but that's all. Bloody marvellous.'

'Gently Bentley,' said a youth with blue eyes looking down at the pavement.

It was a popular expression lumbered on our centre-forward through the Jimmy Edwards–Dick Bentley show, 'Take it from Here'. Every time our centre-forward rose for the ball in a news-paper photograph the caption writers scribbled, 'Gently Bentley' into the text.

'Well he won't be gentle at White Hart,' said the gasman. 'Compton won't get near him. Les'll catch pneumonia out there from Roy's draught.'

'Gently Bentley,' somebody else sniggered.

'Look at those geysers up the front of the queue,' said the gas man. 'Bet they missed getting up their old women last night. Didn't fancy the all night session meself. Had a few pints, got up the old woman and came down here with tea in me belly. We'll get a ticket here, you see. Nothing to worry about.'

One hour to wait before they started selling tickets. The queue had swelled out into the Fulham Road so that people were now standing along the centre of the road. The human mass remained static, pushed occasionally in a more solid jelly by the subtle wriggle of the police horse's backside.

The gas man had youth round him. He looked at us with sardonic acceptance nodding his head at some remark about Chelsea and then offering his own judgements in a loud, unlovely voice.

'What you think the score will be?' said a youth with a face like a weasel.

'Chelsea 3, Arsenal 0.' He hung an 'o' in the morning air and it slowly drifted away. 'Roy'll put two in the net before Mercer's got his tits warm. Mitchell, Billy Gray, Roy and a goal, you'll see. Swindin will be lying there as if he's kicked the bucket with the ball in the net, you'll see.'

'What if they lose, what if they lose,' said the weasel youth.

'Then I'll put me bleeding head in a gas oven.'

We laughed. The gasman became dictatorial, his statements more and more lengthy. With Chelsea playing so well he did not oblige us with one criticism about the club although a year be-fore he would probably have been verbally lynching Billy Birrell and his team for their disorders. But supporters were fickle and there is no criticism when their team is playing extremely well.

'Roy's a better centre-forward than Tommy Lawton,' said the gasman. 'He's got more guts. Lawton was a bighead. Roy gets on with the game and he moves around. He's a bloody marvel.'

The sun came out, first a feeble yellow glow, then brightening up into warm, orange rays; the queue shuffled forward an inch as if the changing weather had itself the power to open the gates of Chelsea Football Club and let us in.

When the gates did open we heard all about it. There were cheers ahead and rattles sounded off clanking in jets of noise.

'Up the Blues,' someone shouted.

'Up the Pensioners,' said the gas man.

'Gently Bentley,' said the youth.

We were moving up, shuffling up, jostling up the Fulham Road past dirty white studios on our left. Above them was the high, ever impending top of the Stamford Bridge terraces and the roof of the stand. People inside the studios were still asleep. One dissipated face with a touch of beard looked at us from a bathroom window and then disappeared. He would have seen a monstrous crowd moving past, head to head, shoulder to shoulder, arm to arm, a masculine crowd with chins up high to see how far there was to go till the turnstiles.

We moved steadily past a man playing 'Music, Music, Music,' on an accordion, the current hit tune of that time. The pile of youths round us whistled in time: 'Put another nickel in . . .'

The gas man rolled along, his shoulders hunched round his chin. 'See you at Wembley, lads,' he said as we came up to the club gates where the mounted police were jostling the huge mass of people. 'See you at Wembley. They can't lose. It will be a Chelsea–Liverpool Cup Final, you see. And Johnny Harris'll be holding up the Cup.'

'What'll you do if they lose?' asked the youth with the weasel face.

'Put my head in the gas oven.'

A man in Wandsworth found dead at 5.33 a.m. leaving a note: 'I did this because the bleeders lost, my bleeders.' The sweet smell of death intermingled by gas. They found him a long time after. He wasn't married despite what he said in the queue.

We were up at the turnstiles and I bought a terrace ticket for the White Hart Lane tie, behind one of the goals. When I went through the gas man had disappeared. Going out of the ground I looked down the Fulham Road towards Walham Green but couldn't see much because of all the faces coming forward.

I walked home in time for Sunday lunch. My parents said it must have been boring to have to wait in the queue for so long. I told them about the man in the queue threatening to commit suicide and they laughed: 'Well, he'll probably be forced to do it. I can't see Chelsea winning,' said my father. He was right.

The story did not have a happy ending. Arsenal and Chelsea drew the first match, 2–2 and the tension was appalling. Roy Bentley did score early goals as the gasman predicted, the first a beautiful lob over Swindin's head, the second a glided header just inside the post. Standing behind the net with my blue and white scarf covered with blood and perspiration, I dreamt of Wembley and Bentley doing the same thing there.

Chelsea were ahead and so much ahead that they became lax against the weight of an Arsenal revival. A minute before half time Freddie Cox swung over an inswinging corner and it plopped into the Chelsea net. In the second half the torture was sealed when Leslie Compton headed in his brother's corner kick, a wave of Arsenal supporters invaded the pitch, and a replay was set for the following Wednesday.

Arsenal won that game in extra time against a Chelsea side weakened by injuries. The goal, again scored by Cox, the tormentor of Chelsea, could have been prevented by a more agile defence. I can still see the ball coming towards me, Medhurst diving, the ball tucking itself into the net and the Arsenal lot running onto the pitch bellowing with joy.

Freddie Cox told how he scored the goal to Desmond Hackett in the *Daily Express*: 'Young Pete (Goring) slipped me a peach of a pass as I stood on the edge of the penalty area. I could see the Chelsea defence lined up, five of them wondering what I was going to do. I wasn't so sure myself.

'Then I realized that Goring and Jimmy Logie were distracting the defence.

'I moved along the line and I couldn't help thinking it was like an officer inspecting a parade. No one moved. I just went on and on. I couldn't believe it.

'Then I saw the goal and I let go with my "swinger" – the old left foot.

'I knew it was a goal. It seemed for a whole second that the game had suddenly stopped dead. The next thing I knew that Reg Lewis was holding me in his arms like a mother nursing a baby.'

So Arsenal went on to Wembley for the fifth time and eventually won the Cup, beating Liverpool 2–0. Chelsea moved into an era of decline. The night they lost that replay I remember coming home on the Piccadilly line and sitting miserably in our kitchen, eating a sausage and trying not to cry. I still wonder if the gasman killed himself at 5.33 a.m.

from THE SOCCER SYNDROME *1966*

Reading – A Supporter's Piece

JOHN ARLOTT

It was not until the question was posed to me that I realized that I have watched football in ten countries, and seen the international elevens of six more. I would argue the case for Kubala, Nordahl, and Doye being included in a European eleven, and I probably follow the progress of the major French clubs as closely as I do that of their English counterparts.

This may sound like the claim of a completely cosmopolitan football follower, but do you, I wonder, remember that cosmopolitan in the O. Henry short story? 'Just put me down as E. Rushmore Coglan, citizen of the terrestrial sphere,' he said, after a conversation which had roamed the world without bias: but he was thrown out of the café fighting the man who dared to speak slightingly of the water supply of Mattawamkeag, Maine – the cosmopolite's birthplace. Thus, while I am prepared to debate the respective merits of the post-war Scottish as opposed to those of the pre-war Hungarian defence, I must confess that I do not go home happily from any game – not even from the Cup Final – until I have heard the result of Reading's match in the Third Division (South) on the same day. It may well be – indeed, I passionately hope – that by the time this book reaches its public, Reading will once more be members of the Second Division and showing signs of mounting to the First, but, wherever they are, their progress will still be my chief footballing interest.

They were a Third Division team when I first saw them, which was, I fancy, in 1923: I remember that the match was against Northampton Town, and that is as far as my memory serves me. Reading, sixteen miles away – in those days a one-and-sixpenny return railway fare – was the nearest club to my home, and a friend of my father's took me to the match: I was nine years old and, as I recall, behaved abominably.

My next match, I can pinpoint exactly: it was played on 2 October, 1926. Reading had just been promoted to the Second Division – leaving behind them, in the Third, Charlton Athletic, Brentford, Queen's Park Rangers, Coventry City and Luton Town. Their opponents on this particular day were Portsmouth, who had been promoted from the Third (Southern) two years earlier and who were, that same season, to win their way to the First Division. They beat Reading – to my great hurt – by two goals to one. A penalty awarded to Portsmouth at a vital moment was taken by Billy Haines – the Portsmouth crowd used to greet him with 'To Be A Farmer's Boy'. He bent down to place the ball, the referee blew his whistle, and Haines, without even straightening up, toe-ended it into the corner of the net while the Reading goalkeeper was still adjusting his cap. I can see that goalkeeper – Duckworth, a Lancashireman – even now, running indignantly out to the referee to protest against the goal: but it stood, and Reading lost.

I remember, too, going after the match, with my autograph album, to the creosoted wooden hut which then housed the dressing-rooms at Elm Park before the present stand and offices were completed just a few weeks later. The first signature in that book, written in a somewhat laboured, boyish hand, was: 'F. Cook' – Portsmouth's Welsh international outside-left. It is fourteen years now since I gave that book to a schoolboy: as I handed it to him, I lifted the cover with my thumb and there it was, all alone on the first page – 'F. Cook' – my first autograph.

The bug had bitten. I was lucky: the Reading side of those days, although it never had a really good record during its five seasons in Division II, held some colourful players. Duckworth, in goal, was a stooping, eager player of incredible courage who would go down at the feet of advancing forwards with great daring. My own particular favourite was Billy McConnell, the Irish international left-back. Tall, rosy-faced, fast, utterly fearless and a terrific kicker, he was of the old school of backs. For four years he was a regular choice for Ireland, refusing one cap – against Scotland – to play for his club, when they were in danger of relegation. A broken leg in 1928 ended the career of the man who was one of the deadliest tacklers of his day.

A few weeks ago, travelling in Wales, I bought a local paper, to find announced the death of Dai Evans, who was a Welsh international left-half in Reading's promotion side. Evans was not a consistent player, neither, I now realize, was he particularly conscientious about his training; but he was a polished player who took the game of football with the natural ease with which it came to him. His transfer to Huddersfield, I always felt, coincided with the start of Reading's slide back to the Third Division.

The 1926–7 season at Elm Park, however, held no thought of relegation. The small, quick, fiery Hugh Davey, Ireland's centre-forward, and Frank Richardson, the inside-left, a treasure for a Third Division side – his socks trailing, fair curls flopping over his face – were eager for goals. Behind them, Alf Messer was a centre-half so dominating that, despite the contemporary Seddon, Hill, and Kean, he came close indeed to England honours. If Evans's transfer marked the beginning of the slide, Messer's move to Tottenham completed it. He was the coolest penalty-kicker I ever saw. He always put the ball about a foot inside the right-hand post at a height of about eighteen inches off the ground: I never saw him fail with a penalty. When Messer left, Tommy Meads, Evans's successor, an immense worker and a fine long-shot, went with him to White Hart Lane and the half-back line, backbone of any side, was gone. But, in 1926–7, Reading were not a selling side.

Their ground was about eighteen miles from my home: it was a cycle ride – a hard one, but a cycle ride – and worth it. Eighteen miles there, eighteen miles back. I can still remember every mile of the route and, given the same circumstances, I would cycle it the same twenty times a year again.

What a season that was – 1926–7. At every opportunity I would see football; I would bury my nose in the football papers which were then so numerous. Alas, that the boy football enthusiast of today has no *Athletic News* which used to appear on Monday morning with a full account of every match in the four English Leagues *and* the Scottish First Division, with due attention to the amateurs and the Irish competitions, *plus* special articles as well. *The Topical Times*, *The Sports Budget*, *Football Favourite*, their names alone bring back their smell and look and feel.

Season 1926–7: Reading fought two replays against Manchester United before they beat them in the third round of the Cup: even Barson could not stop them: what new triumphs, we wondered, lay ahead of last year's Third League Champions? To be sure, they were perilously near the bottom of the Second Division, but Manchester United were a pillar of the First Division: three matches should be enough to crystallize the difference between any two sides – and Reading won that third match. In the next round, they reversed the League result and beat their old rivals, Portsmouth: then Brentford: then they went to Swansea and won there – and they were in the semi-final. Cardiff beat them – as they beat Arsenal in the Final – but the semi-final was a new conquest for Reading.

Season 1926–7. That was the year when Middlesbrough headed the Second Division and, in the process, set up a new goal-scoring record of 122 goals in a season, while George Camsell, their young centre-forward – he had only made three first-team appearances in the previous season – broke the individual goal-scoring record with fifty-nine goals. The match, as I remember, was rearranged because of Reading's Cup-tie commitments and was played, I fancy – I have no means of checking – on a Tuesday evening, though why it should be a Tuesday, rather than a Wednesday – early closing day in Reading – baffles me. It was an awkward day and time, but, if I could raise tenpence – sixpence admission, twopence for a pro-gramme, a penny mineral on the way up and another on the return journey – I would be there. A rush through prep – always a household rule – and there was an hour on my ancient bicycle to cover those hills, along the familiar route. Not one of my friends would come with me, or rather, to do them justice, those who would have done so were stopped by their parents. I was there: I was in. From my reading, I knew this Middlesbrough side off by heart and here, now, in their red jerseys, with the white yokes, were those five goal-happy forwards – Billy Pease, Billy Birrell, George Camsell, Jackie Carr, and Owen Williams – four English internationals in a row and the five of them worth 114 goals that season. But they did not beat Reading; and Camsell did not score. Their only goal came from Billy Birrell. It was a one-all draw when McConnell, way back in his own half, took a huge swing at the ball: it towered high down the middle of the field and dropped towards the Middlesbrough goal: someone went in and shaped to head it, missed, and the ball was in the net – McConnell the scorer of what is still the longest-range goal I have ever seen.

It was a long wait after the game for the autographs but, at length, there they were, complete – and eighteen miles lay ahead. Nor were the autographs my only profit from the match. Camsell was my main interest: he was obviously going to break all goal scoring records that season, and I had gone to that match determined to find out how he was doing it. Five minutes was enough. The offside rule had just been changed to its present form and, with only one man other than the goal-keeper needed between himself and goal when the ball was last played, the centre-forward could lie right up on the deeper of the two backs, with only that one man to race for the through ball and the chance of a goal. As the flow of passes from Birrell and Carr – skilfully varied with long passes to the goal-scoring wingers – came down the middle, Camsell challenged for them: only McConnell's immense speed in recovery and some characteristic Duckworth dives prevented him from scoring.

Until then I had been an indifferent goalkeeper or full-back in school football. Now I had an idea – I was the only boy in the school who had seen the Middlesbrough match, and football styles filter very slowly down to North Hampshire schools. I went to centre-forward. They might call me 'poacher', 'baby-liner', or anything else they liked: if it was good enough for George Camsell, it was good enough for me. I began to score goals – lots of them. I got into my form team, my house team, the school juniors and then the school team all in a year, and scoring all the time. It was my solitary spell of footballing glory. By the next season it was being done much better by better players, and I retired to full-back and obscurity.

I was now interested not only in Reading's League matches, but in the reserve side too. Ask me the names of some of our international sides in the 'thirties, and I shall be hard put to it to recall them: but about the Reading reserve sides of the same period, I have no hesitation at all.

I remember them coming, those reserve players – signed during the close-season to the accompaniment of flattering biographical notes in the local papers. There was an appearance in the pre-season trial match and then an obscure season in – and out of – the London Combination side, and they were gone.

One day, my father took me to see my great-aunt, who lived at Brimpton: at her house we met a satisfying grand gentleman who turned out to be a director of the Reading Football Club. I was tongue-tied, but it eventually emerged that I was a fervent supporter of the club. Would I care to have a stand ticket for next Saturday's match? As easily said as done: producing a piece of note-paper from his pocket, the director wrote on it an order for me to be provided with two – yes, two, so that I could take a friend – tickets for the stand at Elm Park on Saturday next. I could have wished, I seemed to remember, that the fixture had been something more handsome than that with Kettering in the Southern League, but the stand was the stand. I cannot remember where we sat; my solitary recollection of the game is that a man named Bill Collier, a Scottish inter-national, formerly with Raith Rovers, as I subsequently discovered – played a masterly if not over-strenuous game at right-half for Kettering.

No football season can ever be for me such a season as Reading's in 1926–7. The game came as a new impact: it was gladiatorial: yet perhaps because I was always there so early as to be in the front of the terraces, close to the touchline; or perhaps because of the shy remarks – and replies – over autograph books, it was also intimate.

The Second Division of 1926–7 was not without its football greatness. Blackpool were there, with Boy Browell; Manchester City with Jimmy McMullan behind Johnson, and Hicks; Preston had Alex James, Morris, W. T. Roberts; Swansea had Fowler and the unique Lachlan McPherson; Chelsea, Andy Wilson, Miller, and Law; and Jackie Bestall was at Grimsby, yet it was Portsmouth and Middlesbrough who went up.

For that season and all that has come from it, I have something of gratitude in my loyalty to Reading. The loyalty was there then, and an absorbing interest, a fierce anxiety that we should always have our best possible eleven on duty.

One of my great selection anxieties was Bill Johnstone – later to spend several seasons with Arsenal – who, in about 1928, came to Reading from Scotland. I now perceive that he was a skilful positional player, for he was eternally breaking through opposing defences, making or taking so many chances to run clear that he might have broken the goal-scoring record but that his final shots so often missed. Now the great local controversy – Johnstone or Bacon? – broke out. Bacon was a tall man from Derby County, with a shaving-brush tuft of hair growing out from a shallow forehead above a mighty jaw. His chest was like a drum, his thighs hugely tapering, and he had two shooting feet which he threw at footballs as if with intent to burst them. It was on April 3rd in the Year of Our Lord one-thousand-nine-hundred-and-thirty-one – a Good Friday, as I recall, with Reading's relegation virtually certain – that A. Bacon, at centre-forward, realized all his dreams. The match was against Stoke City, at Elm Park, and Bacon proceeded to score six goals against them; six goals of immense excitement. He had a habit of hitting the ball well forward on his instep; not a toe-ender, by any means, but from about the line of stitching joining the toecap to the instep – a point of impact only possible to a man of immensely strong legs and ankles. That day, everything he touched flew at the Stoke goal like a shell. But for some great saves he must have scored twenty, and his last goal was scored from an angle of about one degree to the goal line on the right of the goal and the ball, flying almost vertically into the goal, as I shall never forget, thrust the roof of the net high above the crossbar.

If Bacon is the hero of that story, Johnstone had his day in the 1928–9 Cup competition. In the third round, Reading beat Tottenham and then they were drawn against Sheffield Wednesday, who were already strongly established at the top of the First Division – which they were to head for two consecutive seasons – while Reading were unhappily about the bottom of the Second

Division. Those fast Wednesday forwards bore down, prompted by Jimmy Seed, who was the inspiration of the side, and prompted by the great half-back line of Strange, Leach, and Marsden – all English internationals of the time. Somehow Reading kept them out: men went down like felled oaks and they did not score. Then – and the crammed crowd gasped with disbelief before it cheered – Johnstone scored, and Reading were in the lead. We went on our knees to Johnstone, abjectly withdrew every unkind word we had ever uttered about him and thanked the stars of football that we had him. Did Reading ever come within shooting distance of the Wednesday goal again? If they did, I cannot recall it. I was behind the Reading goal in the second half and the ball seemed perpetually before my face. Why Wednesday did not score, only heaven and Joe Duckworth could tell you – and I suspect that Duckworth would not be too certain. Once Allen broke through and Duckworth dived forwards a full nine feet to push the ball off his shooting foot. It flew to Hooper, and Duckworth, half-way up from his knees, pushed the winger's shot in the air, caught it as Allen charged him, and miskicked it clear to Seed, whose header he turned over the bar. The penalty-area seemed perpetually full of prone and muddy bodies; and Wednesday did not score.

Then it was Aston Villa – Smart and Mort, Walker, and Dorrell, York, Moss – half a team of English internationals and the claret-and-blue jerseys. Nothing, now, was too great. I remember how it rained. There were ordinary chairs on the grass inside the barriers, so that the purchasers of special tickets could sit near the touchline. So heavy was the rain that the legs of the chairs sank into the mud; small boys were passed over the chair-sitters lest they should be crushed: I was aggrieved at being 'not small enough'. It was the end of Reading's Cup for that season and there has never been such another for them since.

Reading's manager in those days was a Scot, named Andrew Wylie, who appeared to have a steady supply of players from his native district, for a vast number of Reading's two teams in those days seem to have come from Falkirk or Bo'ness. In one of the pre-season practices – of 1928–9, I fancy – there appeared a left-wing from that area: Hunter inside and Oswald on the wing. Hunter was short, sandy, unhurried and a superb ball-player. In the trial, he twice or thrice leaped into action, beat some three men and cracked the ball into the net like a character from a story-book. Thereafter, he averaged something less than a goal per ten matches until he went to Sheffield United two years later, and thence disappeared, in a season. He was always, however, a masterly dribbler and a natural constructive player. He fed Oswald with perfect passes: perhaps it was a little unfortunate that the winger was so right-footed that, nine times out of ten, he doubled back and centred with his right foot, but that strong inside foot scored him – and Reading – some valuable goals.

Reading has always been a great club for centre-forwards – Davey, Johnstone, Bacon, MacPherson – who once put a free-kick so fiercely over the bar as to send it out of the ground where it smashed the window of a house and the gas-bracket inside – Harston, Billy Lane, Palethorpe, Newton, Gregory, McPhee, and, since the war, Blackman – with Vigar and Chung promising great things from the reserve and 'A' teams. If MacPherson and Bacon were the two most colourful, McPhee was probably the most dexterous. One of the best buys the club ever made, he was a steady scorer with his head and either foot over a period of ten years. Palethorpe, however, was the most popular. A local lad from Maidenhead United, he had such a following that it was difficult to say whether the crowd at Elm Park were Palethorpe's supporters or Reading's. He was the centre-forward in the club's great season of 1932–3, when they totalled 103 goals, and only some inexplicable weakness in an individually good defence prevented them from getting back to the Second Division. Tall, dark, good-looking and a cheerful trier, Palethorpe lacked just the extra touch of class: with the two clubs he played for after Reading – Stoke City and Preston North End – he was the vital goal-scorer in their successful promotion bids but, once in the First Division – he went also to Sheffield Wednesday and Aston Villa – he was out of his class. His transfer was one of the saddest moves Reading ever made, for they sacrificed both support and opportunity of promotion by selling him.

Never, perhaps, did a side suffer such a tragedy – although one barely noticed it at the time – as Reading did by the outbreak of war. Manager Joe Edelston had at last brought together the side he wanted: cool backs, ball-playing halves, constructively-minded inside-forwards with finishing power. Twice they ran to double figures within ten days and were clear out at the top of the Third Division table when war came. That team went on to win war-time honours, but by the coming of peace it was irretrievably shattered and the chance was gone.

Ever since the war, however, they have been around the top of the league, just thwarted, again and again, of promotion, yet year after year in the first four places. Now – in 1951–2 – under Ted Drake, old friend of obscure but happy days in Southampton – with a strong half-back line, Maurice Edelston making goals, Blackman one of the heaviest scorers in the League and some real talent in the reserves, their run of twelve consecutive league wins has given my perpetual hope new justification.

There is, I find, less open emotion in the directors' box and in the dressing-room than there was on the terraces when I was a boy. Yet there are still times when – like Ted Drake – I cannot bear to look, times when I pray for the end twenty minutes from time, lest our one-goal lead should be taken from us. There are times, when, as a guest in the board room of some mighty First League club, I find that the Third Division results are not read out – they stop at the Second Division. Then it is that I face the superior smiles or the loud laughs and ask, with my heart in my mouth, anxious as ever, 'How did Reading get on?'

from CONCERNING SOCCER *1950*

Part Two

GREAT MATCHES

Yugoslavia v. Russia, 1952

A. J. LIEBLING

On the morning following the opening of the Olympic Games I found myself on a train bound from Helsinki to the much smaller city of Tampere, about a hundred miles north of here, to see a soccer game between Neuvostoliitto, which is the Finnish name for the Union of Soviet Socialist Republics, and Jugoslavia, which is what the Finns call Yugoslavia.

I had some herring sandwiches and an ice-cream cone on the platform at Riihimäki, and discovered that a couple of football experts from English papers of large circulation were on the same train. I met them again in midafternoon on the platform at Tampere, and as we set out for the football field one of them, a thin fellow with a North Country accent, informed me that the Yugos had fair outplayed Brazil in Rio and had far too much experience for the Russians. Our way led through the main street of the town and across a bridge adorned with four huge and explicit nudes. (This explicitness is a feature of Finnish public sculpture; my football man told me that there was only one thing to compare with Finnish statuary in London, and that in a place where one wouldn't ordinarily notice it, high up on a government building.) The two Englishmen lingered to admire the statues, and I went along to the field.

Soon after finding myself a seat in the press row, I was enveloped by Iron Curtain football correspondents. On my left was a merry-looking young woman, red-cheeked, plump, and with amazingly tufted black eyebrows, who told me in French, after a few unsuccessful passes in other languages, that she represented the Bulgarian press agency. On my right was a Russian youth with an ovoid, olive face and grey-blue eye – a knowledgeable and authoritative man, from his appearance, who looked at me in a challenging and disillusioned way, as if to defy me to try any of my capitalistic dialectics on him. I asked him in English if he wanted to sit next to the girl, as they had begun talking across me. He said, 'Don't bother you,' and gazed at me broodingly from under long Circassian eyelashes.

'Who do you think will win?' I asked him.

'Who you think?' he parried unerringly.

'I don't know,' I said, eager to disclaim *parti pris*.

'That's what I don't know also,' he said, and we lapsed into silence. He had a camera that looked complex enough to shoot actinic rays or automatically vend Coca-Cola. He didn't use it once during the game, from which I surmised that it was either a tommy gun or a coop for a carrier pigeon, if not a piggy bank.

The game was to start at seven; it stays light until well after ten in Tampere at this season. Despite the long wait ahead, the field, locally referred to as a *stadion*, was filling up. Tampere has a population of a hundred thousand, and the paid attendance was eighteen thousand, of which at least ten thousand were standees. There were wooden bleachers on both sides at midfield, but most of the crowd stood on banks of earth at the ends. The town band tried its best to fill in the interval pleasantly for us, and succeded very well as far as I was concerned. It played a more extensive version of *The Merry Widow* score than one hears in the usual capsule medley, and was surprisingly accomplished in Sousa marches. The bandsmen wore ordinary civilian clothes, but they all had white yachting caps. I asked the Bulgarian girl if she didn't think they were good and she said that the town was culturally undeveloped. A slip of paper giving the names of the referee and the linesmen was passed along our row; the referee was an Englishman and the linesmen were Finns. Then the Russian team came out for a bit of practice. They were big fellows in red jerseys and light-blue shorts, and they passed the ball about among themselves, kicking it with the sides of their feet and bouncing it off the tops of the heads with considerable adroitness. The Yugoslavs, believers in applied psychology, scorned practice and did not appear on the field until time to line up. They wore dark-blue jerseys and white shorts, and had many more tall men than the Russian side but were in general less chunky. Both teams were well received by the crowd. Newspapermen here have been trying to develop a new science of determining the political tone of an athletic cheer in Finnish, which is a Finno-Ugric language closely related to Estonian. Having lagged in this department, I can report only that the crowd cheered good and loud for both sides. Each team had brought a small but taut cheering section of its own, recruited from its Olympic and press delegations, and these were decidedly partisan. The Russian cheer, as nearly as I could make it out, was 'Bra! Bra! Bra!', repeated as long as lungs and throats lasted. I am not even sure that it wasn't an unusually short, choppy rendition of 'Rah! Rah! Rah!' About the Yugoslav yell I am equally uncertain, but it sounded to me like 'Slahvee! Slahvee! Slahvee!', with a strong accent on the second syllable. This, I guessed, meant 'Slavs', which seemed a likely thing for Slavs to shout. When things were going well, they would also shout 'Haida!' I asked my Bulgarian newspaperwoman what this meant, and she said, '*Ça veut dire, "Allons!"*'

Punctually at seven, the two teams, of eleven men each, lined up, and play began. Soccer, I might point out, is a game whose main object is brilliantly easy to understand, similar in some respects to ice hockey and polo. There is a goal, something like a netted lean-to, at each end of the field. All you have to do is kick the ball into your opponents' net or bump it in with your head, and you get one point. But the speed and intricacy of the play is something else again. Good players pass and dribble almost as accurately as if they were allowed to use their hands. They know how to be almost as rough as if they were allowed to tackle. And they have to have practically super-human endurance, since they play two forty-five minute halves without any substitutions. The weather was favourable to these exertions, being just under sixty degrees, but the turf was wet and slippery. (It has rained several times a day in Finland since the opening of the Games, and when the cold sun does shine through, it does not stay long enough to dry out the ground.) Another thing about soccer is that it is a game whose subtleties the spectator quickly begins to think he understands – the despair of the man who goes down the field for a pass and doesn't get it, the *légerdepied* of the dribbler who seems to offer the ball to his charging opponent and then takes it away, leaving the opponent prone. It was not difficult to keep track of the individual players, since they wore numbers on their jerseys. Two especially caught my eye – the husky, barrel-chested Russian No. 7, named Trofimov, one of those hustling players, always tearing off somewhere at great speed, whom you see in every field sport and who impress you until you realize that they are usually going nowhere in particular, and the extremely tall Yugoslav No. 11, named Zebec, as fine a pantomimist as we have had since the days of the silent movies, who transmitted all his emotions to the crowd by a fine sequence of Yugoslavian gestures and kept leaping high into the air to receive the ball on his apparently cast-iron potato, while the Russians writhed in baffled fury at the lesser altitudes that were all they succeeded in attaining.

For the first half hour, neither side scored, although the Yugos had the ball in Russian territory at least two-thirds of the time. My Russian neighbour with the camera was already making me feel

41

sorry for him, because of the emotional tension I could see he was suffering. He was one of those sotto-voce cheerers, a type I recognised from my race-track experience. They are afraid to cheer out loud because they feel it may jinx the outcome, a feeling whose origins are undoubtedly somewhere in Frazer, if one cared to look for them. 'Cheep, cheep!' he would begin softly when a Russian player got the ball and started a run; then, imploringly and with accelerated enunciation, 'Cheep *cheep!*' as the player hesitated, looking for somebody to pass to; '*Cheep cheep!*' – with wild hope, as the player moved on again; and, finally, 'Cheep *cheep* CHEEP!' But the last 'cheep' was always followed by a gusty sigh – 'Oo – ah!' – as the cove lost the ball.

Ivanov, the Russian goalkeeper, who looked like Chaliapin in a peaked cap, made some splendid stops, once flying horizontally to his right, his body exactly parallel to the ground, as he stopped the ball with his chest and hugged it. (The goalkeeper is allowed to use his hands.) I shouted 'Bra!' and drew a glance of tender gratitude from beneath the Bulgarian girl's right eyebrow. Then a Yugo named Mitic scored the first goal, and I impartially shouted 'Haida!' The crowd cheered unanimously – the special Russian rooting section excepted – denoting, I suppose, either a diminution within half an hour of the Communist faction in the local metalworkers' union (Tampere is a factory town) or simply excitement. Four minutes later, a Yugo named Ognjanov scored another goal. By this time, the Bulgarian girl was crying, although I should have thought that since Russia had put Bulgaria out of the tournament in an earlier game, she might harbour some resentment toward the team. My Russian looked so glum that I feared he would reveal the true nature of his camera and possibly blow up the stadium. Then Zebec, the mimetic giraffe, kicked in a third goal. 'Slahvee!' I shouted happily, and then 'Haida!', for I am always for the underdog when he is on top. That was how the score stood at half time, 3–0. '*Il est bon, votre Ivanov,*' I remarked – unkindly, I'm afraid – to my Balkan colleague. '*Mais il a trop de travail.*' Her sobs prevented her from answering coherently.

The second half opened catastrophically for my neighbours. Ognjanov scored again in the first minute. Eight minutes later, a player named Bobrov scored the first goal for Russia. The man with the camera showed a slight flicker of animation, but he relapsed into his cataleptic state a bit later, when Zebec scored once more for the Yugos. The score stayed at 5–1 until fifteen minutes before the end of the game. Then the Russians scored two goals close together. The Yugos were obviously rattled. The man with the camera began his 'Cheep, cheep!' again, like a robin reappearing with the spring.

Soon, however, the Yugos pulled themselves together and became cagey. They decided to play a defensive game and freeze the ball. The politically unstable crowd was now hysterically on the side of the Russians. I could sympathize with their switch to anti-deviationism, for it was plain to me that, in purest Finno-Ugric, they were shouting, 'Cut the stalling!' I began to discern repulsive characteristics in even the heroic Zebec. When the Yugos had been well ahead, the Russian goalkeeper had come out of his net to snatch the ball virtually off Zebec's toe and Zebec had magnanimously jumped clear over the stooping man's head to avert a collision, landing asprawl on the turf ten feet away; now, in a similar situation, Zebec went into the goalie with both feet and then kicked himself free of the presumed cadaver. The crowd howled its disapproval so vociferously that for a moment I began to fear that Finland had followed the path of Czechoslovakia. The stalling lasted for ten minutes, and then somehow the Yugos lost the touch. Russia scored after eighty-seven minutes of play, with three minutes to go. And suddenly I sensed that everybody, including the Yugos, had the feeling that the Russians were going to get the tying goal. In international soccer, a goal within three minutes is an unlikely proposition (a team seldom gets more than half a dozen goals in a ninety-minute game), but I would have bet even money the Russians were going to get it. And in some mystic way they did, with one minute to play. The marsh-fire of Communism now played incandescently around the periphery of the *stadion* and the welkin rang with the clarion of subversion. It sounded like Ebbets Field in the days of Babe Herman. A Russian named Petrov had banged the ball with his head, which is the way Herman used to field them.

One minute – a panicky one for the Yugoslavs – passed and the whistle blew, ending the regular game with the teams tied at 5–5. I turned to my Russian for information. He had collapsed across the typewriter bench in front of him and was sobbing. I gently touched his shoulder and in time brought him back to an awareness of his surroundings. 'What happens now?' I asked. He sat up. 'Fifteens minutes overtimes this way,' he said, sweeping a hand from right to left. 'Then change sides and fifteens minutes that way' – and he swept the hand from left to right. 'And if it's still tied?' I asked. 'Play again,' he said. I could tell from his tone that he didn't have any doubt that his team would career on to victory, since it was now, as the sportswriters would say, on the crest of a surge. It seemed logical that a team like Yugoslavia, which had allowed four goals in fifteen minutes, was played off its legs. But the two extra periods produced neither scores nor drama, and the game ended at 5–5.

On the way out, I encountered the thin English football man again, and he said that the whole theory of the Yugoslav game suffered from excessive finesse, although he did not phrase it quite that way. I think he said, 'They ran about too bloody much.' 'Let the ball do the work, they always say in England,' he told me. 'Take more shots.' I asked him if he thought the Yugos would win the playoff, and he replied, 'They've had a nasty knock.' He added that in all his life he had never seen such a collapse, or such a rally, depending on how you wanted to look at it.

The two teams played again in Tampere last night, and this time Yugoslavia beat Russia, 3–1. The Russians scored first; it was Bobrov again, according to the score card. But after that it was all Yugoslavia. Mitic, Bobek, and Cajkovski made the goals. Haida! Slahvee! Slahvee!

from THE NEW YORKER *1/8/52*

Blackpool v. Bolton Wanderers, 1953

PAUL GARDNER

Thinking there might be a heavy fog, or an accident, or perhaps a strike – well, so many things can upset railway timetables – I got up at 5 a.m. to catch a train hours earlier than I really needed, with the result that I arrived in London around nine o'clock, leaving me some five hours to dispose of before I had to be at the stadium.

This was 1953, and in those days London on Cup Final day was like a town under benevolent siege. There always seemed to be at least one northern team represented (that year it was Blackpool and Bolton, both from the north) and the supporters flowed in in boisterous little knots, drifting about the streets trying somehow to make a dent in the apathy of the big city. In the narrow streets that used to surround Euston station these working-class fans – they could have been Priestley's Bruddersfordians – were instantly at home, absorbed without trouble into the cheap boardinghouses and the sleazy little cafés, where their broad Lancashire accents badgered the waitresses endlessly, 'Gie us anoother coop o' tea, lass,' and they talked about soccer. Not intelligently, but with the

44

blind partisanship that had caused them to come all those miles to this heathen city, and to deck themselves out with huge rosettes and scarves and hats and even whole suits in their club colours.

'It's Stan's year, lads, it's Stan's year, I bloody know it. I bloody told you so when we beat 'uddersfield, I bloody knew it then, and I'll tell you now, bloody Bolton aren't gonna stop him. Who've they bloody got? Banks? He's a big ox, Stan'll make 'im look bloody daft, he'll wish he'd stayed home with the missus . . . how about anoother coop here, lass?' Solid agreement from all his Blackpool mates. They had a London newspaper in which one of the writers had picked Bolton – 'What the bloody 'ell does 'e know about it?' – the very idea, a London writer daring to give opinions about northern teams.

I sat for a while, a middle-class interloper, listening to them tear Bolton apart until it hardly seemed worthwhile playing the game. As it happened, I agreed with them. I had no ties to either team, but I wanted Blackpool to win. Just because of Stan.

I had first seen Stanley Matthews play maybe ten years earlier, and had never missed an opportunity to see him again. He had shown me, as he must have shown tens of thousand of others, just how superb a game soccer could be. Any game with Stan in it was likely to be a magical occasion. His nickname, said the papers, was The Wizard of the Dribble. In the papers, maybe, but never on the terraces. There it was always just plain Stan. 'Come on, Stan, show 'im, Stan.' And Stan, stooping, balding, his face a blank but always slightly drawn – the only thing about him that suggested anything approaching effort – would show them.

At his feet, the ball was at home, comfortably nestling in absolute security, caressed with soft little touches as Stan shuffled his bowed legs toward yet another hapless fullback. Watch the ball, not the man is considered the defender's golden rule, and you would see them with a mesmerised, almost frightened, concentration on the ball as Stan approached. But how could you not watch a man whose seductive body movements seemed to telegraph his every move? Surely no one could lean that far to his left, unless he were actually going to take a step in that direction? And so the fullback would move, had to move, and all was lost. In one smooth burst Stan would straighten up and sail away to his right, leaving the fullback staring at nothing but air, or falling on to his back as he tried to turn while off-balance.

Then the roar for Matthews as he headed for the goal line, the ball always just that calculated distance ahead of him where he could get to it but an opponent could not. Matthews was not a speedster, but I doubt whether anyone has ever been faster over those first few yards after he had beaten his man. There was never any hope of the fullback, even if he was still on his feet, catching Matthews. Usually, another defender would come running across to cover, but this was just what Stan wanted. A player coming in at full speed to tackle a moving Matthews had the most impossible of tasks. He had to get to the ball at once, and as his foot came in, Stan would pull the ball back and cut inside, or he would push it forward, what looked like just a few tantalising inches beyond the outstretched tackler's foot, which he would step over as though it didn't exist, and complete his enchanted path to the goal line.

There the ball would be pulled sharply back and sent arcing into the penalty area where it would arrive like some gently falling bomb, always out of reach of the goalkeeper, always within reach of the attacking forwards surging in to meet it.

Inevitably, the torment of having to face Matthews invited rough tactics, and Stan was kicked and fouled more than most. The resilient, wiry body bore it all, and the stoic, rather sad face remained as blank as ever. He never had to be cautioned by a referee, and to my knowledge he never retaliated, in a thirty-three-year-long career.

What I and most of England – except Bolton – wanted to see was Stan being presented with a Cup Winner's medal, just about the only honour in the game that he had never won. This was Matthews's third final in six years; twice before, in 1948 and 1951, Blackpool had been beaten and Matthews had walked off the field a loser. Now he was thirty-eight years old and this must surely be his last chance.

The Blackpool fans had it all worked out; it would be 3–1 Blackpool when the final whistle went, and I left them happily plotting Bolton's downfall amid the empty teacups and the greasy plates. Pick another café and you'd have found the same Lancashire accents, wearing black and white, and telling you that Blackpool could put a hundred bloody Matthewses on the field if they liked, it was goals that counted, and 'our Nat', Nat Lofthouse, scores goals, laddie – how many goals has Stan scored lately? And there was a lot of truth in that, too.

I walked into the West End, a different world this, of large smart stores, one where the little groups of fans stood out as foreign elements and defiantly made all the more noise because of it. By one o'clock I was impatient. 'You are advised to take up your position by not later than 2:30 p.m.,' said my ticket, which left me ninety minutes to make a twenty-minute Underground journey. But you never knew, there might be a delay of some sort, an accident. By 1:30 I was at Wembley Stadium, proffering my ticket at the turnstile, holding my breath in case it was rejected as counterfeit (I had no reason to think it was, I had obtained it in the most respectable way, but you never knew . . .).

My seat, I decided, was not a good one, too far to one end, giving an excellent view of one goal but a long-range look at the other. The stadium was already a third full, maybe 30,000 people gathered, mostly behind the two goals. Between them the famous Wembley turf, rich, green and glowing like a massive emerald carpet. A treacherous carpet, though, one that did strange things to players' legs. There always seemed to be cramps and pulled muscles and twisted knees at a Wembley final.

Community singing came next. Led by a military band standing in the middle of the field, we sang popular songs and music-hall numbers until, with the stadium almost full and only fifteen minutes left, we were ready for sterner stuff, *Land of Hope and Glory*, and then the traditional *Abide with Me*, a solid working-class hymn sung with a fervour it would never command in any chapel. There is no real ending to *Abide with Me* at Wembley; the last note slides into a sustained cheer as banners wave and rattles rattle, a cheer that turns suddenly to an amorphous deafening roar of relief and expectation from 100,000 throats as the two teams walk sedately side by side on to the field.

More frustrating preliminaries. The new Queen Elizabeth, crowned earlier that same year, came on to the field to meet the teams – 'As if she bloody cares, one lot's the same as t'other to her,' said a Blackpool neighbour as the pinnacle of Britain's aristocracy and the nobility of its working classes met for a fleeting moment.

Then . . . a whistle, and an ever-changing mosaic of orange shirts and white shirts on the green, all commanded by the movements of a small light-brown ball. Within two minutes, tragedy for Blackpool. Our Nat, got the ball some twenty yards out and shot, an unimpressive effort that looked almost like a miskick. The ball spun across in front of the Blackpool goalkeeper, Farm, who went for it much too late . . . and went in.

While the Bolton fans rejoiced, poor Farm stood in dejected agony, engulfed by the noise his error had caused. Wembley nerves, I thought, something everyone knew about, but something you didn't talk about for fear of inviting the worst. At least there was plenty of time left for Blackpool to reply. But within minutes the powerful Lofthouse was steaming through again, and this time his shot was hit perfectly, a searing drive that had the crowd yelling

'Goal!' the instant it left his foot. Again, Farm hardly moved as the ball rocketed past him, only to crash against the goal post with a solid smack that seemed to echo around the stadium in a moment of quiet as Blackpool's fans were mutely waiting the worst and Bolton's were drawing breath for the final triumphant yell. Blackpool were reprieved with their head on the block, but Farm looked anything but happy. 'Go easy on 'im, Nat, the poor bugger's shell-shocked!' crowed a Bolton voice.

Then it was Blackpool's turn to roar. Down at the other end, where I couldn't really see what was going on, Stan Mortensen ('the other Stan' on the Blackpool team) got the ball in the net. A mistake by the Bolton goalie, they said, so at least the Wembley nerves were striking impartially. But before half-time Farm had let through another shot he should have saved, and Bolton went to the locker rooms leading 2–1, having looked much the better team.

Matthews? He had done little, but then the same could be said of all the other Blackpool forwards. I hoped for better things in the second half, when he would be attacking the goal in front of me. Soon after the restart, Wembley's major jinx struck. Bell, the Bolton left halfback, was injured. In those days there was no such thing as substitution so Bell, barely able to run, was left on the field as a limping passenger in the rather optimistic hope that he might prove a slight nuisance to the Blackpool defenders. Within ten minutes he had done the impossible, leaping high to meet a centre from the right to head Bolton's third goal. Even now, playing against only ten fit men, Blackpool were floundering. They were getting more of the ball, certainly, but their attacks were half-hearted affairs, quickly snuffed by the Bolton defence.

With some twenty minutes left and their team apparently home and dry, the Bolton fans were in full voice, shouting cheerfully, 'Coom on the ten men!', yelling derisively every time a Blackpool attack broke down.

But it was not the noise of the crowd that was to decide the game that afternoon. It was to be the genius of Stanley Matthews. The pressure on the Bolton defence mounted and always the ball was finding its way to Stan's feet, out on the right wing. I could see him cutting and corkscrewing his way through the left flank of the Bolton defence, stopping, accelerating, twisting to avoid desperate tackles, and now it was the Blackpool fans who roared, grasping feverishly at the hope that Stan was destined to get his medal after all, that he *must* bring off the miracle.

Another incredible Matthews run, going past defender after defender, an early centre beautifully judged to lure the goalkeeper out, and in the race for the ball it was Stan Mortensen who got there first to score. Bolton 3 Blackpool 2 – one more goal (and it would be Blackpool's, for Bolton were in deep trouble, burned out as an attacking force) would send the game into overtime. But how many minutes were left? 'Plenty of time, lad, plenty,' said my Blackpool neighbour, but the minutes ticked away and despite all the Matthews magic, the trail of dazed defenders he was leaving after him every time he got the ball and the terrible tangles he was causing in the Bolton ranks, the crucial goal would not come.

I calculated there couldn't have been more than a minute or two left when Mudie, the Blackpool inside left, was brought down directly in front of goal, some twenty yards out. Back came every Bolton player into his own penalty area to defend against the free kick. A wall of white shirts blocked off one side of the goal while goalie Hanson, crouching and rubbing his hands together, guarded the other half. Mortensen, one of the hardest kickers of a dead ball I have ever seen, aimed his shot at the top corner furthest away from Hanson. Either he had spotted a gap in that human wall, or he gambled that someone would move out of the way of his ferocious drive.

Whichever, his shot flashed into the top of the goal, straight and unstoppable. All Hanson could do was to turn and watch as the ball bulged the netting and fell to the grass inside the goal. We were all on our feet now, Wembley Stadium nothing but noise as the late afternoon sun seemed to pick out the orange Blackpool shirts with a suggestively triumphant glow.

Time didn't matter now; the game would go into overtime and Blackpool, running riot against a demoralised Bolton, would be the winner. There was less than a minute to go and the ball had found its way back to Matthews, lurking out on the wing, just inside the Bolton half. With the ease of a skater, Matthews was away on another flexuous run, inside one defender, then past his fullback, racing for the goal line. Barrass, the Bolton centre-half – and a good one – was drawn out of the middle to cope with the danger. The fatal error. Cutting in, Matthews ran the ball straight at Barrass until, just when it seemed the two must collide, there was that diabolical pivot, that almost ninety-degree turn on the run. The move did not get Matthews past Barrass, but that wasn't the idea; all Stan wanted now, having drawn Barrass out to the edge of the penalty area, was room to get the ball into the middle, and he created the space he needed with that one masterful swerve.

Matthews's centre was the final perfect touch. Did he look up to see where he was putting it, or was it just a sixth sense, a soccer

49

sense, that told him what to do? All I saw was the ball flashing low across the face of the Bolton goal, and I remember thinking, maybe saying, 'Christ, no, Stan,' certain that it must be intercepted by a Bolton defender. But Barrass, the key man, was out of position and the ball ran through, untouched, until Perry, the Blackpool left winger, met it at the far post and hit it, firm and low, into the goal.

With under a minute left, Blackpool were sure winners and from the roar even the Bolton fans must have been cheering, not for the goal, but for the man who had turned the game around, who had treated us all to one of soccer's greatest games. The roar was for Stan Matthews.

from THE SIMPLEST GAME *1976*

England v. Hungary, 1953

GEOFFREY GREEN

Yesterday by 4 o'clock on a grey winter's afternoon within the bowl of Wembley Stadium the inevitable had happened. To those who had seen the shadows of the recent years creeping closer and closer there was perhaps no real surprise. England at last were beaten by the foreign invader on solid English soil. And it was to a great side from Hungary, the Olympic champions, that the final honour fell. They have won a most precious prize by their rich, overflowing, and to English patriots, unbelievable victory of six goals to three over an England side that was cut to ribbons for most of an astonishing afternoon. Here, indeed, did we attend, all 100,000 of us, the twilight of the gods.

There is no sense in writing that England were a poor side. Everything in this world is comparative. Taken within the framework of British football they were acceptable. This same combination – with the addition of the absent Finney – could probably win against Scotland at Hampden Park next April. But here, on Wembley's velvet turf, they found themselves strangers in a strange world, a world of flitting red spirits, for such did the Hungarians seem as they moved at devastating pace with superb skill and powerful finish in their cherry bright shirts.

One has talked about the new conception of football as developed by the continentals and South Americans. Always the main criticism against the style has been its lack of a final punch near goal. One has thought at times, too, that perhaps the perfection of football was to be found somewhere between the hard hitting, open British method and this other more subtle, probing infiltration.

Yesterday the Hungarians, with perfect team work, demonstrated this midway point to perfection. Theirs was a mixture of exquisite short passing and the long English game. The whole of it was knit by exact ball control and mounted by a speed of movement and surprise of thought that had an English team ground into Wembley's pitch a long way from the end. The Hungarians, in fact, moved the ball swiftly along the ground with delicate flicks or used the long pass in the air. And the point was that they used these variations as they wished, changing the point of attack at remarkable speed. To round it off – this was the real point – they shot with the accuracy and speed of archers. It was Agincourt in reverse.

One has always said that the day the continental learned to shoot would be the moment British football would have to wake up. That moment has come at last. In truth, it has been around the corner for some time, but there can no longer be any doubt. England's sad end on the national stage now proclaims it to the skies.

Outpaced and outmanoeuvred by this intelligent exposition of football, England never were truly in the match. There were odd moments certainly when a fitful hope spurted up, such as when Sewell put us level at one all at the quarter hour and later during a brave rally that took England to half-time 2–4 down. Yet these were merely the stirrings of a patriot who clung jealously to the past. The cold voice of reason always pressed home the truth.

Indeed from the very first minute the writing loomed large on Wembley's steep and tight-packed banks. Within sixty seconds Hungary took the lead when a quick central thrust by Bozsik, Zakarias, and Hidegkuti left the centre-forward to sell a perfect dummy and lash home, right foot, a swift rising shot to the top corner of Merrick's net. The ball was white and gleaming. It could have been a dove of peace. Rather it was a bird of ill-omen, for from that moment the Hungarians shot ten times to every once of England.

Just before England drew level a sharp move of fascinating beauty, both in conception and execution, between Czibor and Puskas was finished off by Hidegkuti. But the Dutch referee gave the centre-forward offside, which perhaps was charitable as things ended. Yet the English reply when it did come also arrived excitingly, for Johnston, intercepting in his own penalty area, ran forward to send Mortensen through. A quick pass to the left next set Sewell free and that was one all as a low left-foot shot beat Grosics.

But hope was quickly stilled. Within twenty-eight minutes Hungary led 4–1. However disturbing it might have been, it was breathtaking. At the twentieth minute, for instance, Puskas sent Czibor racing down the left and from Kocsis's flick Hidegkuti put Hungary ahead again at close range, the ball hitting Eckersley as he tried a desperate interception. Almost at once Kocsis sent the fast-moving Czibor, who entered the attack time after time down the right flank, past Eckersley. A diagonal ground pass was pulled back by Puskas, evading a tackle in an inside-right position – sheer jugglery, this – and finished off with a fizzing left-foot shot inside the near post: 1–3.

Minutes later a free kick by the progressive Bozsik was diverted by Puskas's heel past the diving Merrick, and England, 4–1 down with the half-hour not yet struck, were an army in retreat and disorder. Certainly some flagging courage was whipped in that rally up to half-time by Matthews and Mortensen, both of whom played their hearts out, crowded as they were, but though it brought a goal it could no more turn back the tide of elusive red shirts than if a fly had settled on the centre circle.

After an acrobatic save by Grosics to a great header by Robb it was Mortensen, dashing away from a throw-in, losing then recovering the ball and calling up some of his dynamic past, who now set Wembley roaring as he sped through like a whippet to shoot England's second goal. But 2–4 down at half-time clearly demanded a miracle in the space left after some of the desperate escapes at Merrick's end that had gone hand in hand with the telling Hungarian thrusts and overall authority.

Within ten minutes of the interval the past was dead and buried for ever. A great rising shot by Bozsik as the ball was caressed back to him on the edge of the penalty area after Merrick had turned Czibor's header on to the post made it 5–2, and moments later Hidegkuti brought his personal contribution to three within a perfect performance as he volleyed home Hungary's sixth goal from a lob by Puskas. It was too much. Though Ramsey said the last word of all for England with a penalty kick when Mortensen was brought down half an hour from the end, the crucial lines had been written and declaimed long since by Hungary in the sunshine of the early afternoon. Ten minutes before the end Grosics, with an injured arm, surrendered his charge to Geller, his substitute, but by now a Hungarian goalkeeper was but a formal requirement.

So was history made. England were beaten at all points, on the ground, in the air, and tactically. Hidegkuti, a centre-forward who played deep in the rear supplying the midfield link to probing and brilliant inside-forwards and fast wingers, not only left Johnston a lonely, detached figure on the edge of England's penalty area but also scored three goals completely to beat the English defensive retreat. But Johnston was not to blame: the whole side was unhinged. The speed, cunning, and shooting power of the Hungarian forwards provided a spectacle not to be forgotten.

Long passes out of defence to five forwards who showed football dressed in new colours was something not seen before in this country. We have our Matthews and our Finney certainly, but they are alone. Taylor and Sewell, hard as they and the whole side now fought to the last drop, were by comparison mere workers with scarcely a shot between them at the side of progressive, dangerous artists who seemed able to adjust themselves at will to any demand. When extreme skill was needed it was there. When some fire and bite entered the battle after half-time it made no difference.

English football can be proud of its past. But it must awake to a new future.

from THE TIMES 26/11/53

Sweden v. Brazil, 1958

GEOFFREY GREEN

The summit meeting of football is over. Brazil are the new world champions and a long awaited ambition has at last come true for them. In the first final between the New and the Old worlds it was they, the lordly representatives of the New, who brought a lustre, a magical quality that dazzled Sweden. It was a climax that had a 52,000 crowd holding its breath in wonder from start to finish here in the Rasunda Stadium – from the moment when Sweden took a swift lead through Liedholm, only to find themselves finally bewildered by a brand of football craft beyond the understanding of many.

Here were dark, expressive sportsmen of a distant continent. When the moment of triumph finally was sounded by the whistle, in an excited, demonstrative and kindly way they broke into triumphal circuit of the soft battlefield scarred by rain, brandishing above their heads a huge Swedish flag – a gesture of appreciation for their reception. The stadium stood to them as if it were the host nation herself who had won, and at the end the King of Sweden himself posed for photographs with the victors while many of them were openly overcome by their achievement.

After twenty-eight years of effort Brazil were the World Champions. To the Briton, perhaps, such scenes might seem far-fetched. But warmth, and an undisguised emotionalism, gushes out of the Brazilians. So it was as Mr Drewry, president of FIFA, presented the gold statuette to Bellini, Brazil's captain, that he said in echoing terms: 'Here indeed was a match to remember, a clean, sporting struggle between two great teams.' Every word was true. None could disagree with that, for here indeed *was* a match to remember. Perhaps one of the finest ever played in history came four years ago in Switzerland when Hungary overcame Uruguay in the semi-final round. This, perhaps, lacked the fire of that other occasion, but for sheer skill it was little behind. The cycles of the game, unfortunately, seldom coincide. If only it were possible to put Puskas and his Hungarians of 1954 on the field with the Brazil of today. But that must be something for one's dreams.

The bones of today's performance were these: at the fifth minute Liedholm, completing a slick penetrating move with Bergmark, Borjesson, and Simonsson, beat two men on a sixpenny piece and shot home low to put Sweden one up. On a slithery green pitch, as glistening as the rooftops of Stockholm after a night and morning of rain, it now looked as if the favourites were in for trouble. The Swedes had got the first blow and the South Americans, so rumour has it, are unhappy in the wet.

But rumour was now put to flight summarily as Vava, at centre-forward after all, with goals in the ninth minute and then again at the half-hour, put Brazil 2–1 ahead by the interval. After that Pelé and Zagallo made it 4–1, and though Simonsson brought Sweden back to 4–2, the swarthy Pelé, leaping like a black panther, headed Brazil to 5–2 as the last seconds of a breathtaking exposition ran out. Brazil, in fact, proved that they could play in the wet.

Thus Sweden, a fine side by any standards, were finally run into the ground by a brand of footballing dexterity that knew no bounds. Strongly and bravely as the Swedish defenders faced the surging tide – Gustavsson, Bergmark, and Borjesson in particular – they were at times left spinning like tops. Gren, especially, Simonsson and Liedholm too worked heroically in attack, threading many a subtle central move. But where they were stifled was out on the flanks and that, if nothing else mattered, finally settled their fate.

Hamrin and Skoglund, their match winners in the past were now blanketed by the majestic covering of D. Santos and N. Santos at full-back and Sweden's sharpest fangs were drawn.

Not so Brazil. Didi, floating about mysteriously in midfield, was always the master link, the dynamo setting his attack into swift motion; and, besides Didi, with Vava and Pelé a piercing double central thrust, they had the one man above all others to turn pumpkins into coaches and mice into men – Garrincha, at outside-right. Rightly has he been called the Matthews of the New World. His methods are the same: the suggestion of the inward pass, the body-swerve, the flick past the defender's left side, and the glide to freedom at an unbelievable acceleration. Poor Axbom stuck to him the best he could, but time after time he was left as lonely as a mountain wind. Garrincha, in fact, and the subtle use made of him by Didi in a swiftly changing thread of infiltration, was beyond control and that was that. There lay the most sensitive nerve-centre of the whole battle and so Brazil stretched out and grasped their ambition.

This Brazilian side was greater than their combination of eight years ago because of its defence: and it was in another world to the side that lost 2–4 to England at Wembley in 1955. England alone held them here in the World Cup. It seems incredible to think of it now, but over the last fortnight the Brazilians have been growing in stature and today they reached their zenith. They showed football as a different conception; they killed the white skidding ball from all angles as if it was a lump of cottonwool. From Gilmar in goal, the giant Bellini at centre-half, right through the team they were fused in swift, intimate thought and execution at changing tempos. They combined the theatrical with the practical and Sweden too often were left chasing dark shadows.

It was in fact a performance of superlatives and Brazil came to life that moment at the ninth minute when Garrincha, receiving from Didi, left Axbom stranded, swept into the by-line for Vava to flash in his diagonal cross. That was 1–1 and a moment later Pelé nearly uprooted the Swedish post with a left foot shot from twenty yards. But there was no holding Garrincha and again, at the half-hour, it was the old echo, Pelé, Didi, Garrincha, the flick, the by-line, the diagonal cross, and Vava striking again at close range. Ten minutes after the change of ends, Pelé with sleight of foot jugglery, flicked up a cross from Zagallo, balanced the ball on his instep, chipped it over Gustavsson and leapt round the centre-half to volley home. Who can live with this sort of stuff?

That was 3–1 to Brazil and the signal for individual exhibition in all corners of the field. Then it was 4–1 as Zagallo, cutting in on a rebound punished a mistake by Bergmark. Liedholm, with a long through pass, put Simonsson beautifully in for 4–2; and there might have been a penalty at each end as Sweden rallied fiercely and momentarily. But all hope was gone, and a swift header by Pelé from Zagallo's cross wrote the last word.

from THE TIMES *30/6/58*

Portugal v. North Korea, 1966

JOHN ARLOTT

Few football matches contain such a range of the startling and the epic as this quarter-final. The North Koreans had made friends in the north-east and their chant of 'Kor-ee-ah' – in the accents of Tees and Wear – had barely been raised, when their 'diddy men' scored. It was the first minute and the first movement. As the Portuguese defence dropped back, Li Dong Woon used what was to emerge as a planned North Korean gambit – he drove the ball hard at the centre of the packed defenders – hoping, no doubt, for a deflection or a cannon which might produce surprise advantage. It bounced off to Han Bong Zin on the right wing: he pushed it inside to Pak Seung Zin who made himself space by backing to the edge of the penalty area and then struck a rising shot into the top left corner of the Portuguese goal. The crowd mixed some laughter with its cheers. Then Yang Sung Kook, having made himself an opening, wasted it by pulling back a pass instead of shooting; North Korea should have been two up within five minutes.

Portugal, however – like the spectators – treated these as inconvenient, but not serious, accidents. They came back along their usual lines, sending the ball high into the goalmouth for Torres' head. But, although he stood a foot taller than the Korean defenders, Torres climbed no higher than Ha Jung Won and Lim Zoon Sum, who jack-knifed into the air like cats on a hot hob.

North Korea, too, were winning their share of the ball in midfield and, in possession, they constantly capitalised on their natural gift of speed in the start. Stroking the ball, angling it, juggling, cross-passing, they reduced the Portuguese defence to suspicion and unease.

Most teams would have been in trouble against such adroit ball-play; and the referee, Mr Ashkenasi, saw to it that the Koreans were not knocked off their game. Still within the first half-hour, Pak Doo Ik slid a neat forward ball to Yang Sung Kook: again the ground pass, precisely to Li Dong Woon who took careful aim and shot the second goal. 'We want three,' called the crowd and, within moments, they had a third. Again it was Yang Sung Kook who made the incision. This time he carried Han Bong Zin's short ball past two defenders with a sidling movement, deliberated to the last possible fraction of a second and coldly directed his right foot drive into the roof of the goal as he went down under the tackle.

North Korea beating Portugal three-nil: Goodison giggled with disbelief. One could feel the waves of incredulity echoing back from the receiving end of every television, radio and telephone cable out of the ground. It sounded like freak: but the three goals had been well made and well taken.

Now Portugal measured up to World Cup stature. Their attacks were urgent, yet free from panic. First Eusebio and then Augusto shot well and hard, only for Li Chan Myung – slim and whippy as a rapier – to curve in the air and make a clean catch.

Eusebio was grafting like three men, but Torres was not winning the ball and Augusto could not 'lose' Ha Jung Won. Only Simoes, switching from left, to centre and to right, was effective. On the half-hour, Eusebio passed to Simoes, moved on, collected the return, jinked along the defensive line, seeking an avenue for his shot and fired it home. In the last minute before half-time Torres burst through on to Simoes' pass and Shin Yung Kyoo, sturdier than most of his colleagues and a hard, fast back, somewhat in the European mould, tripped him. Eusebio sent the penalty kick fiercely and steeply beyond Li Chan Myung's spreadeagled leap.

Portugal undoubtedly received some sound counsel during half-time. They started off with firm efficiency and at once began to uncover the basic weakness in the Korean defenders – they are 'suckers' for the man in possession. So Portugal let them chase the ball, parting with it quickly. Yet this was a fine period for the North Koreans. Small but wiry fit and devoted sharp and quick as needles, they won the ball again and again. If their flaw was fundamental, it had not yet told against them. Then, however, the game was decided by a flash of genius. Again Eusebio sent Simoes cutting down the left and, as the cross came over, hard and low, there was Eusebio lancing in to meet it and crack it home, right-footed, in mid-leap. Level at three-all: half an hour left.

The ball was hardly in motion again before Eusebio, bent upon absolute decision, was on it again, racing down the left wing, taking on three men, beating them round the outside and cutting in on goal, only to be tripped as he was poised to shoot. This time the impact of the trip slowed and altered his approach to the penalty kick, but the ball hit the same uncoverable point in the net.

Now Portugal were in command and could play at their own pace: Eusebio could relax. Yet surely the Koreans, like the rest of us, realised that, at need, he would do it again. Just to make the point, immediately after a foray by Pak Doo Ik, Eusebio picked up a loose ball a dozen yards outside the penalty area and with a long swing of that mighty right foot, struck it through the line of defenders so savagely that it burst through Li Chan Myung's hands and bounced leadenly away from his body.

With some few minutes left, and in case of accidents, Portugal scored through their stock move. Eusebio moved down the left and centred high for Torres, by the far post, to nod it precisely back across the goal where Augusto was waiting to head in.

Korea, gamely and with genuine skills, had achieved as much success as they could have hoped. Portugal had shown themselves as sound in temperament as in technique and Eusebio stood in what, until a few days before, had been Pelé's place.

from WORLD CUP '66 *1966*

England v. West Germany, 1966

HUGH MCILVANNEY

Wembley does not always stir the spirit. As a football stadium it is overrated. The slow, sweaty crush out of the tube station and the long trudge along Stadium Way, where ticket touts and vendors of smelly hot-dogs wait in ambush, are not immediately rewarded. The closer you come to the place the shabbier it looks, twin towers notwithstanding. Under the stands there is the grey, cavernous gloom of most English grounds.

But Wembley is lucky enough to have occasions that work a metamorphosis, that can make grown men persuade themselves that the hideously inconvenient journey from London is an adventure and can transmute the undistinguished concrete bowl into what the more imaginative chroniclers of our time would call 'a seething cauldron'. FA Cup Finals can do that, especially when one of the clubs comes from the North of England and brings its raucous trainloads of supporters to drink at dawn in Covent Garden and spill their beery optimism over the terraces. One wondered if the World Cup could do as much for Wembley. In the event, it did far more. It was impossible to define the atmosphere precisely but it was palpable, and it was unique. It was like walking into an ordinary, familiar room and knowing instinctively that something vital and unbearably dramatic was happening, perhaps a matter of life and death. The people hurrying and jostling and laughing nervously inside had a flushed, supercharged look, but if they were high it was with excitement. 'It's bloody electric,' said one of the doormen. He had found the word.

Down on the field the combined bands of the Portsmouth Command and the Portsmouth Group, Royal Marines, had found the music, a tune for each of the sixteen competing nations. The North Koreans, whose own community singing is probably a little hard to follow, had to settle for a thing called Oriental Patrol. It did not matter much, for the roaring and chanting from the terraces, where the red, black and yellow flags of Germany were in no danger of being submerged among the Union Jacks and English banners, was loud enough to make everything sound alike. It might have been Liverpool's Anfield (England did wear red), and there can be no finer tribute. The weather was to fluctuate unpredictably between bright sunshine and squalls of driving rain, the fortunes of both teams to swing wildly between elation and frustration, but the crowd would remain constantly exhilarated, buoyed up by an incredible flood of incident. When the bands played the National Anthem the English supporters came together in a great chauvinistic choir. *Deutschland über Alles* boomed out in its wake and the battle was on.

The Germans began rather nervously, standing off from the tackle and letting the England forwards move without conspicuous hindrance up to the edge of the penalty area. Bobby Charlton and Peters were able to work the ball along the left at their leisure and there was anxiety in the German defence before the cross was cleared. But that was a tranquil interlude compared with what happened after eight minutes. An intelligent crossfield pass from Hurst set Stiles free on the right and his high centre beat Tilkowski before Höttges headed it away. The ball was returned smartly by Bobby Charlton and Tilkowski had so much trouble punching it off Hurst's head that he knocked himself out. The goalkeeper was prostrate, the whistle had gone and the defenders had stopped challenging before Moore put the ball in the net. The crowd cheered anyway, in the hope that next time it would be the real thing. They had reason to be optimistic, for England were dominating these early moments, running and passing with fine confidence on the wet surface. Without Schulz, patrolling tirelessly behind the main line of four backs, calmly averting crises, Germany would have come under severe strain. Many of their problems came from Bobby Charlton, wandering purposefully all over the field, bringing composure and smoothness wherever he appeared, again making comparisons with di Stefano seem relevant. Beckenbauer, asked to rein in his own aggressive impulses to concentrate on subduing the Manchester United player, was in for a thankless first half.

Yet it was Jack Charlton, carrying the ball forward on his forehead with a skill that would have done credit to his brother, who initiated England's next important attack. He strode swiftly out of defence and his perfectly judged diagonal pass let Peters hit a quick, powerful shot from well outside the area. Tilkowski, already revealing an uncertainty that sharpened the appetite of the England forwards, dived desperately to his left and punched the ball round the post. Hurst met Ball's corner but sent the volley too high. At that point Weber chose to give the sort of agonised performance that had been one of the less admirable characteristics of the German players in the competition. But Gottfried Dienst, the referee, quickly made it plain that nobody was being fooled and suggested it was time to get on with the game. Peters certainly did, surging in from the right wing to shoot only two feet wide from twenty-five yards.

Then, stunningly, in the thirteenth minute England found themselves a goal behind. And it was a goal that anyone who had seen their magnificent defensive play earlier in the tournament could hardly believe. Held glided a high cross from the left wing and Wilson, jumping for the ball in comfortable isolation, amazingly headed it straight to the feet of Haller, standing in an orthodox inside-right position a dozen yards out from Banks. The blond forward had time to steady, pivot and aim his right-foot shot along the ground into the far corner.

There were fears that the Germans would try to make that goal win the Cup, that an open, invigorating match would be reduced to an exasperating siege. It took England only six minutes to reassure us. Overath had been warned for a bad foul on Ball and now he committed another one on Moore, tripping the England captain as he turned away with the ball. Moore himself took the free kick and from forty yards out near the left touchline he flighted it beautifully towards the far post. Hurst, timing his run superbly to slip through the defence much as he had done against Argentina, struck a flawless header low inside Tilkowski's right-hand post. Moore held one arm aloft in a gladiator's salute whilst Hurst was smothered in congratulations. It was another reminder of the huge contribution West Ham were making to England's success in the World Cup.

There were many free kicks but a high percentage of them could be traced to the officiousness of the referee. When Dienst took Peters's name for shirt-pulling, Schnellinger placed the kick carefully for Seeler to outjump the English defence and force in a header. But the ball curved tamely into Banks's hands. Seeler was generally more damaging, both in the air and on the ground, and one through pass in front of Haller demanded an alert intervention from Banks.

At that stage, however, the more sustained aggression was still coming from England. Moore was showing wonderful control and assurance, driving up among his forwards, joining readily in the moves begun by Bobby Charlton. It was unfortunate that Charlton could not be in two places at once. Several of the attacks he conceived in deep positions cried out to be climaxed with his striking-power. Peters, who was his partner in much of the mid-field work, was also the one who went nearest to his cleanness of shot, but so far most of the West Ham man's attempts had been from a range that favoured the goalkeeper, even a goalkeeper like Tilkowski. Thus it was Hurst, with his instinct for being in the right place at the right time and his marvellous ability in the air, who was the most direct threat to the Germans. He proved it again when Cohen crossed the ball long from the right and he rose to deflect in another header which Tilkowski could only scramble outside his right-hand post. Ball turned the ball back into the goalmouth and the desperation was unmistakable as Overath came hurtling in to scythe it away for a corner.

With about ten minutes left of the first half the Germans, quite suddenly, put strenuous pressure on the English defence. They were using the gifted, resourceful Overath to create in mid-field, with Haller between him and the three striking forwards, Seeler, Held and Emmerich. Beckenbauer joined the link-men when he could afford to leave Bobby Charlton, but that was a luxury he rarely enjoyed until the Englishman's selfless running began to slow him down in the second half. Held was the most persistently dangerous of his team's forwards throughout the two hours of the match and it was his determination that began this period of German ascendancy before the interval. Ball and Cohen made the mistake of toying with him near the bye-line and Jack Charlton, who was maintaining the remarkable standard of his World Cup performances, had to come in with a prodigious sweeping tackle to rescue them. It cost Charlton a corner and the corner almost cost England a goal. The ball went to Overath and from twenty yards he drove it in fiercely at chest height. Banks beat it out and when Emmerich hammered it back from an acute angle the goalkeeper caught it surely.

After forty-two minutes Hunt had the kind of miss that was bound to revive comparisons with Greaves. Wilson headed into goal and Hurst again soared above everybody to steer the ball down to Hunt. But the Liverpool man came round behind it rather ponderously and by the time he forced in his left foot volley Tilkowski was in the way.

One of the features of the play was that defensive errors were occurring far more frequently than they had done in most previous games in the series. After Wilson's disaster, the Germans had been slightly the shakier but they could be excused their bewilderment as Bobby Charlton stroked a subtle pass into their midst. Peters could not quite reach it. Then, to stress the hectic, fluctuating pattern of the first half that was just ending, Overath had a bludgeoning twenty-yard shot turned brilliantly over the crossbar by Banks.

The rain came again at the beginning of the second half, falling like sequins in the sunshine. Charlton fell, too, rather more heavily, after being tackled by Schulz, but the claims for a penalty were understandably half-hearted. The first to assert himself was Ball, and it was no brief flourish. From then until the Cup was won he was the most impressive player on the field. In the first half he had worked with his usual inexhaustible energy but had never quite shaken off Schnellinger, who set out to track him everywhere. A redhead and a blond, they were invariably close enough to be advertising the same shampoo. But after the interval Schnellinger, who has held some of the most menacing forwards in the game, found Ball too much. The little man simply went on and on, becoming more impertinently skilful, more astonishingly mobile by the minute. However, in the long period of deadlock following the interval, when both sides were steadying their heartbeats after the tumult of that first three-quarters of an hour, even Ball's dynamism was not enough. Charlton was suffering for the way he had punished himself to mould England's pattern in the first half and, if Hurst was still outleaping the German defenders, Hunt lacked the pace or inventiveness to outwit them on the ground. Both defences were in command, England's closing on the opposition with the consuming vigour of red corpuscles, Germany's blocking the path to goal like a white wall in which the cement was hardening.

Fortunately for England, the wall was not as formidable as it looked. With thirteen minutes to go Ball won a corner, took it himself and saw the ball diverted to Hurst. His shot from the left was deflected across goal by a defender and Peters, strangely neglected by the Germans, came in to take the ball on the half-volley and sweep it in from four or five yards. It was another West Ham goal, and there were more to come.

With only four minutes remaining, England had a chance to crush their opponents. An inspired pass from Ball sent Hurst clear on the left. Bobby Charlton and Hunt were on his right and only Schulz stood between them and the goal. It was a three to one situation, something that should bring a goal at any level of football. But Hunt's pass was ill-timed, slackly delivered and too square. Bobby Charlton was committed to a hasty swipe and the result was a mess.

In the very last minute England were made to pay a cruel price for that carelessness. Jack Charlton was doubtfully penalised after jumping to a header and from the free kick Emmerich drove the ball through the line of English defenders. As it cannoned across the face of the goal Schnellinger appeared to play it with a hand, but the referee saw nothing illegal and Weber at the far post was able to score powerfully. The fact that these German defenders were crowding in on Banks indicates what a despairing effort this attack was. Such an injustice, coming just fifteen seconds from the end of the ninety minutes, would have broken most teams. But England, after a momentary show of disgust, galloped into extra time as if the previous hour-and-a-half had never happened. Appropriately, it was Ball who showed the way with a wonderful run and a twenty-yard shot which Tilkowski edged over the bar. Bobby Charlton followed with a low one that the goalkeeper pushed against his left-hand post.

The Germans looked weary but their swift breaks out of defence were still dangerous. A pass from Emmerich gave Held an opening and only unaccustomed slowness in controlling the ball enabled Stiles to clear. Held compensated for this by sprinting away from all challengers and turning the ball back invitingly across goal. But there was no one following up.

Having lost their lead through one controversial goal, England now regained it with another in the tenth minute of extra time. Ball made space for himself on the right and when the ball went across Hurst resolutely worked for a clear view of goal. His rising right-foot shot on the turn from ten yards hit the underside of the crossbar and when it bounced the England players appealed as one man for a goal. The referee spoke to the Russian linesman on the side away from the main stand and, after an agony of waiting, awarded a goal. The delayed action cheers shook the stadium.

But this match had not yet taken its full toll of our nerves. The hammer blow England had received at the end of the hour and a half was almost repeated in the final minute of extra time when Seeler lunged in and narrowly failed to make decisive contact with a headed pass by Held. And that was only the prelude to the climax. Nonchalantly breasting the ball down in front of Banks, Bobby Moore relieved a perilous situation and then moved easily away, beating man after man. Glancing up, he saw Hurst ten yards inside the German half and lifted the pass accurately to him. The referee was already looking at his watch and three England supporters had prematurely invaded the pitch as Hurst collected the ball on his chest. At first he seemed inclined to dawdle-out time. Then abruptly he went pounding through in the inside-left position, unimpeded by the totally spent German defenders, his only obstacle his own impending exhaustion. As Tilkowski prepared to move out Hurst summoned the remnants of his strength, swung his left foot and smashed the ball breathtakingly into the top of the net.

The scene that followed was unforgettable. Stiles and Cohen collapsed in a tearful embrace on the ground, young Ball turned wild cartwheels and Bobby Charlton dropped to his knees, felled by emotion. Within seconds the game was over and the players, ignoring the crippling weariness of a few minutes before, were hugging and laughing and crying with their manager, Alf Ramsey, and the reserves who must go through the rest of their lives with bitter-sweet memories of how it looked from the touchline. 'Ramsey, Ramsey,' the crowd roared and in his moment of vindication it was a tribute that no one could grudge him.

Eventually Moore led his men up to the Royal Box to receive the Jules Rimet trophy from the Queen and the slow, ecstatic lap of honour began. 'Ey-aye-addio, we've won the Cup,' sang the crowd, as Moore threw it in a golden arc above his head and caught it again. England had, indeed, won the Cup, won it on their merits, producing more determined aggression and flair than they had shown at any earlier stage of the competition. As hosts, they had closed their World Cup with a glorious bang that obliterated memories of its grey, negative beginnings. In such a triumph there could be no failures (the very essence of Ramsey's England was their team play), but if one had to name outstanding heroes they were Ball, Moore, Hurst and the brothers Charlton, the one exhibiting the greatness we always knew he had, the other attaining heights we never thought he could reach.

The Germans had been magnificent opponents and they deserved their own lap of honour at Wembley and the acclaim that awaited them at home. If they were in the West End of London that Saturday night they would have seen some interesting sights. The area was taken over for one great informal party. Some people said it was another VE night, but perhaps that was not the most tactful analogy. At the Royal Garden Hotel, where the English team was spending the night to unwind, there were visits from Harold Wilson and George Brown, who joined in the singing with the crowds outside. Hundreds of people were still dancing a Conga around Charing Cross Station at midnight and nearby, in Trafalgar Square, there was the ritual of leaping into the fountains. For most of the nation, however, it was enough to be bathed in euphoria.

from WORLD CUP '66 *1966*

England v. West Germany, 1970

HUGH MCILVANNEY

When the England party arrived, as inconspicuously as thirty people can, at the back door of the Motel Estancia in Léon shortly after one o'clock on the burning afternoon of Saturday June 13, Mrs Beckenbauer was with the wives of other German players by the swimming pool. Bobby Moore pleased the waiting photographers by walking across to talk with her for a few minutes. As Sir Alf Ramsey and Doctor Neil Phillips joined the trainers, Harold Shepherdson and Les Cocker, in ushering the rest of the group to their rooms around the pool, the scene conveyed a sense of routine calm. There was nothing to betray the private anxiety that already threatened English confidence. Anyone who studied Gordon Banks closely might have noticed that his colour was less than healthy. But the goalkeeper's complexion is never the kind that shines from the pages of holiday brochures and, given a natural expression that is almost orientally impassive, it was unlikely that a casual observer would pick him out from the bunch as a man whose personal distress could spread to leave millions feeling sick.

For an hour or two at least, we could concern ourselves with the historical and psychological factors that must always affect matches between teams from England and Germany. The ultimate question to be answered in the enfeebling midday heat of the following day was whether generations of history could be outweighed by a fortnight of current form. If the alarming inadequacies of England's qualifying performance against Czechoslovakia were compounded by the effects of travelling to a city that was about 1,000 feet higher and appreciably hotter than Guadalajara, there would be little chance of interrupting West Germany's confident advance towards the semi-finals of the World Cup. But when the English and the Germans meet on any competitive field echoes of previous battles, more distant and more bitter than the Wembley final of 1966, sound in the blood. This may be regrettable but it is inescapably real, and there is no doubt that the unique tensions that pulse beneath the surface of these occasions have done more damage to Germany than to England. The Germans carried into the quarter-final the knowledge that their only victory in previous full internationals with England was in Hanover in 1968. And then they needed an untidy, slightly fortuitous goal to beat an English side deliberately weakened in recognition of imminent exertions in the European Nations Cup. Of the other ten meetings, England had won nine and drawn one. The Germans, however defiantly they insisted that they were broken in the final of four years before by an illusory goal, would be obliged to ignore more omens than Julius Caesar on assassination day.

Yet when one encountered an economics adviser from Brazil who wanted to bet two hundred dollars on West Germany the only surprise was his name: Pedro MacGregor. MacGregors have been known to go in at worse than evens against the English, but they are rarely recruited from Brazil. The justification for the boldness of Pedro, and for the smiling, relaxed optimism that greeted anyone who drove through a wilderness of scrubland to visit the Germans at their spa hotel sixteen miles outside Léon, was in the contrasting courses Sir Alf Ramsey and Helmut Schoen had found themselves taking to a place in the last eight. Ramsey's men had come to Léon with the disconcerting awareness that their best display in Group Three matches brought a defeat. The achievement of losing only one goal was put in unimpressive perspective by their failure to score more than two, including one from a dubious penalty. In the meantime, West Germany, after making a melodrama of beating Morocco, had settled to a virile rhythm and thrashed Bulgaria and Peru. The Germans' scoring record was ten against four and, despite the irresolution of their opponents compared with those faced by England, the figures reflected a willingness to go after goals and a capacity for getting them.

The exuberant spirits of the German camp at Comanjilla were exemplified by Schoen's excuse for being late for a Press conference before the quarter-final. He had to change after being tossed into the thermal swimming pool by two of his more boisterous players. 'How would Sir Alf Ramsey take that?' we were asked archly by Wilfried Gerhardt, whose intelligence and unofficious competence as a Press officer raised him to the level of respected helper at the manager's right hand. Sitting under the palm trees bordering the pool, Schoen, a tall, bald man with a quiet articulate manner, admitted that he had come to Mexico with no more than 'an idea of a team', having had his preparation eroded by the bad winter and the extended league season that kept his squad in Europe until May 19. But he was satisfied that they were now a cohesive and vigorous force. By persuading Beckenbauer to operate with Overath in midfield, leaving Schnellinger or Schulz as sweeper, and convincing Muller that it was no disadvantage to play with the legendary Seeler, Schoen had given his side a solid base from which he could exploit the exciting form of his wingers, Libuda and Lohr, and the dramatic interventions (through carefully planned substitution) of Grabowski. The wingers' main function was to feed the aggressive appetite of Muller. Playing an unequivocal centre-forward game – with Seeler switching tirelessly between the middle three and the front line – Muller took seven goals to emerge as clearly the leading scorer in the Group matches. He had shared the same honour with Tostao of Brazil in the qualifying stages of the World Cup. Anyone tempted to think Muller merely adept at punishing weak defences had to consider his 138 goals in five years of German league football and especially his record-breaking thirty-eight in the 1969–70 season. In Germany they say there should be a law against him in the penalty area, where his thick, heavy-thighed physique does not stop him from demonstrating a swift, economical agility on the ground and in the air. His positioning is inspired and, if his control is moderate, he is one of that rare breed of apparently ordinary forwards who become giants when presented with the remotest chance of scoring a goal. The English strikers, who had found scoring about as easy as ski-ing on marmalade, were sure to envy Muller. It went without saying that the English defence would worry about his presence. Now, on the eve of the match, however, everyone was suddenly absorbed by the likelihood of another man's absence.

Gordon Banks did not take part in a light training session at the Guanajuato Stadium on the Saturday afternoon and Ramsey admitted that the goalkeeper had stomach trouble. He was, in fact, suffering from the complaint described, with grim facetiousness, as Montezuma's Revenge, a condition that usually brings bouts of nausea and the need to sprint for the lavatory with exhausting frequency. The illness must have hurt Neil Phillips almost as much as Banks. Having protected the players with unremitting care through nearly two months in Latin America, guarding them against every foreseeable hazard, down to the ice that arrived automatically in their soft drinks, the doctor found the enemy's first serious victory flattening one of the most vital men in the party. Phillips was not likely to endorse the views of those at home in England who suspected a plot to put Banks out of the match, least of all the theory of one well-known figure who muttered that the CIA had an interest in keeping the Brazilians happy. But he could be forgiven for cursing his luck. There seemed a chance that it had changed when Banks passed a good night and rose on Sunday morning to do a little light practice with a ball. He was officially in the team when the players assembled for the pre-match meeting in Ramsey's room. While the meeting was in progress, however, the goalkeeper suddenly took a turn for the worse again and it became clear that he could not play. With less than an hour to go before the party left the motel to travel the few hundred yards to the stadium, Peter Bonetti learned he was about to play in a World Cup for the first time. It was a bitter irony that an ambition so long cherished should be realised in such unfavourable circumstances. Perhaps some players would prefer to be thrust unexpectedly into that kind of challenge, without time to brood on its implications. But it is reasonable to suppose that most would benefit from a more gradual psychological preparation, from having time to cleanse the shock and personal excitement of the promotion from their minds, leaving their concentration keen and uncluttered. No one could fail to sympathise with Bonetti as he lined up under the high, hard sun with a number 12 on his back, knowing he was the only one of the twenty-two who had never before experienced the unique pressures of the World Cup. Five of the England men beside him had worn the same red colours at Wembley in the final of 1966. None of them had any doubts about Bonetti's talent – he was by all acceptable standards of comparison among the best half-dozen goalkeepers in the tournament – but they could not escape a slight twinge of uneasiness over the absence of Banks' relaxed, rather shambling figure. Through the early matches of the competition, indeed as early as the short tour of Colombia and Ecuador, he had confirmed that his gifts were unimpaired, still without equal in the game. It was simply impossible to believe that anyone in the history of football had ever done the goalkeeper's job better. And beyond his great worth as a member of the team, Banks was a potent talisman. True, his finest save, the miraculous interception of Pelé's header at the Jalisco Stadium, had not averted defeat but there was a persistent feeling that this big man, apparently capable of catching mortar shells, could make his side nearly invulnerable. Banks shares with Moore the remarkable distinction of drawing from fellow internationalists the effusive tributes that normally come from star-struck fans. And Moore himself gets about as close as he ever can to rhapsodising when he talks of the goalkeeper. On their way to keep a date with Pelé after the Brazil match, Moore and Bobby Charlton agreed that they had never known anyone in football quite like Banks. 'He is the only keeper I know who never wants to play in another position, even when we are having a little practice game,' said Charlton. 'Most of them are desperate to play out of goal, to show you what they can do on the wing or knock in a few goals. They often fancy themselves on the ball. But Banksie just wants to stay in there and let you try to beat him. He would have you shooting at him all day. We all lined up on the edge of the area this morning and hammered shots at him and we couldn't put one past him. He was unbeatable. He loves that. If one does get by him, even in a little kick around like that, he gets needled with himself. Starts muttering and trying to work out what went wrong. He thinks you have no right to score against him.' The Germans had managed it twice at Wembley four years earlier but they were unlikely to be depressed by the thought that now, as the screeching of their supporters' klaxons became louder and the red, black and yellow flags isolated the Union Jacks on the terraces, Banks lay in a darkened room along the road. He would follow the match by means of a delayed transmission on television, trailing far behind its breathless fluctuations.

There was a stuttering start when the referee had to replace the unsatisfactory ball with which the Germans kicked off. Less than a minute had been played before the change but it was time enough for Hottges to give Lee some harsh treatment. The discomfort inflicted on Newton immediately afterwards was more legitimate. Lohr's speed, used first individually and then as the cutting-edge of a one-two manoeuvre, twice left the full-back straining in pursuit. Moore's alertness doused the threat in the second situation. The England captain was giving instant evidence of his commanding form and when Muller pushed the ball through his legs, obliging Labone to clear, one felt that the German should receive some sort of prize for his nerve. There seemed no likelihood of any other reward for Muller. When he took to drifting away from the spearhead position, withdrawing or going wide in an effort to pull the central defenders out of their places, he found a wary response. Labone stayed back to block the way through the middle, alternating with Moore in picking up Muller as he came within menacing range. With Newton repeating the pattern of previous matches, swiftly overcoming a nervous beginning to play with assured brilliance, the defence soon asumed a look of solidity. England, as usual, had a minimum of four men in the midfield and if this inevitably left the front line under-manned there was obvious compensation in the subduing effect on the German builders, Overath, Beckenbauer and Seeler. Harassed by the vigorous mobility of Mullery and Ball and the swooping interventions of Charlton, they had little opportunity to develop the measured passing moves that should have fed the wingers and Muller. They might have been swamped entirely if Peters had equalled the efficiency of those alongside him. But he was again a lifeless imitation of himself, questioning with every tentative gesture the wisdom of Ramsey's insistence on using him in all of England's games. Even the sight of Hurst at his most effective could do nothing for Peters. Indeed the first of many breaks marvellously engineered by Hurst was ruined the moment Peters joined him. There was a faint stirring of hope when the familiar slim shape slipped, almost unnoticed, behind Maier in anticipation of Newton's inswinging centre. The goalkeeper, possibly distracted, dropped the ball but recovered it. With that chance gone, Peters sank back into vagueness.

The fact that Lee was the least impressive of the other England players ensured that the burden on Hurst was huge. Still unable to reproduce the electric aggression of his home form in these crudely alien conditions, Lee was permitting his frustration to express itself in petulance, complaining about collisions he would hardly acknowledge if things were going well. He may have been entitled to grumble, however, when he had his name taken following an incident with Maier. Lee closed with Maier after Hurst headed Charlton's centre across goal and the goalkeeper went down as if he had been hit with an axe. Later the forward claimed he had merely patted Maier teasingly on the cheek. If so, the referee, Angel Coerezza from Argentina, made certain the joke misfired. Before the match many of us had felt, remembering 1966, that there was an unnecessary risk in asking an Argentine to be referee. Apart from the open wounds left by the circumstances of England's victory over Germany in that World Cup final, it had to be recalled that most Argentines remained convinced that they would have beaten the

English at an earlier stage and gone on to win the Cup if their captain, Rattin, had not been wrongfully ordered from the field. That the referee who dismissed Rattin was a German added to a welter of ironies calculated to make the head reel. And all this was made more disturbing by Coerezza's performance in the Aztec Stadium the previous Thursday, when he allowed the host nation to ease into the quarter-finals by awarding them a penalty which neutrals present agreed was one of the most ludicrous they had ever seen. Fortunately, he was showing no such malleability here. Some briefly suspected that he was being influenced by the Mexican support for Germany when he reacted favourably to Overath's histrionic allegations against Ball and gave a free kick. But that misconception was rapidly corrected when Muller, who had re-treated far into his own half to foul the same English player, had his name noted under Lee's in Coerezza's book. Ball was irritating the opposition in more ways than one at this point, once almost getting a destructive pass through to Hurst. Schnellinger and Overath combined to give Seeler scope for retaliation, and for a change the old warhorse found himself free of Mullery's smothering presence. But the shot was shut out by Moore. A long ball from Schnellinger soared over Labone's leap and set Muller chasing but the ball ran too far left and, though a chip by Beckenbauer did give the forward a shot, he had still to do his first real damage. A fairly simple punching save above the heads of Seeler and Muller was the only notable effort required of Bonetti so far. Maier, admittedly, had not been called upon to be much more energetic but there was far greater substance in the attacks that did reach his area. Hurst, collecting and shielding the ball with flawless economy and aplomb in the tightest positions, constantly alarmed the German defenders. The memory of his three goals against them in 1966 seemed to have doubled his flow of adrenalin. It was difficult to think of any other forward in the tournament, apart from Tostao and, of course, Pelé, who could have achieved half as much in advanced isolation – and even Tostao rarely functioned as far ahead of the main body of his attack. With half an hour played, England were in control and gaining the confidence to back Hurst by sending other players through from behind, as Ramsey had promised they would do in the sudden-death state of the competition. Ball climaxed one progres-sive dribble by edging the ball right to Charlton, who promptly swung at it. When Hottges put his foot firmly in the way both crumpled. The referee awarded Charlton a foul but it was a doubtful one.

German satisfaction at surviving that free kick without cost did not last long. In the thirty-first minute England took a deserved lead with a magnificent goal. The build-up began when Cooper, deep and wide in his own left-back position, pushed the ball inside to Mullery. Having sent it forward to Lee, Mullery moved on to a short return in time to hear Newton's intelligent call from far out on the right, near the halfway line. Mullery's left foot carried the ball crisply in the air across the width of the field for Newton to bring it down and stride ahead. As the full-back did so, Mullery was already committed to a surging diagonal run and he met the angled centre as it fell on the edge of the six-yard area opposite Maier's left-hand post. Mullery said later that all the time he was running he was waiting to be blocked or diverted. 'I couldn't believe they would let me run as far into their box without interference. I kept thinking, "Any second now I'll be clattered".' But he was not and as the ball dropped his right instep made perfect contact ('I knew I'd got it just right – it was a great feeling') to sweep it high past Maier's left shoulder. It was Mullery's first goal in over thirty internationals for England. He could not have wished for a better or more important one.

Muller, finding Moore's regular attentions too much for him, was inclined occasionally to push like a Japanese wrestler but when the Englishman uncharacteristically complained the referee advised him to get on with the game. Overath received a similar admonition after voicing his opinion of a free kick given for a foul by Libuda on Cooper. It almost took the misdemeanour to remind us that Libuda was on the pitch. Cooper, maintaining the excellence of his performances in Guadalajara, made it hard to realise that this was the winger who had wrought so much havoc in the Group Four matches. Seeing Beckenbauer reduced to a succession of long, meaningless shots and Lohr become steadily more innocuous on the left-wing, we were forced to conclude that the weight of history was going to prove stronger than recent form. Seeler, with the sweat glistening on his bald head, was still pumping his short, thick legs all over the field and the great Overath continued to probe hopefully for weaknesses, like a doctor struggling with a difficult diagnosis. Vogts was fast and enormously aggressive from full-back. Having seen his inaccurate drive needlessly headed back by Labone, he stayed upfield to meet the corner with a dangerous header. But there was no concealing the apprehension that had spread through the German team. Their main tactic now was to lift long speculative passes forward from midfield in the manner of a quarter-back in American football. They did not trust themselves to keep possession for a controlled, concerted assault. The shouts of 'Uwe, Uwe' that had urged on Seeler and his men in the first half hour were significantly muted before the two sides headed gratefully for the comparative cool of the dressing rooms at the interval.

When they came out again both teams applauded the announcement that Bobby Charlton was establishing a record by playing his 106th match for England, one more than Billy Wright's total. The other information conveyed by the public address system was that Schulz was replacing Hottges. Predictably, however, Schulz lined up in the middle of the defence, concentrating on Hurst. Fichtel, who had been given the unpleasant job of marking Hurst in the first half, switched to left-back to fill the gap made by the departure of Hottges. Schnellinger's responsibilities were still mainly those of sweeper. With Moore usually managing to repel Muller before he could move close to Bonetti's goal, Labone was similarly free for general policing duties in the England defence. Mullery, having another of the faultlessly reliable matches that made the World Cup a personal triumph for him, gave first priority to watching Seeler but used his overspill of vitality to drive on the English forwards. Their healthy urgency appeared to have carried England into the semi-finals of the World Cup when they scored another goal after only five minutes of the second half. Moore dispossessed Seeler and passed to Ball, who steered the ball to Hurst. As Hurst pressed through powerfully in the inside-right position, Newton made a furious run on the outside, checking momentarily and then accelerating fiercely again to outflank the defence. Just when it seemed that Hurst might hold the ball a fraction of a second too long he passed with perfect timing and Newton, from near the bye-line, clipped a sharp centre just beyond the far post. Peters, rediscovering his gift for materialising as an executioner, forced the ball past Maier. Some British Pressmen stood up in the stands, faced the German supporters and shouted 'Auf Wiedersehen'. At the time it struck us as a logical if slightly offensive comment. But strange things were about to happen.

The Germans were in urgent need of stimulation and Helmut Schoen was lucky in having a man at hand who could provide it. Jurgen Grabowski had already earned the reputation of being the most influential substitute in the World Cup. Schoen had made a habit of introducing him at crucial points and he had never failed to galvanise the side. This match was no exception. As soon as Grabowski took over from Libuda, in the fifty-eighth minute, the course of the game was profoundly altered. The hard, low shot he struck immediately from the right was only a hint of what was to come. Cooper stopped that effort but Grabowski's runs became increasingly troublesome as the back tired in the heat. Whereas Libuda had a standard technique for evading tackles, his replacement exhibited endless variety, going past defenders on either side with killing fluency. Enlivened by Grabowski's example, the whole German team began to generate a mounting rhythm. Beckenbauer, always at his magical best when riding a tide created by others, emerged excitingly from his detached mood of the first hour. His best shot so far cannoned off Moore's head before going wide. But there was hardly more than twenty minutes left. Surely it was too much to expect the Germans to penetrate the strongest defence in the world, not once but twice, in such a short time. It would have been, if that defence had not suddenly revealed a mortifying weakness. Bonetti, so long insulated from the pressures of his unique situation by England's overall superiority, was now asked a relatively simple question. His response was fatally hesitant. He was like a boy who goes into an examination knowing every answer, then sits staring at the hypnotic blankness of the paper, forcing his mind to focus and his hand to move only when it is too late. Beckenbauer's goal in the sixty-eighth minute, the goal that transformed this match and perhaps this World Cup, was the result of a shot that would not have given the goalkeeper a moment of anxiety on a normal day. Beckenbauer was a little fortunate to find room for it in the first place. He had tried one from short of the eighteen-yard line on the right wing and seen Lee fall in pain as he took the ball between the legs. The rebound went to the German but when he swerved to his right, outside Mullery and into the extreme corner of the England penalty area, he seemed to be a negligible threat. Both Lee and Mullery recalled afterwards that they stopped worrying when he turned away from the target, especially when they were aware of him shooting early from that inauspicious angle. To us on the sidelines it appeared that the right-foot shot was a reflex at the end of the run, something to round it off rather than a determined, optimistic attempt at scoring. 'He shot because there was nothing better to do,' said a Brazilian in the Press stand. Given the angle and the unfrightening speed of the ball, those accustomed to the excellence of Bonetti's goalkeeping waited for him to take two brisk steps to the side and pick it up or at least fall firmly on it. Instead, he dived in a slow arc over the ball and left it to travel on into the side of his net. The impact of that goal was immense. Apart from encouraging the Germans to hope that their rally could give them more than an honourable exit, it hit the English with the full chilling realisation of what it meant to be without Banks. 'With a two-goal lead, you would have felt you could let them come and shoot it at Banksie, that he could have held them out on his own,' one of the players said later. That blissful illusion of impregnability merely created yet another burden for Bonetti to bear on the most unpleasant afternoon of his career.

The alarm that was being kindled in England was not stifled by Ramsey's decision to substitute Bell for Charlton within a minute of the goal. Bell had been warming up on the touchline before the blow but seeing one of their most feared enemies withdrawn at that point could only raise the Germans' morale, persuading some of them that they could detect panic in the opposition. Charlton himself was not a happy man when he reached the bench. 'They're pissing about too early,' he said as he sat down.

However, Bell did make a spirited entrance. Taking a pass from Moore, he struck a low shot that Maier saved and then, served by Ball, broke on the right to precipitate one of the crucial moments of the match. Hurst dived brilliantly to meet Bell's low centre at the near post, leaving Schulz and Maier flailing around his ankles, and flicked his header for the other side of the goal. It looked guaranteed to go in or at worst bounce back off the upright (Lee confessed that he waited, hypnotised, for it to come off the post, instead of following up) but at the last second it bobbled over the bye-line. English hearts dropped further when Muller, finding himself one-to-one with Newton, beat him and steadied for the shot. But when it came, Bonetti dropped skilfully on the ball.

There was no time to savour the relief. With eighty minutes played, Peters was belatedly taken off and Hunter shunted into the competition for the first time. That Ramsey ignored the possible implications of an injury already suffered by Newton, who was on the ground when the change was made, indicated that he was extremely anxious to introduce Hunter in place of an attacking player. His idea, presumably, was that the most vigorous challenger in British football should win the ball from the Germans in midfield, above all from the ubiquitous Grabowski, and hustle them out of their growing confidence. The idea soon looked sick. Hunter had been on the field only a few seconds when England lost another goal. The substitution apparently extended a period of disruption in the defence and there was a hectic flurry of abortive clearances on the right-hand side of the penalty box. At last the ball fell conveniently free in front of Labone and he seemed sure to lift it out of harm's way. In fact, he swung at it hastily and slid it straight to Schnellinger. The reaction was a quick, left-footed cross aimed high towards the far edge of the six-yard area. There Seeler slipped behind Mullery – into a position that may have been offside – and he leapt for a typical backheader. He did well to make solid contact and could not be choosey about where he placed the ball, obviously being content to guide it into the mouth of the goal. The generalised menace was made murderously specific by Bonetti, who stranded himself in the no-man's land half-way between his line and Seeler. The ball lobbed over the goalkeeper and under the bar. England felt they were the victims of something close to a black miracle. The Germans, who had pushed them into extra-time with a late goal in the Wembley final, were doing so again. Indeed they almost did worse. In the nine minutes that remained (there were barely two after the equaliser in 1966) Beckenbauer's left-foot shot swept just wide of a post and Lohr's high header from an Overath free-kick was sufficiently near to make a few Englishmen close their eyes.

The Germans surge carried over into extra-time, led first by Lohr and then by Beckenbauer, whose drive from twenty-five yards was touched over by Bonetti. There followed three corners in quick succession, five in two or three minutes, and the English wariness was blatant. Grabowski was veering and spurting like a power-boat among paddle steamers and even a fresh Hunter, though pounding around strongly, could not subdue him. No one was more distressed now than Labone, but he did manage to move upfield for a shot from Bell's low cross. A marvellously persistent run in on the bye-line by Lee brightened England's prospects a little more but once the change of ends had put Bonetti back in his unlucky goal pessimism swiftly took over again. A centre from Ball that went through Maier's hands should have brought England more than a corner. Another centre, this time high and diagonal from Grabowski deep on the German right wing, should have brought England less than defeat. But this unsubtle stroke killed them. As the ball fell beyond the far post, Lohr rose and forced the tired Newton to head across goal. Muller, so ineffective for so long, had started to move towards the far post but now, with spontaneous perception, he spun round and overtook the ball on its return journey. He was unhindered as he hoisted himself off the ground for a muscular volley. The cameras caught Bonetti in a helpless pose that might have been mistaken for supplication. There were eleven minutes left and England filled most of them with furious aggression. Lee jockeyed the ball round Schnellinger on the bye-line and pushed it across to Hurst to score but the goal was inexplicably disallowed. Lee was not off-side and we had seen no foul on Schnellinger. Argument being pointless, England resumed their assault. Mullery, hammering the ball on the run, saw it rise inches too high and Ball, coming in on Hurst's downward header, could not keep his shot from going wide. Appropriately, Newton, who had contributed much to his side's two goals, provided the last flourish by galloping on to Ball's pass and blasting the ball towards Maier. The goalkeeper was beaten but the ball stayed fractionally outside his posts.

So history had repeated itself, with an agonising twist for England. Here it was Beckenbauer who rolled over ecstatically on the turf, much as Ball and Stiles had done at Wembley. Here the German supporters brought their flags and their jubilant klaxons crowding into the centre circle. It was for England to find consolation in the memory of that first hour and of some splendid performances by their players. And to reflect on what might have been, what must have been if Gordon Banks, or for that matter if the real Peter Bonetti had been in goal. . . .

from WORLD CUP '70 *1970*

Rapid Bucharest v. Tottenham Hotspur, 1971

HUNTER DAVIES

I looked for crowds all the way to the ground, but there were none. We saw one supporter, carrying a red banner, who waved and held up four fingers to the coach – meaning Rapid were going to beat Spurs 4–0 and therefore win the tie. It was the same sign the players had had since Monday whenever people saw them in the street, especially during the training session. As at Nantes, every fan was good at spotting Chivers, with Peters a close second. Football is the national sport in Rumania and every match is televised live. They have a daily sports paper, like *L'Equipe*, which is more than Britain has. I'd met their reporter at the training sessions and he knew the name of every Spurs first team player.

We arrived at the ground at 12.30, just an hour before kick-off, and even there the streets leading to it were deserted. I thought perhaps there had been a mistake. The kick-off had originally been going to be two. Now it was one thirty. Perhaps it had been changed again. Someone said perhaps the match was over. It felt eerie, arriving at a huge deserted stadium. The players seemed on edge and keyed up. With every match they play, home and abroad, they're accustomed to crawling through dense traffic, often with police escorts to keep back the crowds.

77

At the players' entrance, a crowd of uniformed police stood waiting, silently. We went inside the stadium, which was like a grand but rather old fashioned hotel. There were long corridors full of large vases and potted plants. The players couldn't believe the dressing-room. It was exactly like someone's front parlour, only larger. There was a green carpet in the centre (the first dressing-room I'd ever seen with a carpet), and in the middle of that a small circular table with a potted plant on top. At the edge of the carpet was a row of elderly chairs arranged round the walls. It looked as if the room had been cleared ready for folk dancing. There was no sign of showers or lavatories. Someone finally found them, across the corridor and further down, two showers, neither with soap. In a corner of the dressing-room was a pile of faded towelling dressing gowns, presumably for players to put on when they padded down the corridor for a shower.

Having inspected the dressing-room, everyone went back along the endless corridors and down a huge tunnel leading to the pitch. The tunnel was even bigger than Wembley's, big enough to drive a couple of lorries down. In the middle of it ran a narrow wired-in cage which led out onto the pitch itself. This was to protect the players, before and after their march into the lion's den.

The stadium still looked deserted, till we got out onto the pitch and were greeted by a blast of kettle drums and shouts. There could only have been a couple of thousand Rapid fans, all crowded into a strip of the terraces beside the tunnel, but they went mad, shouting, screaming, roaring. The Press had to go across the pitch to get to their box on the opposite side and they too were screamed at as they crossed. Geoffrey Green, as ever, rose to the bait and waved his fist back at them, which led to even louder roars.

Back in the dressing-room, the players stood around, putting off the time before getting undressed. It was very quiet. It wasn't just the strangeness of the room and the stadium, but nervousness. It was the sort of silence which nobody remarked on, being too aware of it. Ralph Coates was the first ready. He stood in the middle of the carpet, doing exercises. The bump could be seen on his thigh where his ham string injury still hadn't completely cleared up. Mike England, with his ordinary clothes on as he wasn't playing, took down his trousers and bent over while the doctor gave him an injection, a pain killer, to help his infected toe. Cyril Knowles, the biggest fearty in the team when it comes to injections, looked the other way.

Bill was going in and out, busying himself but not talking. Johnny Wallis went round giving out kit and bandages. Eddie silently rubbed oils into Gilly's body and massaged Steve's legs. The five reserves got changed into their playing gear, going through all their usual rituals of rubbing and massaging, elaborately stretching their socks, testing their leg muscles, even though the chances were against them playing. When they were ready, they sat huddled in a corner in their blue canvas tracksuits. They whispered and nudged each other. Joe Kinnear *looked* like a reserve, hunched and rather self-conscious, not the big strapping, self-assured star who'd begun the season.

'No complaints?' said Johnny, half to himself as he went round asking everyone if they wanted anything else, more bandages, tie-ups, more oils. Nobody wanted anything. 'I can't get over it.'

Three of the reserves in the corner suddenly started giggling – Terry Naylor, Joe Kinnear and Jimmy Pearce. Mike, standing silently in his good clothes beside them, asked what the joke was. 'What does a midget do in a football team,' said Terry Naylor. 'He takes short corners.' All three of them collapsed, unable to stop giggling. All the players, the real players, the ones who definitely knew they would have to go out there and perform, stared at them blankly, unable to take in even the stupidness of the joke.

'Right lads,' said Eddie Baily, clapping his hands. 'Fifteen minutes to go.' It was time for Bill's pep talk but he seemed to have disappeared from the dressing-room.

'I want you to go over the top, get the bayonet right in and twist it.' It was Eddie's usual wartime metaphors. They exchanged looks behind his back.

'Where's all the chewing gum,' said Martin Peters, coming back from a short walk to the lavatory.

'I put twenty packets on that table,' said Johnny Wallis, pointing to the centre of the room. The little table was now covered with his medicine and equipment. The potted plant had been placed carefully on the carpet underneath.

'Yeah,' said a voice. 'And seventeen of them are in Cyril's pocket.'

Everyone was ready. Chivers, Gilzean and Ray Evans, the last to get changed, had had their ankles strapped and were now stretching their feet, easing themselves into their boots. Bill reappeared, holding a piece of paper. He'd got the team sheet. Earlier he'd been saying that three of their regular players wouldn't be playing. Now he'd got the news that Dumitru, Rapid's best player, had made a recovery and was in the team after all. He hurried on to tell everyone that the tactics would still be the same, 4-4-2 once again. In the midfield, the two on the outside would have to take their winger leaving the two in the middle to mark their two front runners. When a midfield man went for the winger, the full back had to give him cover, and vice versa. Pete Collins, playing centre half in place of England, was told to have no worries. He would be able to beat Dumitru in the air. Bill went over each person's role quickly, player by player, except for Pat Jennings. Chivers and Gilzean were told they would have to work very hard, to keep at it, even on their own.

'Above all,' said Bill finally, when there was only five minutes to go, looking up and round at everyone, 'I want no retaliation. You've got to keep your tempers. It'll be hard, but you'll be penalised if you step out of line. So no retaliation.'

There was a knock at the door. It was opened to reveal the Italian referee standing there, spruce and shining. He didn't come in and made no attempt to inspect anyone's boots. He asked for the captain. Martin Peters came forward. The referee shook his hand, still standing in the doorway, and then turned and walked away. There was a pause of about ten seconds, while everybody looked at each other, then a whistle blew in the corridor and everybody started talking, banging, slapping, wishing each other as usual the best of luck and shaking hands. At the doorway Bill's face came to light and life as he threw off his twitches and his expression of panic.

Rapid were already on the pitch. They'd been warming up for almost twenty minutes, to the delight of the crowd, which now numbered about ten thousand. Their noise was deafening, yet nine-tenths of the vast stadium was empty. The terraces were uncovered and were simply layers and layers of concrete, going up miles into the sky. When the weather gets bad in Rumania the football season breaks for the mid-winter till the spring thaw begins.

I sat on the bench beside Bill and Eddie and Broderick, the Thos Cook's man who'd taken it upon himself to help Johnny Wallis the trainer with the kit. The five substitutes in blue sat at the other end, away from Bill and Eddie. Some of them had put cotton wool in their ears, knowing that sitting beside Eddie in a match can lead to deafness.

Eddie was up and shouting from the first kick, screaming at the ref for fouls he'd spotted. Bill just hung his head in silent fury. Five minutes later Bill himself was on his feet, tearing towards the touchline, shouting and screaming. Gilly had been brutally and openly punched in the kidneys by the Rumanian number 4, unseen by the referee who was at least fifty yards away.

As they stood shouting, ignored by the referee, it happened again. This time the number 4 took a running jump at Gilly, going through the air and bringing both his upturned boots down against Gilly's legs. It had again been completely unprovoked, yet once again, Gilzean did nothing in reply.

Slowly, Gilly shook his head and moved out of reach of the number 4, shrugging his arms to Bill on the touchline, signalling there was nothing he could do. A younger, less experienced player would certainly have retaliated. Yet Gilzean, miraculously, had just stood there, taking it.

Bill and Eddie were hysterical. I thought they'd both have heart attacks. The powerlessness of their position was making them froth at the mouth. It had been Gilly's brilliant back header in the first minute of the match at Tottenham which had led to their downfall. There had obviously been instructions this time to get Gilly.

Play moved on, the number 4 had to run for the ball, and Gilly escaped, limping. Bill and Eddie collapsed back on the bench, their heads in their hands, moaning.

Spurs soaked up all the Rumanian pressure, slowly but surely, and all their fouls and kicks. Chivers was being brutally kicked, on and off the ball, but being bigger and stronger than Gilly, he was managing to shrug them off, so far.

The Rumanians created several good chances, only to be saved by Jennings, Collins and Ray Evans, which made their policy of fouling seem all the pettier. If they'd concentrated on playing they might even have scored. Their policy of physical aggression betrayed cowardice, not confidence.

Spurs at last managed a good move, but Coates shot wide. Rapid had the best opportunity of all. Ene picked up a terrible back pass by Perryman and was through, with only Jennings to beat. Pat dived at his feet and Ray Evans cleared the rebound. There was no score at half-time.

Rapid had had more chances, but had wasted them. Spurs had taken everything thrown at them and were becoming more confident all the time. By keeping their heads, they'd given nothing away. Gilly was limping but worst of all Perryman had badly injured his shoulder. He'd come off for a few minutes midway through the half, after a bad tackle on him had resulted in an awkward fall. The doctor had treated him on the touchline. A bone had become dislocated in his shoulder, but had gone back into place. Steve had insisted on going back on, though he must have been in considerable pain.

In the dressing-room at half-time, Bill and the doctor examined Steve. Terry Naylor was told he was going on instead. Terry left almost immediately, going out on the field to warm up. Johnny and

Eddie attended to all the other bruises. Gilly and Collins had both been kicked in the chest and needed their ribs strapped.

Bill said they were doing well, keeping cool, but they must keep the game even quieter and give nothing away. He told them to watch out for the quick one-twos near the penalty area. Several times Rapid had got through that way. He told Ralph to head for the wings, to give himself space along the touchline, beating his man when he could, but without losing the ball.

Bill's criticisms were mild, nothing compared with what both he and Eddie had been shouting from the bench in the heat of the game, unheard by the players on the pitch. Peters, Coates and Chivers had all come in for unprintable abuse as each in turn made some mistake or failed to take a chance which Bill thought they should have done. Eddie particularly had kept up non-stop screams at Chivers, shouting as usual that he wasn't trying hard enough. Bill finished by complimenting them on not retaliating.

In the second half, Spurs gradually got on top. It became obvious that Rapid knew they could never score four goals, and their tackles and fouls became even worse. Eventually Gilly had to go off and was replaced by Jimmy Pearce. It was Pearce who got the first and vital goal of the match. Chivers was put through by Pratt but the goalkeeper blocked his shot. Jimmy hooked in the rebound.

Once again Jimmy had come on as a substitute late in a game and scored the vital goal. But this time he went off just as suddenly, sent off, after only twelve minutes on the field. He got into a tussle with their number 2, out on the wing. They both aimed blows at each other, though neither connected. Jimmy's swing was a joke punch, ending it by scratching his head, hoping the referee thought he really had only been scratching his head. Immediately they were surrounded by other players, all tugging and pushing at each other. Bill and Eddie joined in from the touchline, screaming and shouting at the referee, an action which could have had them severely penalised in an English League game. Jimmy was given the red card, and so was their number two, and both left the field.

As a piece of brutality it had been nothing compared with what had gone before. Neither Jimmy nor the Rapid player had been vicious, simply squaring up to one another. But Jimmy had made the mistake of appearing to retaliate, using threatening behaviour which until then the Spurs players had avoided, despite continual provocation. After that the Rapid players kept up non-stop fouling to the end, knowing they hadn't a chance. Cyril Knowles eventually got in his bit of retaliatory fouling and had his name taken. In all, three Rapid players had their names taken, plus the one sent off. The worst, and most farcical, incident concerned their eccentric goal-keeper, Raducanu, after Jimmy's goal. He was so furious, maintaining Chivers had been off side, that he ran a good thirty yards and threw the ball viciously at the referee, scoring a direct hit on his back. Amazingly, he wasn't sent off but merely cautioned. As usually happens in a match full of fouls the referee appears to turn a blind eye to the home team, as if he fears the crowd will storm the barriers and lynch him. Where we were sitting, two bottles did come over the wire fence behind us and smash into pieces at our feet.

But the referee did award a penalty to Spurs, when Coates was brought down from behind. Martin Peters, the penalty expert, missed it. The goalie had moved before the ball was kicked, which is illegal, and had come a good couple of yards out from his line, but all the same, Martin's shot went weakly past the left hand post.

Just before the end, Chivers scored, a brilliant and typical individual Chivers' shot. Up until that moment, Eddie's screams had been constant and terrifying, shouting that Chivers was letting the team down, the club down, he wouldn't have him in his side, he was useless, etc. Eventually, Chivers himself had heard some of the oaths when he came near. He could be seen quite clearly swearing back at Eddie.

Chivers beat two men by swerving out to the edge of the penalty area and shrugging off their brutal tackles, then he began to home in on goal. Almost on the goal line, he shot, scoring from the narrowest of angles. Everyone on the bench was in the air, cheering and clapping the best and only piece of individual play in the whole sordid match.

The subs immediately all turned to Eddie, watching him, wondering what he had to say now. After all his terrible abuse, Martin had done it once again, proving Eddie wrong.

'The bugger,' said Eddie, sitting down, mopping his brow in a state of bemused hysteria. It was almost as if he couldn't stop his abuse, as if he still wasn't aware that the object of his hatred had produced a piece of genius. Slowly he came to his feet again and ran to the line, clapping and cheering, shouting to Martin that he'd done it, he was brilliant, he was great. Martin obviously heard every word this time but he studiously ignored him, deliberately turning his back on him. Eddie sat down, drained but satisfied.

When the final whistle blew, Bill and Eddie ran forward onto the pitch to help the team off, putting their arms round them, congratulating, commiserating, asking if they were in pain. In the dressing-room, there was a controlled but excited noise, not the excitement which a brilliantly played match would have brought, just a general loud noise as everyone in turn said it was the worst team they'd ever played against.

'Now be careful with the Press,' said Bill Nicholson, going to the middle of the room. 'They're bound to ask you what it was like. Just be careful what you say.' There was a pause as everyone stopped talking and listened.

'But as far as I'm concerned,' Bill continued, 'it was the dirtiest team I've seen in thirty years. If this is European football, I'd rather have a Combination match. Diabolical. I've never seen such dirty fouls.'

Even the players were a bit taken aback. There was nothing anyone of them could possibly have said which was stronger than that. (Later, when the first pressman, Bernard Joy, was allowed in Bill repeated the same remarks – that Rapid was the dirtiest team he'd ever seen. Nobody bothered to try to get quotes from the players, not when they had a manager saying such things to them, all on the record.)

Bill went round inspecting the injuries as the players began to undress. As they each padded back, wet and exhausted, with their dressing gowns wrapped round them, the old fashioned parlour turned into a hospital casualty ward.

'What about that miss then Ralph,' Bill said to Coates, going back to his normal self, unable to forget the chances missed despite all the achievements.

'What?' said Ralph, obviously hurt. 'What about the penalty I got you? You forget that, don't you.'

'Never mind,' said Bill, smiling, playfully punching him. He went to the middle of the room and told everyone he was proud of them. That was the phrase he used: proud of them. The players looked amazed. It was the first time he'd used such words all season.

'Yes, I'm proud of you. You showed them how to do it. You didn't retaliate. We've had the last laugh. Well done.'

Steve Perryman, in his street clothes, had his arm in a sling. He and the doctor had missed a lot of the second half, staying in the dressing-room to attend to his injury. He'd been given a pain killing injection, but the pain was still there.

Peter Collins carefully unwrapped the plaster and strapping from his ribs. In the second half, he'd been punched in the stomach. Phil Beal was being treated for a calf injury. Knowles had an ankle injury, plus a knee injury and he'd also been kicked in the arse behind the referee's back, which he said had annoyed him most of all. Everyone smiled. Steve said that in the first half, when he'd been clearing a ball on the touchline, one of the players had grabbed him by the balls. In Steve's case, not wearing underpants, it must have been very painful.

Gilzean was getting both legs and his back attended to. Jennings was nursing his arms where he'd been trodden on. Chivers was rubbing his head. He had bruises all over his body but the most painful was his head where he'd been punched.

There was no tea or any refreshments but the groans didn't last long. They could do without tea, fuck them. They certainly had no intention of having a drink with the Rapid players, as they'd been invited to before the game. They just wanted to get away. Everyone was pleased that we were flying home at once, not spending another night in Bucharest.

The trip home was very noisy, with the drink and food flowing freely. The players talked excitedly and hardly played cards. Perhaps card playing is an escape, when players don't want to talk to each other or think about the game. Everyone was very excited and pleased.

Every newspaper except one carried horrifying accounts next day of the match. Peter Batt in the *Sun* said it was 'the most shameful exhibition of thuggery I have ever seen by the brutes of Bucharest'. Norman Giller in the *Express* said Spurs were 'hacked and kicked about like rag dolls'. Jeff Powell in the *Mail* said it was one of the most 'savage matches in the riot-torn history of European football' and was 'another bloody chapter in the Rumanian catalogue of brutality'.

Even the *Daily Telegraph* reporter, Robert Oxby, let himself go, describing it as 'the most cynical exhibition of deliberate fouling I have ever witnessed'. The *Guardian* headlined it as a 'Kind of War' and their reporter Albert Barham talked of 'sly cynical fouls ending in pure viciousness'.

Only Geoffrey Green in *The Times* avoided any emotion, though he talked about the 'fur flying' and quoted Nicholson, as everyone else did, on Rapid being the dirtiest side he'd seen. He managed to stay relatively calm in his report, pointing out, which nobody else did, that in the first half Rapid had three good chances and if they'd scored, the game might have been very different.

It's difficult to avoid prejudice, following one team and concentrating on what they do. Naturally, this leads to seeing life through their eyes, but a newspaper reporter is supposed to be unbiased. With a foreign trip, when it's a British team against the rest, then chauvinism always comes into it. It's much easier to let yourself fly, calling a foreign team the dirtiest in the world. It's relatively safe. No reporter, or manager, would ever use such words about another

British team. There are no come-backs when you slander a foreign team.

All the same, notwithstanding and nevertheless, it was a brutal display. Spurs didn't play much good football, apart from Chivers' goal, but their calmness and maturity in the face of constant provocation was a lesson for every team. I would never have believed they had such strength of character. It had been their manager's last instruction, on leaving the dressing-room, and they'd resolutely stuck to it.

from THE GLORY GAME *1972*

Argentina v. Holland, 1978

ROB HUGHES

In the end, they got there.

Time, like almost anything else in Latin America, often has to be expanded to get results, and this World Cup finale, like those of 1934 and 1966, went deep into extra time. . . .

The stadium seethed with the ecstatic sound that grew so familiar to our ears with each Argentine triumph: 'Vamos, vamos, Argentina' – 'Go, go, Argentina.' . . . And whatever deficiencies this Argentine side contains, it at least was by far the most attack-conscious of all the sixteen nations here. But, whatever sympathies there are for the Netherlands, which at times yesterday had to play against the Italian referee as well as the boisterous crowd of nearly 80,000, it would have been the worst irony that the Netherlands failed four years ago with an inspirational game of flair and then succeeded here with a style and a mood that were sour beyond comparison.

When play started, against a blizzard of tickertape and patriotic singing, the Netherlands began with two cynical fouls by Jan Poortvliet and Arie Haan. As expected, the Dutch clamped down heavily on the rampant Argentine wingers, Daniel Bertoni and Oscar Ortiz, and marked centre-forward Leopoldo Luque like a second skin.

Strangely, however, the Dutch plan was not total man-to-man, and it left Mario Kempes, the extra forward who sneaks in from behind relatively loosely marked. And the Netherlands paid for that.

It was Kempes who ran into space in the Dutch area to open the scoring after 37 minutes – a time when the crowd had been subdued to a hush, the Argentine attack blunted by the Netherlands' deliberately containing strategy. Kempes kept his head superbly, dashed on to a pass twelve yards out, and neatly prodded the ball beyond the onrushing goalkeeper, Jan Jongbloed.

Before and after that goal, the first half had been a dampened one, stodgy in the image of this [World Cup] tournament itself. The Netherlands' collective technique, its determination not to allow superior individual Argentine skills the time or room to flourish, its aim to wear down the home team, were all too frustratingly clear.

And yet the half produced chances – three to the Dutch, who broke with speed and caught the Argentine defence too advanced, chances from which the reflexes of goalkeeper Ubaldo Fillol denied first Johnny Rep then Robby Rensenbrink. Rep also headed fractionally wide.

Argentina, of course, did not stand idly by. Its captain, Daniel Passarella, found time enough and determination enough to hurl himself at the Dutch goal on four occasions: at 14 minutes Jongbloed saved his curled free-kick, after 24 his left-foot volley squeezed narrowly wide, at 35 his header was flicked over the bar and, in the 43rd minute, Jongbloed safely gathered another header.

Why, with all the Dutch technical and tactical awareness, did not one man in 10 just once pick up the big Argentine skipper at free kick and corner situations? It seemed almost tactically insane for a team managed by Ernst Happel, a man many claim to be the world's tactical master. But then who is running this Dutch side – Happel or his No. 2, Jan Zwartkruis?

Some say one, some the other, and meanwhile a leading Dutch club manager with players in the squad told me: 'It's neither. It's the players.'

Those players, self-governed or not, produced after halftime the fight-back that characterised their World Cup: in round one, they struggled and wriggled against their own poor form, in the second round they came from behind against both West Germany and Italy, and yesterday at River Plate Stadium they determinedly did so once more.

With the aid of tactical changes (by Happel, one presumes) they gradually wore away at an Argentine side that dangerously relied on its always uncertain rearguard and, led by the magnificently brave Johan Neeskens, a man who fought off serious injury to play here at all, the Dutch knocked at the door hard and long before, nine minutes from the end of normal time, substitute Dirk Nanninga launched himself at full gallop to head in a cross from René Van der Kerkhof.

A stunning goal, one that justified the substitution of Nanninga for the moody Rep, and, which came when the Netherlands was so desperate it had centre-back Ernie Brandts permanently in the forward line. On the stroke of the 90th minute, the Netherlands almost won the match, a long, long through ball from captain Ruudi Krol being kicked against the outside of the post by Resenbrink.

Not only was the referee, Sergio Gonella of Italy, inclined to favour Argentina, fate too was against the Dutch. They never recovered. Argentina, the team we thought may have expended too much energy playing every game at nerves end, found from somewhere deep reserves of energy.

In the 13th minute of extra time, Kempes shot the second goal to become, very deservedly indeed, this tournament's premier scorer with six goals. It was all his own work, a run that again proved the folly of loose-marking him: a wriggling, pacey dribble through two defenders, then a quick piece of reaction to push the ball over the line after Jongbloed rushed at him desperately and partially deflected it.

Plenty of time was left for a side as resilient as the Dutch, but for once there was nothing left in their souls, their socks and their heads were down, defeated, and they knew it. Jongbloed kept them in with a remote chance by saving magnificently from Luque but, with the Dutch inevitably trying, if heavily, to attack, Argentina exploited the space at their backs when both Kempes and Bertoni ran for a pass, almost collided, and Bertoni finally sealed the result by shooting in the loose ball from 12 yards.

The Argentines had found more stamina than the Dutch and it was that quality that decided, in the end, a World Cup that had from start to finish shown up mediocre playing skills with sheer determination and application.

Rhetorically may we ask: would it have been different if either Johan Cruyff or Willem Van Hanegem – the two inspirational Dutchmen who watched this cup in Europe – had been here? No team in this World Cup found their like.

from INTERNATIONAL HERALD-TRIBUNE 27/6/78

Italy v. Brazil, 1982

Rob Hughes

Barcelona. It feels like losing a friend, one who has insisted on giving, giving, giving but who has taken little in return.

Brazil is out of the 1982 World Cup. The team that restored the old values of soccer as a *players'* game is gone even before the semi-finals. And we have to admit it: Italy, which knocked Brazil out Monday, deserved, that day, to do it.

Brazil's fall was at least in character with all it had achieved here. By playing with unrestrained attack, it lifted every opponent to response in kind. And by leaving its own goal relatively unprotected it played with a cavalier, almost Corinthian risk.

'I already said Brazil could be beaten,' said Tele Santana, the coach who liberated its style, 'and now you have seen the result. My players had freedom to play with creativity as they saw fit. We started in 1980 to choose the best players in Brazil, and you saw the way we played. . . . But one has to win.'

The victory ethic is the final judgment on a team's value, although I believe that, for once and even in these times, the soccer world knows Brazil has cleansed the sport's whole image, has reopened far beyond its shores the love of attacking play that had stagnated under negative coaching.

So how could it lose — and lose to Italy, whose sterile defensiveness had only survived the first round on a technicality against Cameroon?

Foremost, because of the Italians' sheer courage. Here is a nation that has long submerged its beautiful talents beneath a defensive neurosis and a cynical will to kick the opposition into surrender. But Italy deceived us all.

It beat Argentina by attacking in the second half and it beat Brazil by attacking almost from the start. It is also as if the Italians have to be forced to use their unquestioned skills.

Marco Tardelli was Italy's first inspiration at this World Cup. So often the defensive marker, so often the villain whose opponent cannot walk after a match, he already had one yellow card by the time Italy met Argentina. So, rather than risk the almost inevitable booking by asking him to stop Maradona, Italy freed his considerable inventive talents. Claudio Gentile kicked Maradona instead.

Gentile was booked against Maradona and booked again early in the Brazil match for an horrendous foul on Zico. By booking him,

89

Abraham Klein, the superb Israeli referee, served notice on Italy that defensive butchery was out: Play the game.

And how Italy played. Giancarlo Antognoni, revelling in the space Brazil allows, reminded us that he is a survivor of an almost extinct Italian breed of classical creators, delicate as porcelain but devastatingly inventive when the mood and stage are right.

But Brazil has creators to spare. Where Italy mastered the favourites was in two positions , goalkeeper and goal-scorer.

Brazil gave – and I mean gave – Paolo Rossi five attempts at its goal. He scored three times, one a header and once from each foot. Two of his goals came after mistakes by Toninho Cerezo, whose manager was to say: 'Our defeat was not a case of tactical errors but of individual mistakes.

'Paolo Rossi is a great player. He is intelligent. He knew how to find the gaps, how to get into the spaces we left. And he punished our mistakes.' Some say that Brazil's soccer is too naive, that the charges of fullbacks Leandro and Junior leave those gaps.

They do, of course, but the philosophy that has thrilled millions who thought the game was dying is to *outscore* opponents, and Leandro and Junior, one playing almost as a winger the other as an inside forward, are integral links in that ambition. They stretch, they surprise – and if we loved them for it last week, why criticise them now?

Where the adventure was lost was not in the goals conceded but in those Brazil failed to score. Serghino, the big, black, erratic spearhead, was partly responsible. He looks what he is, a substitute; Brazil's real scorer, Reinaldo, is back home, a near-cripple after nine knee and ankle operations. His nation of 115 million could find no adequate replacement.

None, certainly, that could beat Dino Zoff three times. Twice they did so, on marvellous goals from Socrates and Roberto Falcao, but the third would not come. Not even when defensive anchorman Oscar came up in the dying moments to send in a thrusting header that the Brazilians claimed was over the line before Zoff, with unbelievable reflexes for a 40-year-old veteran, dived on the ball.

'The header did not cross the line,' said Italy's goalie and captain. 'I saved it. I know it did not cross the line.' Zoff drew heavily on a cigarette. He has played 104 internationals and says, as if ordering the groceries. 'The last two games form part of Italian soccer history.'

Not taking history nearly so unemotionally was Zoff's boss. Enzo Bearzot, Italy's long-suffering manager, crossed paths with Santana

as the Brazilian coach was leaving an interview room and Bearzot
was entering.

Bearzot hugged the beaten adversary in a way we would all have
liked to. Even an Italian, and especially Bearzot, loved Brazil's
World Cup.

But the Italians do show their feelings in a physical way. At
Monday's final whistle, Bearzot rushed to the centre circle and
threw his arms around Gentile. Bearzot's face was smothered and
his sunglasses shattered. Suddenly, the face that has worn a
thousand haunted looks in the name of Italian soccer opened into a
huge, beautiful and ironic laugh – ironic because Bearzot, more
than anyone, should have known that no one tangles with Claudio
Gentile, the smiling butcher of Turin, without paying a price.

But Bearzot's Italy had, for 90 minutes, been admirable – the
game he talks rather than the one his men usually play. No one will
thank them for getting rid of Brazil, but we will be thankful if the
Italians' artistry can keep on rising above their anxious cynicism.
Show us it can, Enzo. Show us.

from INTERNATIONAL HERALD-TRIBUNE *June 1982*

Brighton v. Manchester United, 1983

DAVID LACEY

The 1983 FA Cup Final produced all that was asked of it except a
definite result. Having experienced only one draw at Wembley in six
decades, the competition has now had three in succession and of
these the latest must surely be regarded as the best.

Whether or not Brighton and Hove Albion and Manchester
United can now repeat the eventful fluctuations and compelling
climax of Tottenham Hotspur's replay against Manchester City
two years ago is a matter for conjecture. Certainly the elements of
another exciting encounter at Wembley on Thursday are there, not
because either team is especially accomplished but because, on
Saturday's evidence, the chemistry seems about right.

In their two hours of yomping across a sodden field, Brighton and
United managed to create a montage of the images and emotions of
several of Wembley's better finals. The match was seldom dull,

rarely lacked interest and not only refused to follow its predicted course but, once started, laid a number of false trails.

For a second or two on Saturday, it looked as if everybody was going to be spared another few days of speculation. In those moments Brighton's hands stretched out for the Cup over a prostrate Manchester United, only for the prize to move tantalisingly out of reach.

The match was into the last half-minute of extra time when Case sent Robinson ploughing towards goal with one of his firmly struck early through passes. Robinson outpaced Moran and leaned a shoulder into the Manchester United defender to ward off his challenge. He then turned sharply inside McQueen and spotting Smith to his right, unmarked and onside, squared the ball to him.

Smith had only Bailey to beat from a range of just over 10 yards. Being a habitually careful player he allowed himself a touch of the ball before shooting, by which time Bailey had come off his line to narrow the angle. Smith intended to shoot towards the far left-hand corner of the net but instead put the ball too close to Bailey who saved it with his legs, in the manner of Pat Jennings, then fell on the slippery object as it threatened to squirm in behind him. Twenty seconds later the match ended.

Maybe some Brighton supporters went home telling each other that from such a distance Mrs Fitzherbert would have scored. In these circumstances everyone is an expert afterwards. For instance there were those who thought that Robinson should have shot of his own accord, even though he could see that Smith was much better placed.

The argument that had Smith shot sooner the FA cup would now be reflecting Sussex sunshine for the first time in its history carries more weight. Then again, after Montgomery of Sunderland had made his astonishing save to deny Lorimer a goal for Leeds 10 years earlier – same end, similar distance – it was said that had Lorimer placed his shot, like Smith, instead of trying to blast the ball through the back of the goal he would have scored.

There is more substance to Smith's version of the incident. He said that because of the wet pitch the ball ran to him slowly and that he had a fraction too long to think about shooting. The more one watches the replay of the pass, the shot and the save, the more it takes on the properties of a dream sequence.

Anybody who has ever dropped a crucial catch, fluffed an important putt or indeed missed a winning goal, will sympathise with Smith. Wembley has not seen such a sad moment for an individual since Don Fox failed to convert a match-winning penalty for Wakefield Trinity with the last kick of the 1968 Rugby League Challenge Cup final, his foot slipping on an equally wet surface.

Yet in a way this ultimate twist to the plot was a fitting denouement to a game which had more than once produced the unexpected just when it seemed that the obvious was about to happen. Not for the first time a match at Wembley, taken out of the seasonal mainstream of English football, made nonsense of the participants' contrasting League positions. At times, it is true, United did look like a side which had just finished third in the First Division but seldom if ever did Brighton wear the expression of one just relegated to the Second.

Manchester United displayed that fitful form which had been largely responsible for frustrating their ambitions in the League for another season. They had some excuse for this: the ball seldom ran smoothly on the saturated, lumpy pitch; they badly missed Coppell, who when fit would have put much more pressure on Brighton's inexperienced left-back, Pearce; and when Grealish and Case began to out-tackle and outmanoeuvre Robson and Wilkins the absence of the suspended Moses was particularly noticeable. Unlike Foster, the Brighton captain for whom the final represented the last half of a two-match ban, Moses will also miss the replay.

Less easy to explain was the square, ponderous state of the United defence which at one stage in the first half simply fell apart whenever Brighton fed the ball diagonally into the penalty area. McQueen and Moran, who in the Milk Cup final had resisted Liverpool so solidly until both were injured, now looked strangely vulnerable.

Their discomfort was thrown into sharper relief by the excellence of the Brighton centre-backs, Stevens and Gatting, who went into the match cast as foils for the talents of Stapleton and Whiteside but emerged their equals.

Stevens, assuming Foster's responsibility for organising the Brighton defence, was acclaimed by both teams as the game's outstanding player. His positioning could scarcely be faulted, his interceptions were consistently well timed and it is hard to remember a wasted clearance. Bobby Robson has already noted Stevens's potential as an England player and it is surprising not to see the defender included in the party for Australia.

The imminent reappearance of Foster for the replay gives Melia something of an organisational problem. Well though the centre-backs played on Saturday, he can hardly ignore Foster, having gone to the High Court in a vain attempt to get the ban lifted or at least delayed. If Ramsey is fit, as he expects to be, Gatting will probably move to left-back in place of Pearce but should Ramsey be unable to play on Thursday then Stevens may move to right-back with Foster and Gatting in the middle and Pearce retained. Switching Stevens at this stage would be a gamble. Perhaps Mr Justice Vinelott should be consulted.

Had it not been for later events, the injury to Ramsey less than a minute before United drew level early in the second half might have remained the major controversy. A high tackle by Whiteside, his boot digging into Ramsey's leg and an awkward, twisting fall left the Brighton defender hobbling so badly that an immediate substitution might have been the wiser course.

Instead Ramsey struggled back into the goalmouth as Duxbury crossed to the near post for Whiteside, diving in low, to nod the ball across the goalmouth. Moseley was beaten, Stevens could not reach the ball and Stapleton lunged in front of the despairing Ramsey to score. While the move was worth a goal, the fact that Brighton had a defender limping at the time left a niggling doubt about its merit.

Manchester United could argue that two late lunges by Case on Wilkins – as with the Whiteside tackle neither was adjudged a foul – were equally culpable. All one can say is that Wilkins stayed on to prove an important influence while Ramsey left the game.

For a time in the first half the baleful marking of Wilkins by Case and Grealish's careful covering of Robson seemed destined merely to delay the inevitable. United were making sure that Davies, the young Welshman brought into the side to fill Coppell's role, saw plenty of the ball. He began promisingly but lacked the awareness to make full use of his undoubted skills. Even so the rhythm of United's play was looking ominous for Brighton.

Melia's team did not make a serious expedition into their opponents' half until the 14th minute. Then, being Melia's team, they scored. Howlett floated the ball at a fine angle through the defence and with Bailey half-committed to going to his right, Smith sent a gentle header into the opposite corner.

Moseley having made a series of excellent saves, the best to hold a shot from Robson that came at him through a thicket of legs, Brighton came in at half-time confident that the spirit of endeavour which had beaten Liverpool could see them through another 45 minutes. However, with just under 20 minutes remaining all this had changed. United, after wearing the slightly offended air of gentry required to mingle below stairs, appeared to have re-established a proper order of things.

More pertinently, they had also taken the lead. At times Muhren's contribution to the match was as distant as it had been in the Milk Cup final but in the 71st minute he sent a beautiful pass from the left dipping across to Wilkins in space on the right. As Wilkins turned inside towards the 18-yard line Albiston sprinted through the middle anticipating a pass and this prompted Moseley to leave his line. Wilkins spotted the goalkeeper trapping himself in no-man's land and curled a marvellous shot out of Moseley's reach into a far corner of the net. It was a rare goal in more ways than one: Wilkins has scored only three times in two seasons for United, twice against Brighton.

Four minutes from the end of normal time Brighton forced a corner on the right. Case sent the ball low to Grealish who was waiting outside the penalty area, he pushed it forward and in one smooth movement, with the defence standing still, Stevens gained control and brought the scores level. Seldom can a goal in a Cup final have been better deserved.

There is a line of argument which suggests that Smith's miss represents the end of Brighton's remarkable Cup run, that if their name had been on the trophy from the start Bailey would have been beaten. Maybe so, but it was the other Moses who failed to make the promised land after an epic journey – and he does not play for Brighton either.

from THE GUARDIAN *23/5/1983*

In the replay, Manchester United beat Brighton, 4–0. Editor.

Part Three

THE STARS

G. O. *Smith* – *Corinthian*

C. B. FRY

Corinthians and Cricketers, full of interest and information about an important period in the history of field-games, is in the nature of a Pindaric ode in prose. Its central subject is one man – his fame and prowess in football. But the select personality is a theme song, as it were, that introduces, among kindred topics, a great Public School, a great University, a great Club, and a great formative area of what is now a great national and international entertainment. Some would say an industrial entertainment . . .

The elegant and blameless football now seen on occasions, e.g. at Wembley, did not come from the Midland and Northern industrial towns, though of the skill a good deal did, but from the now supposedly obsolete Old Boys teams. Indeed, but for the Old Boys clubs – Carthusians, Etonians, Westminsters, Salopians, Reptonians and the like – the world of soccer would never have seen the Corinthians, in their day the greatest of all amateur football clubs yet known or likely to be known.

This epoch-making club came into being through the selective and organising ability of N. L. Jackson. He saw that if he avoided cup-tie competition he could skim off the cream of the Old Boys clubs into a quasi-international amateur team. This he did, and in 1886, he being on the Selection Committee, ten Corinthians and one professional appeared at Hampden Park to represent England v. Scotland. There has never been a stronger England team.

But let us now consider G. O. Smith, our hero, and his compeers, if any, and his times. A genius in football he was. Like all geniuses he rose on stepping-stones of his real self by taking infinite pains in terms of his natural gifts.

He came up to Oxford from Charterhouse with as big a name as any Freshman ever in Association football. He was not alone as a Carthusian eminent – E. C. Bliss, E. Farquhar Buzzard, R. J. Salt and C. D. Hewitt were all Blues with him. In the 1893–4 Varsity match when I was captain we had the strongest team that ever played for either University, but we lost.

The ground was frozen at Queen's Club and was more suited to skating than football. We had five internationals, but not for skating. G.O. played extremely well all the same, and he was as good a centre-forward then as ever afterwards. A gem.

His rating as the finest man in his place who ever played for England is generally accepted. But such rating cannot be proved correct. *De gustibus* comes in. So do changes of conditions of play. Anyhow he was the cleverest centre-forward I saw between 1888 and 1903 – my years of first-class football. Clever is not the word. He was inspired.

He was of medium height, slight and almost frail in build. He was a quick mover but not a sprinter. He was uncannily prehensile of foot and almost delicately neat. What made him was his skill in elusive movements, his quickness in seeing how best to bestow his passes, his accuracy and his remarkable penetrative dribbling. He swung a marvellously heavy foot in shooting – always along the turf and terrifically swift.

The yarn that he was a weak shot in his early first-class seasons is just a yarn. I played often with and against him, and he was as straight and hard a shot as I have ever met except perhaps only Steven Bloomer of Derby County, on one of Steve's special days. G.O.'s was every day.

The Corinthian players of the eighties used to say that Tinsley Lindley of their great forward-line was at least as good a centre. Theirs was a great line – Bambridge, Cobbold, Lindley, Brann and either Aubrey Smith or Spilsbury. Lindley, like G.O., was slim and elusive, with a knack of slipping in unexpected shots, but he did not shoot as hard as G.O.

G.O. was, you might say, an epitome of Charterhouse football. He was an emanation of a hot-bed of skill in the game produced by a long tradition and a fast sandy field where delay meant loss of the ball and inaccuracy a troublesome bounce.

Charterhouse, originally buried in London near Smithfield Market, was transferred to Godalming by Dr Haig-Brown. . . . There were many fine footballers bred on the hill at Godalming. The brothers Walters, A. M. and P. M., were the best pair of backs who played for England in my time; C. Wreford Brown and Blenkiron were two excellent centre-halves; and among the earlier Carthusian footballers were two fine cricketers: Major E. G. Wynyard, DSO, and Sir C. Aubrey Smith, the actor and film hero. Yet the strange thing was that Charterhouse cricket, though of course good, was not at that time up to the standard of the football. They had no cricket master at all. I was a classical master there for two years and only just escaped being taught by the head boy, Lord Beveridge. But I did not teach cricket – I was not allowed.

G.O. in his schooldays was a great run-getter, but he had a peculiar short-handle lean-down style. He was a formally correct off-driver and cutter with an excellent defence, but although he scored a famous match-winning century for Oxford v. Cambridge he was not a good model for the average young batsman. Not upstanding enough and not free enough in his driving. No left arm swing. In fact he batted like a very good putter at golf. Nevertheless, a useful man on any side, he would have collected stacks of runs in Australia.

By the way, he had curiously fine grey eyes and grey eyelashes such as any girl would envy. He read History at Oxford and the Keble Dons thought well of him. I guess he taught well as a schoolmaster; he was kind, quiet, and peculiarly patient.

He is worth reading about, as also are many of his contemporaries, and much of his conspicuous context.

from Introduction to CORINTHIANS AND CRICKETERS *1955*

Stan Mortensen

Alan Ross

Slighter, and also fairer, than Stanley Matthews,* for his grandfather was a Norwegian sailor who married and then settled in South Shields, Mortensen, 'the other Stanley', has something of the same magnetism. Partly, perhaps, it is because he has the coolness and flair for the dramatic, essential to the big-match temperament; partly it is the result of flawless technique, that in turn allows a player to conserve his energies and to dispense the graces of his craft without apparent effort.

It is inevitable that these two players should be mentioned together, for, though their methods are as different as could be, they understand each other, and this mutual confidence has produced the most remarkable partnership in post-war football.

Mortensen is not an inside-forward of the 'fetch-and-carry' type, nor is he an architect on whose blue-print the other forwards build. He is the high-quality opportunist, with positional instinct, uncanny powers of anticipation, the ability to do the unexpected at great

* *For a portrait of Matthews in action, see 'Blackpool v. Bolton, 1953', on page 44 above.*

speed, who not only can alter the whole balance of the game in a few minutes but who has the directness and goal-sense to finish his own moves off. Matthews may draw the opposition by sheer virtuosity; Mortensen goes through them before they are aware of an opening.

He is neither particularly fast nor strong; but what mark out his genius are phenomenal acceleration, clever changes of pace, balance, and a singleness of purpose that enables him to score goals when the way seems solidly blocked. If Matthews dominates a match, calling up the thunder on the wings for all to admire, Mortensen is the lightning that strikes immediately after. Like many great inside-forwards, he often appears idle; yet just when it seems he has written a match off and a false security is settling on the opposing defence, he is suddenly away on his own, jinking his way through in short bursts or turning up from nowhere to hurl himself head-first at the ball and flick it into the net.

His reputation is entirely post-war. In 1938, after some success in South Shields school football – 'I was a poor boy,' he has written, 'brought up in a happy home' – he was invited to sign for Blackpool. By the outbreak of war he was some way off the League side. 'I was made aware of the fact that I was fortunate to stay on the staff.' He joined the RAF, and his Wellington bomber caught fire and crashed during operational training. Mortensen had enough stitches in his head to deter most people from heading a ball for life. But he was soon back playing for Service teams, and during this substitute war-time football he suddenly found himself. 'I was developing. It came just like that.'

Since then Mortensen has become, at centre-forward or inside-right, one of the brilliant players of our time. He scored twenty-one goals in his first fifteen representative games and was never on the losing side. Till this year he has been a fixture in the England team. He began the season quietly; now he leads the First Division goal-scorers once again. The future, and at international level the barometer is rarely steady, might break either way. Meanwhile, like Matthews, he hankers after a Cup Winner's medal.

from THE OBSERVER 22/4/51

Bobby Charlton

ARTHUR HOPCRAFT

Everyone who follows football has his favourite player; even the players do. The selection is bound to reflect something of the nature of the one who is doing the choosing. The favourite is not necessarily being named as the greatest player of all. We may admit, reluctantly, our favourite's weaknesses. What we are saying is that this particular player appeals to us more than any other. It has to do with his personality, his style of behaviour, perhaps importantly the way in which he compensates for his deficiencies. He is the player who may disappoint sometimes with a ragged, off-form performance, and yet over the years stays clear and bright in the memory. He is the player we bring to mind first when we ask ourselves what football looks like when we enjoy it most. The man I name for this role is Bobby Charlton.

The flowing line of Charlton's football has no disfiguring barbs in it, but there is a heavy and razor-shaped arrowhead at its end. It is the combination of the graceful and the dramatic which makes him so special. There are few players who affect a crowd's responses as much as he does. Something extraordinary is expected of him the moment he receives the ball. He can silence a crowd instantly, make it hold its breath in expectation. A shot from Charlton, especially if hit on the run from outside the penalty area, is one of the great events of the sport, not because it is rare, which it is not, but because the power of it is massive and it erupts out of elegance; he is never clumsy or desperate in movement; he can rise very close to the athletic ideal.

The persistent complaint I have heard made against Charlton, the one which keeps him out of the lists when some people name the handful of the world's greatest players, is that he avoids the fury of the game, that where the hacking and elbowing are fiercest Charlton is not to be found. But this is like dismissing Dickens from the world's great literature because he never went to gaol for throwing bricks at politicians; like denigrating Disraeli on the grounds that he was a third-rate novelist. Charlton's courage is geared to his special talents. I have certainly never seen him fling himself headlong across his own goalmouth to head the ball away from some opposing forward's foot. But I have seen him summon his speed and use his swerve to score goals when defences were swinging their boots at him with intent to hurt. Charlton has been felled so often in his career that he could not possibly have stayed so compellingly in the game for so long if he lacked nerve. I do not object at all that he has never been sent off the field for kneeing someone in the groin.

It is true, I think, to say that although he became an England international player when he was twenty it was in later years that he gathered full resolution for the game. He was never less than an excellent player, but he was past twenty-five before he became a great one. He flowered fully, and gloriously, for the World Cup in 1966, appropriately scoring England's first goal with a veering run from near the centre-circle and a characteristic shot taken in mid-stride. He scored another like it in the semi-final against Portugal. They are the kind of goals he will be remembered by. They are a great player's goals.

Yet Charlton is not just a scoring specialist. Being so fast and possessing the best body swerve of his generation, he made his name as a winger. In his early years as a professional his great merit was his ability to run past the defender from the left touchline and go diagonally on the back's inside to hit the ball at goal with either foot. This was the young Charlton, with most of his weight in his legs, whose speed and control of the ball were aimed almost exclusively at scoring goals. By his late twenties – he was twenty-eight in the 1966 World Cup – he had moved to a deep-lying centre-forward or inside-forward position, as the fulcrum of the attack. His accuracy with the ball at great distance was now used to shift, in one sudden pass, the point of action. These passes, especially if preceded by one of his sidesteps and a burst of acceleration, could turn the fortune of a game instantly. A moment's work of this calibre from him, perhaps at the edge of his own penalty area, could take his side out of an alarming defensive situation and have it menacing the other goal immediately. I saw him do this once against Liverpool and the moment stunned that ferocious crowd into silence.

Charlton makes his own rules for dealing with a football. He is a player to admire but not for younger ones to copy. When he strikes the ball he often has his head up high, instead of looking down over the ball as the coaches teach. He will flick at it with the outside of his left foot when leaning back looking at the sky. When players on his own side are unaccustomed to him they often find that the ball comes to them, having miraculously been 'bent' round some obstructing opponent, spinning violently and therefore difficult to control; only the best can take advantage of such passes, as Denis Law, George Best and Jimmy Greaves (in the international side) all have. Charlton does not dribble with the ball in the sense that Best does, patting it between his feet, nor does he run with it as if it is tied by elastic to him, as in the case of Pelé, of Brazil, so that it bounces against his knees, thighs, stomach, ankles as he moves. Charlton kicks the ball close to the ground in front of him, often a long way in front, and runs like a sprinter behind it, almost as if there was no ball at all. No boy could possibly be taught such a method of playing football.

This run deceives defenders. They see the ball coming towards them, with Charlton well behind it, and they think they can reach it before him. Suddenly, just as they commit themselves, his right shoulder dips, his whole weight goes momentarily on his right foot, flat on the grass, and then he has sped past them the other way, kicking the ball in front of him as he goes. His own speed, coupled with the defender's impetus, often means that he is ten yards clear before the defender has turned. To be beaten by Charlton's swerve is to be beaten for good. If the defender anticipates the swerve and turns in the right direction Charlton will clear the tackle expertly like a hurdler.

There is delicious exhilaration in watching movement like this. Crowds will him to repeat it, and if he gets the ball and pauses as if gathering himself for such a run the whole sound of the stadium changes from its baying or grumbling into an excited purr. If he decides the moment is not right, and releases the ball quickly with a merely sensible short pass, there is a deep groan of disappointment.

He has his bad matches, when his touch deserts him and the casual flicks and lobs skim away erratically, sometimes presenting the other team with the initiative they had lost. In games like these his shooting at goal can be laughably wild, and yet there is seldom laughter; the communal embarrassment is the same that settles around a wrong final note from the recital platform. Charlton hates these lapses. He reacts to them with something close to self-revulsion, like a man discovering a flea in his vest. He shakes his head wretchedly, apologises to the company, and on his very worst days may keep clear of the ball for a while. More often he tries to compose himself, trapping the ball and striking it with an unusual, elaborate care. It is only now that he looks awkward. When Charlton is keeping his eye intently on the ball, as every good player is supposed to, then he is at his least effective. He is not a player's player, in the sense of being reliable, even though he is entirely professional in his attitude to the game; he is certainly a spectator's player, in the sense that he is a sight to watch.

His dejection in failure, even in the momentary kind, is more easily understood when Charlton has been met off the field. There is a natural diffidence in him, a sense of anxiety not to show himself up in public. His shyness was brought home to me first of all when he was twenty-one, unmarried and living in lodgings. I had some fairly harmless questions to ask him for the newspaper I was working for at the time, and the whole interview was conducted on the doorstep, with Charlton holding on to the doorknob, not being in the least obstructive but blushing and leaving words trailing indistinctly and ambiguously in the air. He said at the time that he had always found it hard to answer any questions about himself. Seven years later, when he was a much better player and going bald, he was still far from casual in conversation even in his own home, only showing a marked step forward in self-confidence when he was holding one of his children in his arms. He has done a good deal of talking to youth clubs and at sports clubs functions in recent years, yet there was a distinct nerviness in his voice when I heard him deliver a few impromptu sentences in a hospital's broadcast at half-time in one of Liverpool's midweek matches. He smokes more than would be expected of a man who is still one of the fastest movers in international football in spite of being thirty years old.

He gets the star footballer's profusion of flattery. His name is chanted to raise the spirits of ticket queues in the rain; vivid, coarse girls have to be held off by policemen when he gets in and out of the Manchester United coach; small boys write him letters of charming clumsiness and kick footballs with his autograph on them; he has been European Footballer of the Year, and a poll of referees has voted him Model Player. His wife is pretty, so are his two daughters, and he lives in a rich man's house in a rich man's neighbourhood. He is the classic working-class hero who has made it to glamour and Nob Hill.

from THE FOOTBALL MAN *1968*

Alfredo di Stefano

GEOFFREY GREEN

I was once invited to a reception at the Argentine embassy in London on the occasion of a visit by their national football team to play England at Wembley as a warm-up on their way to the 1974 World Cup in West Germany. Among those there to greet his countrymen was that fabulous player, Alfredo di Stefano, a wanderer who had left his homeland a quarter of a century earlier in a search for happiness and job-satisfaction. As a man and a player he found both in Madrid where he became a naturalised Spaniard.

Football had been known to change many lives – some for the better, others for the worse. We recognised each other across the crowded room from times past and duly fell into conversation. 'You were always my number one player of the world,' I said. 'Had I ever been in a position to choose a side from the four corners of this earth you would have been first and Pelé second.'

He smiled and bowed with a hint of irreverence. 'You would have been wrong,' he replied. 'The best player in my opinion was Suarez, the Spanish inside-forward. He was the real master. The Italians realised it when they persuaded him to Milan.' It was no good arguing the point with him.

He seemed to me to be the most *complete*, all-round player of the lot. Pelé, of course, cannot be surpassed in the matter of goals scored. Yet di Stefano himself was no slouch when it came to putting the ball in the net. After all he is still the highest scorer in the European Cup. However, as a deep-lying, artistic and creative centre-forward he was totally involved in whatever was happening in every corner of the field.

However, he did not strut arrogantly across a pitch like some peacock. He had a swift, short stride with a high-stepping knee action and he moved lightly with bouts of timed acceleration like someone stepping over burning coals or broken glass. He possessed peripheral vision; his eyes darted here and there hungrily as his mind measured and calculated every situation. Many were the memorable performances he left to posterity in the all-white strip of Real Madrid, without question the outstanding club of the 1950s and early 1960s.

For five years in succession – 1956 to 1960 inclusive – Real Madrid won the European Cup. By 1960 their attack had been joined by Ferenc Puskas, once captain of Hungary who had fled his country following the crushing of their revolution by Russia. At once he set up a marvellous, instinctive partnership with di Stefano which reached an apogee at Hampden Park in 1960 when Real beat Eintracht Frankfurt 7–3 in the European Cup final. Puskas scored four goals and di Stefano, also doing most of the spade work, claimed three. So enthralling was their play that at the final whistle 135,000 Scotsmen stood motionless for a quarter of an hour roaring their heads off.

To give Real their full European Cup record for those five magic years, home and away ties, we find the following figures:

Played	Won	Drawn	Lost	Goals For	Against
37	27	4	6	112	42

Born in Buenos Aires in July 1926, the grandson of an immigrant from Capri, Alfredo di Stefano built his remarkable staying powers through cross-country running. His father was a half-back for River Plate and it was with that famous Buenos Aires club that Alfredo first made his name. He joined them at sixteen, made his debut a year later and played seven times for Argentina. Then, in common with other Argentine professionals, 'illegally' left the country to play for Milionarios of Bogotá. Colombia, at that time, was not a member of FIFA, the International Football Federation.

In 1953 he made his peace with River Plate and was transferred to Real Madrid, where he played till his retirement. Married with three children, he indulged in athletics, basketball and pelota to keep fit and enjoys going to the opera. Well-built, he was an astonishing dribbler, explosively quick off the mark and a free goal-scorer.

Above all, he has always played first and foremost for the team despite his exceptional abilities – an ideal example to younger players. He made a mockery of coaching manuals since he was completely one-footed – his right. That was his individual touch and he was better with that one foot than most are with two.

I cannot help returning to the old argument – Pelé or di Stefano, who was the greater? During the World Cup of 1974 in Germany I became involved one night in a discussion with Brazilian journalists. Again I voted for Stefano because of his *all-round* qualities. The others would not agree. 'Di Stefano,' they said, 'was manufactured on earth. But Pelé came from heaven . . .'

from PARDON ME FOR LIVING *1985*

The Magic of Pelé

PAUL GARDNER

Why Pelé? Why, from the millions all over the world who play this game of soccer, does Pelé stand out as the greatest of all, perhaps the greatest player in the history of the game?

Simply because, in soccer terms, he is a genius. All of soccer's myriad skills, from the simplest touch of the ball to the most intricate dribble, seem to flow from his supple body with never-ending clarity, freshness and perfection.

The body itself seems almost purposefully designed for soccer: stocky but lithe, powerful but fast, balanced to perfection on legs that look like tree trunks but that operate with the finesse of a ballet dancer. Pelé himself has frequently said that his skills are God-given, that he was born to play soccer. A characteristically modest remark that makes light of Pelé's own devotion to his sport, to the tireless way that he has polished those gifts.

Technically, then, Pelé is close to soccer perfection. But there is more to the man than that. Another vast dimension made up of the awe and mystery that are inseparable from genius. A dimension that blends his gifts as a player, his role as a legend, and his qualities as a man to make up the magic of Pelé.

Pelé: The Soccer Player. Anyone who has seen Pelé in action – even someone who knows little of soccer – recognises that there is something electrically exciting about his play . . . more, about his mere presence on the field. Pelé brings a palpable feeling of tension and excitement to every game that he plays in, a feeling that hovers over the crowd like a flash of lightning waiting to flash.

Whenever Pelé takes possession of the ball, the pulse of the game hastens. Suddenly those marvellous skills have taken charge. The ball, until that moment a bouncy sphere with a will of its own, comes to Pelé and is instantly tamed. It is plucked out of the air with one decisive leg movement, or it is chested to the ground with an athletic curling leap, or it is firmly stopped with an imperious foot movement. Whichever, it belongs now to Pelé, nestling docilely between his feet as crowd and opponent alike await the next move.

And that next move might be almost anything. Here, perhaps, we are close to the essence of Pelé genius as a player. His total unpredictability. His constant ability to surprise, to do the unusual, the unexpected and at times the utterly impossible.

With no real weakness in his skills. Pelé can do virtually anything he wishes with the ball. A short pass, a long pass, made with right foot or left foot, but always with clinical accuracy. A shot on goal – thunderous and powerful, or delicately flighted to deceive the goalkeeper. Or a sudden surging dribble, taking the ball past two or three opponents in a burst of twists and turns and breath-taking ball control.

The physical ability to do all these things is remarkable enough. But to that Pelé adds the skill to do them all supremely well and the mental sharpness that tells him instantly which of them is the right one for any given situation.

This knack of knowing the right move when you have the ball, and of sensing what your opponents are doing, of anticipating their moves when they have possession, is known in soccer terms as 'reading the game.' A neat enough term, but just not adequate to describe what Pelé does. He is not merely reading the game; he is writing it, controlling its every nuance, its whole structure, making it happen the way he wants it to happen.

Two examples of the Pelé magic in action: first, an incident from the Brazil vs. Uruguay game in the 1970 World Cup competition. Brazil is on the attack. The Uruguayan fullbacks have been drawn out of position and from the Brazilian left-wing the ball is pushed through into the middle. Into a gaping space where the Uruguayan fullbacks should be. Instead, there is Pelé coming through at full speed, moving on to the ball. The only Uruguayan player who can hope to beat him to the ball is their goalkeeper, Mazurkiewicz, who comes racing out of his goal.

Pelé, Mazurkiewicz and the ball arrive at about the same moment right at the edge of the penalty area. Pelé swerves to his left, as though to move the ball that way. Mazurkiewicz dives to intercept . . . and finds himself clutching nothing but air. Pelé's move was a fake, a fake that fooled not only Mazurkiewicz but everyone in the stadium and the millions watching on television all over the world.

In fact, Pelé did not even play the ball. He ran to the goalkeeper's left, but allowed the ball to run on, so that it continued rolling exactly where Mazurkiewicz would have been if he hadn't dived. As Mazurkiewicz scrambled on his hands and knees to turn around, Pelé raced past him, met up with the ball and turned to chip it towards the goal . . . and, agonizingly, inches wide. No goal – but an exquisite piece of soccer that everyone who saw it will treasure forever.

The second example of Pelé's skills comes from his first game with the New York Cosmos, an exhibition against the Dallas Tornadoes.

PAUL GARDNER

His team is down, 2–1, when Mordecai Shpiegler moves in from the right wing and lofts a soft, curling centre into the Dallas goalmouth. As the ball begins to drop, there is simply no inkling of danger, a whole bevy of Dallas defenders is waiting to clear it. And then, almost too late, there is Pelé, running forward, leaping high, twisting that muscular frame violently in midair, crashing his forehead decisively into the ball.

The Dallas goalkeeper and one of his fullbacks, both standing on the goal-line, have no chance to move as the ball flashes past them, a streaking white bullet that goes into the goal in the top corner, just under the bar. It almost looks as though they have forgotten that they are there to prevent goals, as though they are content to stand, rooted to the spot in jaw-dangling admiration at the perfection of Pelé's header.

Pelé has started his re-born career with yet another memorable goal, a worthy addition to his fabulous total of 1,220.

Pelé: The Legend. To understand Pelé's role as a soccer legend one has to go back in years, back first to 1958, the year in which the World Cup, soccer's world championship, was played in Sweden.

Once again Brazil had qualified for the final rounds, as it had done for all five previous World Cups, dating back to 1930. Yet the World Cup had never been won by Brazil. For Brazilians, a people with a passionate love for the sport of soccer, the failure was a national tragedy, a source of humiliation and shame. What, exactly, was wrong? Their team was always among the favourites, always glittered with marvellous players . . . and always lost.

The most bitter of moments had come in 1950 when the World Cup was played in Brazil itself. Brazil had swept through to the final in almost truculent fashion. Then, with the whole country poised on the crest of a nationalistic fever, waiting for the inevitable victory, Brazil had gone down, 2–1, to little Uruguay before over 200,000 stunned fans in Rio's giant Maracana Stadium.

That black afternoon was to hang like an incubus over Brazilian soccer for years. At the next World Cup, in Switzerland in 1954, the Brazilians fielded what many thought was their best-ever team. Yet they lost to Hungary in the quarter-finals – a violent game that was dubbed the Battle of Berne and brought more shame for the Brazilians.

The world passed its verdict on Brazilian soccer: limitless talent but no discipline, unmatchable artistry but uncontrolled nerves.

The slur was felt by every Brazilian, felt with the keenness that

111

doubt brings. Was it true? Worse still, was it true not only of Brazilian soccer, but of Brazilians themselves?

In 1958 this mood of doubt affected every Brazilian as, not wanting to despair but hardly daring to hope, they followed the progress of their team in Sweden. A fine 3–0 win over Austria was followed by an unimpressive 0–0 tie with England ... and immediately it was crisis time again. Was Brazil faltering? Was it to be the same old story? Team changes followed, and for the next game, against Russia, three new players were brought in, including the young forward Pelé.

It seemed like a desperation move. There was already some doubt about Pelé's physical fitness, but in any case surely his age, a mere seventeen years, must count against him in the nerve-shattering atmosphere of the World Cup?

But suddenly, almost by chance it seemed, the Brazilians had found their team. The Russians were beaten, 2–0, and the talk began about the remarkable seventeen-year-old who played with the skill and the poise of a veteran. Three games later Brazil, at long last, were world champions. The hero of the final game, scorer of two goals in a 5–2 win over Sweden, the player who was chaired off the field by his teammates, was Pelé, weeping freely on their shoulders.

A wave of emotional relief swept through Brazil. Their soccer – their nation, it seemed – had been vindicated. Soccer, the Brazilian sporting religion, had found its Messiah: Pelé, the chosen boy-man who had led his people to their rightful place as the world's number one soccer nation. The Pelé era had begun.

Four years later, in Chile, Brazil repeated as World Champions. Pelé, injured in the second game, played only a minor role, yet his mere presence seemed to be all that Brazil needed. Covering that 1962 World Cup was a young English journalist named Clive Toye – who was later to become general manager of the New York Cosmos, the man responsible for bringing Pelé to the United States. Said Toye: 'You know, looking back to Chile, it's hard to realise that Pelé played in only 1½ games. His name was on everyone's lips, his presence was everywhere. It was almost as though he *did* play in every game.'

The 1966 World Cup, in England, was a disaster for Brazil. An aging and constantly revised team was beaten in the preliminary round and Pelé – mercilessly kicked by opposing defenders – vowed he would never play in the World Cup again.

By 1970 he had changed his mind. In Mexico, at the age of twenty-nine, he played perhaps better than he had ever played as he led an irrepressible and inventive Brazilian team to victory for the third time in his four World Cups.

But that was it. Pelé retired from the Brazilian national team in 1971. Despite a public outcry in Brazil, despite all sorts of emotional pressures and financial inducements, Pelé stuck to his decision not to play in the 1974 World Cup. The Brazil party travelled to Germany for the finals . . . but for the first time since 1958, there was no Pelé. The Pelé era had come to a close. Brazil did not play badly – they took fourth place – but that was not good enough for Brazilians. If only the Pelé era had lasted a little longer, if only he had played, even at thirty-three years of age . . .

The Brazilians have given Pelé a nickname, or perhaps it is really a title – *O Rei*, The King. But he is in many ways seen as a God rather than a King. He is still the Messiah, and ever since 1958 a detectable aura of religious respect and mystery has hovered around the name and the man Pelé.

Pelé: The Man. It is the large eyes that you notice first – they seem to be pressing forward, almost bulging out of the face . . . and you remember the stories of Pelé's fantastic peripheral vision on the soccer field. They move slowly and beautifully, conveying one minute an infinite, far-away sadness, the next a warm intimate happiness. The Pelé smile is sudden, gripping, irresistible, and very, very real.

There is nothing false in the public image of the man. He has never courted fame, never behaved outrageously, never relied on gimmickry, never sought publicity. He was born in 1940, just one of millions of poor boys from poor black families in Brazil. He has become Brazil's best known citizen and one of its richest. Sudden fame, sudden wealth, temptations that destroyed the career of George Best, another great soccer player from a poor background. But Pelé has coped, and he has survived.

Somehow he saw, or sensed, early on that there had to be two Pelés, one private and one public. He kept his personal life as private as he could. He quietly courted a white girl and when he announced that they were to be married, the ceremony was not allowed to become the circus it could so easily have been.

In public Pelé played soccer as most of us had never seen it played before. Off the field, in all sorts of situations, from meeting the Queen to simply chatting with an excited crowd of fans, he behaved with a firm, quiet dignity.

Is there, anywhere in the world, a young boy who can say that Pelé refused him an autograph? Those four magical letters have been written a million times on everything from expensive menus to the skin of a grubby outstretched palm. Always written with care, never scribbled, always with a smile. Journalists have been treated with courtesy and candour in the midst of frenetic, shouting mob scenes where panic and flight would have been the first reaction of most athletes.

Candour? Well, yes . . . though there persists the feeling that the private Pelé – perhaps the real Pelé – is by now so well protected that he is virtually beyond reach. Only the eyes, those wonderful great expressive eyes, tantalise and hint at a mystery just beyond reach.

Sometimes, looking at that distant sadness in the eyes, you think: this is still a frightened boy from a poor family, wondering if he's dreaming, dreading that he's going to wake up, a boy who doesn't really believe anything that's happened to him.

Then the smile, the lovely soft laugh. The introspection and the mystery vanish in a moment and the charm of Pelé, the magic if you will, dominates everything.

from THE COMPLETE HANDBOOK OF SOCCER *1976*

George Best

GEOFFREY GREEN

At one stage in the late 1960s there were four Bests who were appearing currently on the stage of the Football League – an Irishman, an Englishman, a Scot and a Bermudan. One was a goalkeeper and three were forwards. But only one of them was THE Best. Born in Belfast in 1946, a child of Gemini, he was christened George; he stood 5ft 8½ins in height; was frail-looking at some 10½ stone and was always the one to catch the headlines.

Thumb through the glossy magazines or the humblest football rag, the odds were he would be staring out of a page, fixing attention with luminous eyes, a lush Beatle hair-style and a quizzical expression which suggested that while he alone may know the hundredth name of Buddha, it was all a bit of a joke anyway. Words, words, words: analysed, x-rayed and photographed, it has all been told before about this phenomenon of a football scene. In a few years he became a cult of youth, a new folk hero, a living James Dean who was a rebel with a cause. The cause was clearly defined – the welfare of his club and country and to prove himself the greatest player in all history.

The rebel in him was two-fold and contrary – the creator of a new image for football – yet one who turned back the clock in a search for individual freedom in an age of conformity and method within the game. He was a son of instinct rather than logic. He was touched, mauled and buffeted by the crowd off-stage and on the field. Yet he did not suffer an inflated ego nor a wounded sense of revenge. Like breathing in and breathing out, it was all merely part of the business of life.

Certainly there were flaws in his complex psyche. There could come the sudden upsurge of angry retaliation to something brutal; sometimes a childish taunting provocation, the figurative thumbing of the nose at some frustrated opponent; a mischievous irreverence; he was difficult to pin down in personal affairs. A pied piper in one sense, he was an elusive pimpernel in another. He was a Leonardo da Vinci who wantonly threw away his paint brushes and his genius. Yet he was generous, a lost child who loved to do tricks. One of these was to drop a penny piece on the toe of his shoe, then flick it up into his top breast pocket. He never failed.

People persistently inquire his place in the hierarchy of the game. Where does he stand in relationship to Stanley Matthews, Tom Finney and the rest of the cavalcade of the past? Everything is relative from age to age. The genius of one would be the genius of another. Once Reuben Bennett, the coach of Liverpool, a Scotsman, remarked to me: 'Wee Patsy Gallacher, of Celtic, was as good as Pelé and Eusebio rolled into one.' 'And,' laughed the Liverpool players around us, 'to think that he weighed no more than eight stone when wet!' They had heard this claim a hundred times.

Once I put the question to Arthur Rowe, the architect of Tottenham's fine 'push and run' days in the early 1950s, and to Blanchflower, later his captain who carried forward the White Hart Lane spark into the 1960s: 'Place in order of preference Matthews, Finney and Best.' Rowe at first hedged: 'Diamonds are diamonds, rubies are rubies and pearls are pearls,' he replied evasively. But when Blanchflower voted for Best, Rowe was inclined to agree.

Blanchflower's reasoning ran: 'Stanley was a supreme dribbler who would tax even the most ruthless, sophisticated defences of today; but he was primarily a provider. Finney was perhaps a better all-rounder than Matthews. He could play anywhere in a forward line and besides that was a free goalscorer. But George Best gets my vote. A master of control and manipulation, he was also a superb combination of creator and finisher; he, too, could play anywhere along the line. But more than the others he seemed to have a wider, more appreciative eye for any situation. He seldom passed to a colleague in a poor position. He was prepared to carry the responsibility himself.

'But basically, Best made a greater appeal to the senses than the other two. His movements were quicker, lighter, more balletic. He offered the greater surprise to the mind and eye. Though you could do nothing about it, you usually knew how Matthews would beat you. In those terms, he was more predictable to the audience. Best, I feel, had the more refined, unexpected range. And with it all there was his utter disregard of physical danger. Think of his ability to beat giants like Ron Yeats, well over six foot, in the air. He had ice in his veins, warmth in his heart, and timing and balance in his feet.' I would second Blanchflower's opinion.

Genius is a much overworked word. Yet when Best, after a stuttering homesick start, first settled down at Old Trafford as a skinny schoolboy of fifteen, Manchester United felt that they were in the presence of an evolving genius with an individual expression. From the first, the word went out from Sir Matt Busby: 'Don't try to change this boy's style. Let him develop naturally. The rest will come in time.' Now Busby draws on his pipe and says: 'George Best was possibly the greatest player on the ball I have ever seen. You can remember Matthews, Finney, Mannion and all the great players of that era, but I cannot think of one who took the ball so close to an opponent to beat him with it as Best did.'

As for Best, his own hero remains di Stefano, of Real Madrid. Voted Footballer of the Year both at home and in Europe concurrently in 1968, Best was the sharp point of the attack in the centre; the figure 11 on his shirt meant nothing. A marked character, the hatchetman tracked his every stride, and if anything is certain it is that he will not play to his fifties like Matthews or Billy Meredith.

Yet his dedication was complete in his earlier days, his nerves non-existent. Once, before a big European Cup tie, he was calmly drinking Bovril with me at a crowded bar under the Old Trafford stands while other players, already changed, were anxiously living out the last tense moments before the kick-off in the dressing-room. With only twenty minutes to the whistle, he had to be reminded that he was playing and still unchanged. Whereupon he departed, to perform in a kind of radiance, destroying the opposition as he has done so often. Benfica, among others, will always have cause to remember him.

Best himself was a gipsy at heart. His mother was more than partial to drink. I do not think that George ever took drugs, although he became virtually an alcoholic. Yet he was a dear person and we always remained friends. He gave a house-warming party in the Wirral one fabulous Saturday night. There were so many policemen round the house it was like trying to get into the Kremlin. I had a camera with me and took some pictures – which nearly caused a scene. Best had an exclusive contract with the Express Newspaper Group and one of their photographers saw me with my camera. He went up to Best and said: 'Who's that guy taking photographs?'

'Oh, don't worry about him,' Best replied, 'He's an artist, he's just doing it for fun.' And that was the end of it.

When he was playing for Fulham in the 1970s he took me out to lunch one day at some Italian dive in the King's Road and we sat there until 5 p.m. while people paid homage to him. He told me that he was still up to his old tricks – womanising, drinking and so forth. He had just been to America where he had a house near the beach. But he said that he rarely reached the beach because, to get there, he had to go through a bar – and that was that as far as the beach was concerned. He always stopped at the bar – 'on the edge of the penalty area' so to speak.

from PARDON ME FOR LIVING *1985*

Terry Venables

PETER BALL

'I think we can grace the occasion,' says Queens Park Rangers manager Terry Venables of Saturday's FA Cup Final. 'I hope we do.' If so, then Venables' team will have done him a favour. For incredible as it would have seemed two and a half years ago, Venables' image as the shining light of English football has of late come under considerable suspicion.

Thirty months ago Crystal Palace were challenging at the top of Division One in their first season back in the top flight, and their shrewd, bubbling young manager was pointing the way forward for English football, which, apparently, no longer had to be based upon the old-fashioned values of character and competitiveness. English central defenders could break from the back and look comfortable if they popped up in a striking role, and if you did the right things, worked extensively on developing young players' technique, and added your own sharp tactical brain into the mix, then there was no reason why English teams couldn't play like the Continent's finest.

Venables' beliefs were being proved where it mattered – on the field – and if he was far too shrewd to dub his team 'The Team of the Eighties' he had plenty of admirers to do it for him. Doubters were few and tended to keep their own counsel. The distinguished ex-manager who angrily reported back to his club after a scouting visit to Crystal Palace: 'Team of the Eighties? Cheats of the Eighties more like!' did not express that feeling publicly.

With the televised serialisation of his 'Hazell' novel (co-authored with Gordon Williams), a young team around the top of the first division, and his inclusion in Ron Greenwood's squad of coaches, Venables was unquestionably the man of the future, the new breed of football man: aware, sophisticated, articulate, the man to lead English football out of the dark ages.

Of course the team could not sustain the overblown praise, and by the end of the season had slipped back to thirteenth. Which was still a testimony to Venables's genuine talents as coach and manager, that he had taken an ordinary team so far. But in persuading the critics that they were better than they really were, he perhaps made a rod for his own back.

Next season saw things quickly change. Despite the arrival of QPR's goalscoring sensation Clive Allen (via Arsenal in exchange for England full-back Kenny Sansom), the side started badly. With the club's financial situation steadily worsening, the directors panicked – or at least Chairman Ray Bloye did. 'We never had board meetings,' recalls Venables, 'because the Chairman ran things. And then suddenly we were having all these board meetings, with everyone being asked for their opinions, and people chipping in with "why did you pick so-and-so?" and all these criticisms.' Suddenly the man of the future was, at the first hiccup in his managerial career, finding himself being sniped at instead of supported.

Jim Gregory, Chairman of QPR and an old friend, had long been an admirer of Venables. He had already made periodic attempts to prise 'Venners' away from Palace, approaches which Bloye had previously dismissed with the statement that Palace would want a £1 million transfer fee to release their manager. However, this time Bloye told Venables he should talk to Gregory. The writing was on the wall.

Even so, says Venables, he turned down Gregory, pointing out that if he left the club so early in the season when they were at the bottom of the table, he would have been setting himself up for hostile criticism. Bloye, though, seemed less than convinced that Venables should remain. On the morning of yet another board meeting, Venables phoned the Vice-Chairman and asked: 'What can I do to keep me at the club?' By the afternoon he had learnt that Palace had already approached two other managers to replace him and he decided, quite reasonably, that his position had become untenable. He resigned and joined QPR.

The criticism followed. Palace fans, who had seen their manager apparently desert them, were less than enchanted when he returned to take several players with him. And when the 'revelation' was published that Venables had put up the money for an agency representing several of the players in question, darker questions began to be put. In a game rife in the last few years with rumours of greed and corruption, was Venners the latest idealist to be found with his finger in the till? There were plenty ready to believe it.

Venables made no attempt to avoid the issue. 'Perhaps I made a mistake, but I do believe that clubs should handle players' outside interests, and this was a step in that direction. Anyway what did people think? That I was using the agency to tap players? That's absurd. If I want to tap a player I can get you to do it, I can get my trainer to do it, I can pick up a phone and do it myself. And I've never taken a penny out of the game that wasn't legal. For the record, I actually lost money over the agency.'

Despite the ring of truth contained in Venables's statements, his switch of clubs still smacked to many of opportunism. After three further managers including Malcolm Allison in the one season and Bloye's sale of his shares to a consortium headed by Ron Noades, the club crashed into the second division. Venners, it seemed to his critics, had seen the right moment to launch his personal lifeboat. Tommy Docherty, an old sparring partner, encapsulated it in his expression: 'A Rubber Dinghy Man.' If Terry Venables is a 'Rubber Dinghy Man', it was a characteristic he inherited early, if unwittingly. The day after his parents moved from the house in which he was born, taking baby Venners in tow, it was bombed.

The move was a short one, exchanging one Dagenham home for another, and Venables remained there until he was twenty-three. Like many an East Ender who has made it, he then moved to Loughton in Essex, a more salubrious neighbourhood, but one still close to home. Despite the dark looks which betray his Welsh mother, he remains an East Londoner through and through. As a player, the quick, short passing and the bouncy strut revealed his background in every stride.

If Dagenham and the East End did not provide an academic education – surprisingly, Venables didn't go to grammar school, football being a greater priority than books – it left its mark in other ways. The villains and people on the edge of villainy who people Venables' books were the product of rich source material, even if the telling of them reveals his own natural talent and bright, sharp humour. (For the time being, the writing has been put aside – 'as a player I had the afternoons free, which I don't now, and I had to have Gordon Williams there to bully me into doing it' – but he expects to return to it when he finishes in football 'in about five years . . . though that depends on what happens; I said five years ago I'd leave the game before I was forty').

The Cockney wit is still there. Discussing another manager over lunch, Venables remarked that the unfortunate's nickname among his players was 'Mogadon'. *'Mogadon!'* he exclaimed with a pained expression. It would be the worst thing you could call Venables, not that anyone is ever likely to.

So too is the taste for the verbal scrap.

He is readily roused by slurs on London football and particularly on the character of London footballers. QPR & Spurs' presence in this year's cup final, the second time in three years that two London clubs have contested the final, has provided him with ammunition and he has used it with relish. 'Well, if you're attacked you've got to have a go back,' he says characteristically.

Very characteristically, in fact, for as a fellow London manager remarked: 'What you've got to understand about Terry is that he likes to think he's very sophisticated but deep down there's a good old East London backstreet scrapper.'

And then there is the keen intelligence, a handy weapon, especially on those occasions when he is making a not very good case. After hearing his defence of Omniturf, made in typical Venables style by a witty analysis of all the faults of this dreadful surface called 'grass', a pro responded with amusement, yet with doubts: 'Well, it was right. But it wasn't right.'

At thirty-nine now – 'Just thirty-nine! At our age it's important to say that, isn't it?' – the dealing in stock and shares, the Mercedes, a taste for large cigars, and the noticeably thickening waistline may reveal a successful, even sophisticated man, but the roots are still much in evidence.

As a player Venables was always looking for the little ploy which gave an opening, putting him a step ahead of slower-thinking opponents. He was a great man for free kicks, which he worked on with considerable effect during his later years at QPR, with his willing lieutenant Gerry Francis. Together they developed a number of tactics, several of which involved using the opponent's defensive wall to their own advantage.

Fooling the wall was Venables's own speciality. In one match against an Italian team at Chelsea in the mid-1960s, Chelsea were awarded a free kick just outside the box. There was the usual kerfuffle about the placing of the wall. Venables made great play of marching out the requisite ten yards but as he reached the wall, who were watching him with idle contempt, he spun, the ball was played in to him quickly, and before the Italians realised what was happening it was in the back of the net. After that, the match deteriorated rapidly, until finally an Italian was sent off for scything him down.

That incident summed up much about Venables. It was sharp thinking – although probably rehearsed, it was clearly at his instigation rather than his manager's, Tommy Docherty – it was funny, and it paid off. A typical piece of Cockney cheek. And it certainly wasn't illegal; the illegalities were all on the Italian side. Yet as a fairly neutral onlooker, I felt some sympathy for the Italians, felt sure that if I'd been on their side I'd have been outraged and attempted immediate violent retribution. Somehow 'it was right, but it wasn't right'.

That response continues to arise with Venables' teams, and they pose the most serious question about the man. He is shrewd, good company, with the quality which sets him apart from his friend, and in many ways his mentor, Malcolm Allison, that of being a good listener as well as a good talker.

Less brash and much more modest than his image sometimes suggests, he has the great talent for putting across strong criticisms without upsetting people or provoking big headlines. He is a man of substance in all respects. His idealism about the game, his belief in skill, his belief that English football has to be open to new ideas and new approaches, is undoubtedly genuine, and his teams bear it out.

Nevertheless there are doubters who question whether good values are all his teams represent. 'Cheating' might have been too strong a description, but the search for the little advantage is not to every taste. Nor is their ebullient, brash style. As one solid pro of impeccable judgement put it: 'Terry? Well, all that Crystal Palace and QPR thing, it's not to my taste. It's a bit flash, a bit spivvy. I don't think in the end people like that come out on top.'

Is that right, or is that just Northern suspicion of London style? Saturday will be revealing. In many ways Spurs and QPR are similar teams; and although very different men, both managers have very similar beliefs about football. The dour, quiet Yorkshireman and the extrovert Londoner have both been influenced by the Dutch and German teams of the 1970s, and that influence is revealed in their teams. Both are pragmatists, something which Venables' admirers sometimes close their eyes to, although he would certainly not deny it, and both teams can look after themselves when things get rough. But there perhaps is the difference. Burkinshaw the Yorkshireman has gone for the bluff hard men, the 'honest cloggers' if you like. Venners's lads are less straightforwardly aggressive, a bit niggly and petulant, although as a bloodbath at Rotherham recently proved, when the scrap began they knew how to hand it out. But then, for all the sophistication, what else would you expect from an East London scrapper?

Postscript As it turned out, to say that QPR graced the 1982 Cup Final would be an exaggeration. It wasn't that sort of match, but Rangers held their own and emerged from the replay with most of the credit for their spirited but unavailing search for an equaliser after falling behind to Hoddle's early penalty. The Tottenham fans showed their sympathy at the end by cheering their opponents off. Venables' image had been restored, if it had ever been in doubt, while Tottenham received most of the flak that was going for their failure to illuminate the occasion.

That Venables deserved praise for his tactical resource in thwarting a much more talented side was unquestionable. Whether it went beyond that is more debatable. The Tottenham point of view, expressed by Steve Perryman in his autobiography *A Man for All Seasons*, was put more forcibly at the time. 'I don't think Terry fancied getting a very public belting on an occasion like that, which could have happened with a second division team against us if they'd tried to take us on,' said one player, 'so they set out, very effectively, to stop us playing. They only really had a go at us when they were behind, and I think Terry was happy to lose 1–0 with a lot of credit.' Personally I doubt whether Venables has ever been happy with a defeat in any circumstances, but that part, the analysis, paying due credit to his pragmatism, strikes me as about right.

There was soon further evidence to support the view. After the Final, Venables went off to Spain to join Ron Greenwood's phalanx of coaches. While there, a chance conversation with Bobby Robson, who revealed that he had turned down the Barcelona manager's job partly because of the language difficulties, struck a chord. Venables began to learn Spanish.

Back in England he also picked up the threads of his success story again, taking Queens Park Rangers to the second division championship and then establishing them in the first division with marked success. Controvery continued to rage about the omniturf pitch. Publicly, Venables would not concede an inch, defending it constantly on the grounds that it helped good players and sorted out bad ones, especially defenders who were used to getting away with careless lunges. Privately such an astute man must have known he was defending the indefensible.

In 1984 QPR were firmly established as a first division team. How much further they could go with little money and small gates was questionable. Briefly it was suggested that Venables would buy the club when chairman Jim Gregory decided that he had had enough. But that did not happen. Instead he went to Barcelona. César Menotti, the Argentinian World Cup manager, had left, the latest in a long line of managers defeated in the effort to give the club the Spanish championship. This, an awesome task in itself, was made no easier when Maradona, the fans' idol, quickly departed in Menotti's wake, yet it proved a masterstroke for Venables. His ability to get the best out of awkward customers was demonstrated as the German Schuster and the Scot Archibald, Maradona's replacement, fitted in perfectly and Venables' tactical and organisational acumen, given at last the type of skilled players he exalted, worked like a dream.

Apart from an embarrassing 4–1 home defeat – after a 4–2 away victory in the first leg – by Metz in the first round of the European Cup Winners Cup, Venables had a triumphant season, bringing Barcelona the desperately coveted championship for the first time in eleven seasons. Lionised and feted, Venables was granted the freedom of Barcelona. His Spanish lessons had paid dividends, although characteristically he still uses a hardly-needed interpreter when meeting the press.

A measure of his achievement is that it was a task which had broken some of the greatest names in European football management. El Tel's stature as a football manager was established beyond reasonable doubt.

from TIME OUT *21–27/5/82; postscript 1986*

Fast Forwards – Trevor Brooking and Mike Channon

FRANK KEATING

There is just a month between them: Trevor Brooking was born in October, 1948, and Mike Channon in November. There is just one England cap between them: Brooking has forty-seven, Channon forty-six. In the admittedly dreary dozen or so years since England had a national soccer side that seemed to know exactly where the goalposts were, the two of them, more often than not, could display a singular turn of talent. They were often seen to be smiling; and when they were fouled they didn't foul back.

From the top of the stand of a murky, phosphorescent teatime, you would half-close your eyes to a squint and still tell them from the others by their gait – something you cannot do with too many mundane midfield men these days. Both were gallopers: Channon was the thoroughbred, classic, short sprinter; Brooking, who had a caressing touch on the ball, lolloped more like a stayer. Neither, alas, had quite the flamboyant nature nor the cruel competitive edge to take a game by the throat and throttle it to submission. But often and gaily they decorated many people's Saturday afternoons.

In 'Close Network'* I suggested that, if fathers care about such things, they should summon their sons and go to see Pat Jennings – at thirty-eight, three years older than these two forwards – keep goal for Arsenal just once more before he picks up the gloves from the back of his net for the last time and clatters down the tunnel for ever. The same applies here. Hurry, hurry, while such stocks last.

The 1983–84 season was Brooking's last. And no Dame Nellie Bugner he. Channon says he feels like frolicking for a few years yet, but old athletes' bones are brittle and there's no knowing how long they can keep up the chase. And if his zip goes, then surely will his zap.

Brooking joined West Ham as an apprentice in 1965, a year before Hurst, Moore, and Peters helped win the World Cup for England. He arrived with eleven O-levels and A-levels in Economics and Accountancy. Before the Sixties were over he had set up his own firm in the plastics trade. It has flourished. He has no remote desire to try his hand at soccer club management. He has his feet on the

* See page 149.

ground. A shrewd East Ender. His mother and father met when they both worked for the Co-op at Barking. Dad later became a police sergeant. On those faraway Fifties Saturdays every available police-man for miles around was not drafted with their handcuffs to Upton Park. After the boy's tenth birthday Sergeant Brooking would take him, hand in hand, to stand at the North Bank terraces for every home match. 'There was a friendly, family atmosphere, and a tingling, wholesome excitement. If I had a son of ten today I wouldn't take him near it. It's so sad.'

Later, on that same field, the lumbering jogtrot was actually deceptive. It allowed Brooking a placid, not to say serene, journey to the right place at the right time. For all his schemes were born of a sharp, clear awareness. When he was fouled he looked pained, not for himself but for the juvenile boorishness of his marker. He once scored the winning goal in a Cup final with a genuflecting header – such an unlikely event that it kept all Essex warm with delight throughout the bad summer that followed. And he could occa-sionally hit some screamers with either instep, especially with his right. Once, in Budapest for England, a twenty-odd yarder clamped itself to the net stanchion and the poor Hungarian goal-keeper took a minute or two to prise the thing away.

Channon, too, has logged some dramatic whizzbangs in his time, not least for Norwich City. He also played for Manchester City in a side that could, and should, have been an enlightening one. But it is always as a Southampton Saint that he will be remembered. Nothing really, but when he first played for England in 1972 I recall being charmed by the fact that he had a broad Wessex accent. Somehow, you don't associate the growly burr and the buzz with top flight soccer. To go with it was a hale and handsome, boyish, countryman's face; and a trim, lithe figure, and a speed that blistered off the mark; and then sometimes, in the sternest hullaba-loo, the broad, toothy smile.

He was born at Orcheston, a farming village on the Plain. Around full moons, on a clear night, you could see Stonehenge. It was equidistant, thirty miles each way, between Swindon and South-ampton. The boy was still in single figures when Dad took him to the local derby at Southampton's Dell. He couldn't see a thing, and doesn't think he enjoyed it much. But his father did, and in future when they went, they stood at the back of the terracing so son could sit on father's shoulders.

At Amesbury School, he played for Wiltshire Boys. After a match against Hampshire on the little Walled Meadow in Andover, two of the few grand old legends of Wessex football, Bert Head, the manager of Swindon, and Ted Bates, his counterpart at Southampton, met, with smiles, to haggle. Ted won, and the scrawny fifteen-year-old sprinter found himself in digs in Southampton within days.

Channon is still the countryman, the wide-eyed Jude enjoying the bigtime only while it lasts. His hobby has turned into a small business: he owns and breeds racehorses.

Trevor Brooking in his pinstripes and patent leather briefcase, might well exchange every one of his England caps to be named Young Plastics Businessman of the Year. Mike Channon would certainly swop every one of his, to own a Derby winner. So far, in the Classics anyway, they cannot run as fast as he could.

from LONG DAYS, LATE NIGHTS *1984*

Bryan Robson

HUNTER DAVIES

The minute England had qualified for the [1982] World Cup finals in Spain, the people who like to pick Ron Greenwood's team for him, of whom there are twenty million, immediately pencilled in the name of B. Robson. After all, he was the only player who had appeared in each of England's eight World Cup qualifying matches. In the past two years he has been England's most consistent player and about the only one not to suffer the personal abuse which was thrown at the team in that period.

That, plus the fact that he is the country's costliest player would, you might have thought, have made him a household name, if not a household face. Yet few people outside the game have heard of him. Even among the football faithful up and down the terraces, it is probably only the followers of Manchester United and West Bromwich Albion who could tell you very much about him. It is as if he had got to the top in disguise, coming through on the wings, so silently that nobody realised.

The *lumpen*-mass of professional footballers, toiling away every Saturday afternoon in our ninety-two league clubs, know they could never be Kevin Keegan even in their wildest dreams. They haven't got the German for a start – or his gift of the gab, or his skills, or his workrate in the television studios. But in their more realistic reveries they could possibly be Bryan Robson.

While Kev is an exotic, Bryan Robson is the archetypal English player, perhaps, the best example of what our native game thinks it is all about, the very model of a modern member of the team.

On the pitch, he's never flash. He's not the star who catches the eye like Hoddle or Brooking, whose skills are obvious for all to see, but the solid core every manager admires.

Off the pitch he's equally unobtrusive, quiet, softly spoken, rather hesitant and unsophisticated, with none of Keegan's social graces — although he has picked up bits of the outward camouflage accepted by all star players these days, such as a gold bracelet, two rings and a gold chain. Could this be the influence of Ron Atkinson, his manager at Manchester United and West Bromwich and a friend to all jewellers?

'No. That was my wife, not Ron. She bought all the jewellery for me.'

He met his wife Denise at a local pub in Birmingham six years ago. She was having her twenty-first birthday party, so he bought her a drink, when he heard she was twenty-one. 'It wasn't really like me, chatting up a strange bird.' She was a typist, but had her own car which was handy, since he hadn't; nor could he drive at the time.

They have a sixteen-month-old daughter Claire and a second child due this June, about the same time as the Princess of Wales's, and as the World Cup. They are house-hunting in Cheshire at the moment, looking for something in the £100,000 range. They fancy something Georgian; 1982 Georgian, of course.

His background is almost an Identikit version of the English player. If you were making up his life, writing it like painting by numbers, where would you have him born? The North-East, of course, where so many of our football greats have come from.

He was born in Chester-le-Street, County Durham, on January 11, 1957. His father is a long-distance lorry driver who these days spends a lot of his time abroad, lugging juggernauts through France and Italy. Bryan was christened Bryan, with a y, because his father was already Brian. He has an older sister Susan and two younger brothers, Gary, eighteen, now with West Bromwich, and Justin, sixteen, now with Newcastle.

He lived for Newcastle United as a boy. On Saturdays, when his father was at home, he and his sister Susan were taken to St James's Park, queuing up outside even before the gates opened at one o'clock. Bryan was very small as a child and his dad liked to get him settled on a wall, at the front of the terrace in the Wing Paddock, before the crowds arrived. In the 1960s, Newcastle were still getting 30,000–40,000 gates.

He collected programmes and hung team pennants on the bedroom wall of his council house, read *Tiger* and *Roy of the Rovers*, just like everyone else. He went to a comprehensive school at Birtley where, he says, he was quite good and liked history and geography, and if football had not come along he likes to think he could have got a few O levels.

Football did not come along with a rush. He got into the district team, playing for Chester-le-Street, but never made the County team, let alone the English schoolboy team. (This again is typical: few who play for England schoolboys ever last the pace and become top professionals.)

He was not very disappointed at the time not to play for Durham: he was captain of his district team, which included four boys who *did* get into the County team. Looking back, it could have been his smallness – or perhaps local politics, certain schoolmasters favouring certain schools.

One night when he was thirteen there was a knock at the door of his council house and a gentleman was standing there who said he was a scout for the Burnley football club.

'Me Mam and Dad couldn't understand him. They didn't know what scouts were. It was a bit of a shock, like.'

The scout had been that day to watch Bryan's school team play another school team because he had been tipped off about the other team's goalie. The goalie had turned out useless, but he had been impressed by B. Robson and got his home address – they were not on the phone – from a teacher.

It led, during his next school holidays, to a week's trial at Burnley, which he didn't really enjoy. He was put in digs, with one other boy, but left to his own devices, having to find his own way to the ground and back each day for training. The afternoons he whiled away on the putting green in the local park or at the pictures or just hanging about feeling lost. He couldn't understand the local *patois*, nor could they understand him. He would ask for a 'Coäk' in a caff, and they wouldn't know what he was on about.

Not long afterwards other scouts from other clubs started contacting him. He thinks the word must have got around that he'd been to Burnley (then in the First Division) so they all had a second look, even the ones who might have dismissed him earlier.

He was invited to West Bromwich for a similar week's training – but this time he loved everything about it. 'They just seemed to look after us better. It was all organised. All the lads were put in a hotel together and a mini bus picked us up, took us to the ground and brought us back. Our dinner would be fixed for us and we'd be given tickets for a match, if there was one in Birmingham that night, or the pictures. Nothing seemed too much trouble for them. They kept you involved.'

By the time he was fifteen and able to leave school, four clubs had given him some sort of trial (Burnley, West Bromwich, Coventry and Newcastle) and eleven in all had expressed some sort of interest; but from his first visit to West Bromwich, he had decided they were the club he liked best and he told other clubs accordingly. 'I could have gone on trials to many other places, and I think now I should have done. That's what I've told my younger brothers. Until you actually sign for one, go everywhere.'

He was given no extra inducements at fifteen to sign apprenticeship forms for West Bromwich, which again is probably typical (although in some cases underhand payments, or gifts to parents, do occur). The only perk from any club was from Newcastle United, who regularly sent his father free tickets for their matches, even after Bryan had told them he preferred West Bromwich.

The day he travelled through to Birmingham with his parents to sign the official forms turned out to be a bit of an anti-climax. 'They told me, just before I signed, that Newcastle had been on the phone and would still have me if I wanted to go. They said it was up to me. I couldn't believe it. It was as if they weren't bothered whether I signed or not. But I said, Oh no, I wanted to come to them, so they said fine, sign here.'

When he arrived at West Bromwich in 1972 he was only 5 ft. 2 in. and weighed just seven stone. That was the main reason why nobody, least of all West Bromwich, had been exactly panting for his signature, although they all admired his skills.

'It was West Bromwich's chief scout, Paddy Ryan, who used to cheer me up when I got depressed. "I've seen your Mam and Dad," he used to tell me, "and they're normal height. You'll be OK."'

All the same, for the whole of that first year at West Bromwich he hardly played any football. He got his £6 a week as an apprentice, swept up the dressing-rooms and cleaned the first team's boots in the time-honoured way, but he was given little chance to play football.

'It was for my own good, I suppose. They didn't want me knocked about by some big lads. I played only about fifteen games in the whole year. I was in digs on my own, which is what I wanted. If you share with some other lad then every evening it's "What shall *we* do, where shall *we* go?" I wanted just to be on my own, make up my own mind what to do. But I was very homesick.'

At the ground, during training sessions, he was given lots of weight exercises to do. In his digs, his landlady was instructed to build him up, as if preparing a fighting cock.

'Every morning for a whole year I had a raw egg with milk, sherry, and sugar mixed in. It tasted awful at first but I got used to it. It was just the sight of the raw egg that put me off. Then every evening, after my tea, I had to drink a bottle of Mackeson. It was strange. I'd never tasted beer before.'

It must have worked – or something must have worked, if only his Mam and Dad's genes. Today, he is a tough and fit-looking 5ft. 11in., weighs 11 stone and is known for the fierceness of his tackling.

On his first game in the Reserves, away to Everton, he got bounced so hard by Bob Latchford that he ended up on the cinder track, a mass of cuts and bruises. 'No, I didn't say anything to him. He was a star. I was only sixteen.'

He didn't have a lot of confidence during the next season or so and there were various changes of management at West Bromwich, which didn't help. But the worst blow to his progress from the Reserves into the first team came in the 1976–77 season when he broke his leg not once but three times.

'It happened first against Tottenham, when Chris Jones kicked me as I was tackling him. It wasn't his fault. I came back too quickly, in just eight weeks, and on my first match back, in a Reserve game, I fractured the same leg in the same place.' He recovered from that, but just towards the end of the season, against Manchester City, he broke his other leg and was out for fifteen weeks.

'I lost about a year in all before I was back to peak fitness. It didn't affect me psychologically. I never go into a tackle thinking I might get hurt again. The worst part was that it happened before I established myself. When you're established, and you get injured, everybody is waiting for your return and you get your place back quickly. But when you've never been there, you just get forgotten. You've lost all that time.'

It was the arrival of Ron Atkinson as manager in 1978 which confirmed him in the first team. He became a regular for the next three years and also played for the England Under-21 and Under-23 teams. When Ron Atkinson moved on to Manchester United, in the summer of 1981, Bryan Robson soon followed him, after a saga chronicled in the sports pages for weeks, with accusations from West Bromwich, that he was letting them down, unsettling the team, and the papers saying he was being greedy.

'I'd been there eight years and I felt I needed a change. They didn't seem to me to be thinking of themselves as a big club. When good players like Stapleton or Francis were for sale, you never heard of West Bromwich making offers. I wanted a big club with big ideas.'

There was also talk of personality differences between him and the new West Bromwich manager, Ronnie Allen; but Bryan will say nothing about this. He has never been one for giving public opinions. 'I don't like people slagging each other off. I don't believe in criticising others. I just want to get on with my own job.'

West Bromwich asked £2 million at first and finally settled on £1·5 million – plus 15 per cent VAT and 5 per cent to the FA pension fund. Players no longer get a cut of transfer fees, but they do arrange their own terms and wages, helped, in Bryan's case, by an accountant and lawyer. 'I let them get on with it. While they went through the forms, I went for my medical. The price was ridiculous. We shouldn't have got to that state. No footballer is worth that sort of money.'

Other players have suffered with big prices on their heads. Steve Daley, perhaps the best known recent example, seemed almost to be diminished once he went to Manchester City for a record £1 million.

'I did have Steve Daley at the back of my mind when I went to Manchester, but I was determined to dismiss all thoughts of the money. I told myself it was nothing at all to do with me. I hadn't set it. It was the two clubs, not me.

'Instead I thought of what the pressures must be like for a *striker* who has cost over a million. As a midfield player, I felt no real pressures. I can go twenty games without scoring, and nobody will get at me.'

Since Robson's arrival Manchester United have greatly improved, shooting up the league. But he doesn't feel he is quite into his stride yet. At West Bromwich, in his last two years, he averaged, by his own standards, four good games out of five. In his first ten for Manchester United, he felt only three were good, one poor, and the rest average.

'It's hard to explain why a footballer sometimes doesn't play well. Nobody ever *wants* to play badly. Every professional always tries hard, whatever the critics might say.

'Some days it's because you're trying *too* hard. You rush in, play too quickly, make a mistake and your confidence can go. You have to steady yourself, slow down, read the game. Some days your touch is just not on. Then you have to say: "Well, I can still help the team, I can still run and still defend."'

He gets very upset by those who call today's footballers greedy. It wasn't the money that was the main attraction of Manchester United, whatever the West Bromwich fans (the ones who sent him hate letters) might have thought. In the end, his old club offered him a contract for five years which in basic terms was not far from United's.

'It seems that everyone in life can go out and work hard, earn as much money as they can to give their family a better life – except footballers. When it happens to them people call them greedy. Pop stars, golfers, tennis players, they get real fortunes compared with footballers, yet nobody accuses them in newspapers of being greedy.'

What happens, of course, is that disaffected managers, who have either lost or failed to get a star player, turn round in their ghosted columns and accuse players of holding them over a barrel.

At West Bromwich his earnings were modest until last year. It had taken him a long time – from £6 to £28 as a professional, to £45 in the reserves and then to £75 when he got into the first team. Now, at his England peak, and with the country's most glamorous team, he should earn £60,000 a year from football. His non-football earnings are almost non-existent, so far. (Keegan, on the other hand, gets £100,000 a year *outside* football.)

The first and obvious differences between West Bromwich and Manchester United is the crowds. Home and away, if you play for United, you play to huge crowds who cheer you, regardless, all through the match. At West Bromwich, Bryan got ten to twelve fan letters a week. Overnight, after arriving in Manchester, the mail has jumped to a hundred a week, from all over the world: Tahiti to Norway, Canada to Sweden. He answers all of them. He doesn't mind the postage, which he pays himself, but sending signed photographs is proving expensive.

Then there are the facilities. Some of them might seem rather trivial, but even after three months, Bryan could still hardly get over them. 'Do you know we get flip-flops and dressing gowns provided by the club? Really. The training ground is terrific. At West Bromwich you just got changed, went home, and that was it. Here, after training, we can have a sauna, then we can put on our flip-flops and dressing gowns and just wander round, casual like. There's a restaurant and a place where you can sit and talk to people, friends or the press. On the team coach they provide a real meal, you know. Steak and roast potatoes I had last week. We never had that on the team coach at West Bromwich. And there's a video. I get a free club car, a Granada 2·8 Ghia. It's really good. And every time you go to

Old Trafford, no matter what time of day, there's always a sort of buzz. You really *feel* you're at a big club.'

He felt he played well in his first England game, against Eire, but was upset to be left out of the vital European match against Italy. 'I'd had an ankle injury. I tried hard in Australia with the England team to impress Ron Greenwood that I was better, but he didn't pick me. I watched the lads on television before the Italian game. They'd had tea with Mrs Thatcher at Downing Street and I felt really sick that I wasn't one of them as I saw them all coming out. It really hardened my attitude. I realised you can't take anything for granted.'

Since he returned to the team, he has remained – and has now got fourteen caps and played ten games on the trot. Everyone tells him he is now a fixture, definite for Spain, but he refuses to accept it. He says he has to keep turning it on every week to keep his place.

The rituals with the England team are completely different from normal league matches. For a start, he has never seen Ron Greenwood give a specific team talk. 'He spends the time the England team are together picking off players individually and going through their specific jobs at a personal level. There's a relaxed, almost casual approach, but nothing is left to chance.' Even the chosen team is given out rather informally while the players are in tracksuits at training.

'I find it easier playing for England than in a normal league match. There's an extra spark, pulling on an England shirt, unlike the Saturday week in, week out, sort of game. I find I get more space. The opposition in internationals allows you more time than in League matches. Physically it's easier. But it's harder to get the ball back once you lose it.

'If we'd lost the Hungary match, we would have been lynched. I'm not kidding. We would have to hide for four years, or emigrated.'

For England, he has been playing mostly in the middle of the mid-field, which is where he prefers to play and where he played at West Bromwich. In the Manchester United team he has been operating on the left of the middle, leaving Ray Wilkins to be the middle man, which has taken him some time to adjust to. He is naturally left-footed, which helps. He has also operated very effectively as a sweeper for England (going back into defence, to sweep up), which he thinks is an asset and hopes will give him a better chance of keeping his England place. In the years ahead, when his legs tire, he sees himself going permanently into the defence.

His main rival for England defensive mid-field position is his club colleague, Ray Wilkins. Brooking, Hoddle and Devonshire are really competing among themselves to be the mid-field creative man. Robson does create chances, and is at his best when going forward having won the ball in a tackle, and then surging past his man; but his combination of strong defensive tackling (which Brooking, Hoddle and Devonshire don't possess) and his eagerness to go forward when the chance presents itself makes him an almost perfect *team* player, able to help at the front and the rear . . .

Footballers are very fond of regular habits. Robson feels lost if he isn't wearing a Number 7 shirt for Manchester United. That was always his number at West Bromwich, too. His other bit of superstition is a champagne cork with a two pence piece on top, fixed in the wire, which he takes to every match. . . .

'I don't like being flashy or living an extravagant life. I'm not really an individual player. I always think what's best for my team-mates, but I do want to do more things now. I want to do charity things, help children particularly. If you get close to the top you have a sort of duty to help the less fortunate.'

He then went off to book an appointment to have his hair done. He was due for another perm. It is not as distinctive a perm as Mr Keegan's, more a subdued version. But there again, Mr Robson is a more subdued person. But a very worthy one: I'd have him in my team.

from SUNDAY TIMES MAGAZINE 31/1/82

Part Four

THE GALLANT ART OF
GOALKEEPING

Keeping Goal at Cambridge

Vladimir Nabokov

Of the games I played at Cambridge soccer has remained a wind-swept clearing in the middle of a rather muddled period. I was crazy about goalkeeping. In Russia and the Latin countries, that gallant art had been always surrounded with a halo of singular glamour. Aloof, solitary, impassive, the crack goalie is followed in the streets by entranced small boys. He vies with the matador and the flying ace as an object of thrilled adulation. His sweater, his peaked cap, his kneeguards, the gloves protruding from the hip pocket of his shorts, set him apart from the rest of the team. He is the lone eagle, the man of mystery, the last defender. Photographers, reverently bending one knee, snap him in the act of making a spectacular dive across the goal mouth to deflect with his fingertips a low, lightning-like shot, and the stadium roars in approval as he remains for a moment or two lying full length where he fell, his goal still intact.

But in England, at least in the England of my youth, the national dread of showing off and a too grim preoccupation with solid teamwork were not conducive to the development of the goalie's eccentric art. This at least was the explanation I dug up for not being over-successful on the playing fields of Cambridge. Oh, to be sure, I had my bright, bracing days – the good smell of turf, that famous inter-Varsity forward dribbling closer and closer to me with the new tawny ball at his twinkling toe, then the stinging shot, the lucky save, its protracted tingle. . . . But there were other, more memorable, more esoteric days, under dismal skies, with the goal area a mass of black mud, the ball as greasy as a plum pudding, and my head racked with neuralgia after a sleepless night of verse-making. I would fumble badly – and retrieve the ball from the net. Mercifully the game would swing to the opposite end of the sodden field. A weak, weary drizzle would start, hesitate, and go on again. With an almost cooing tenderness in their subdued croaking, dilapidated rooks would be flapping about a leafless elm. Mists would gather. Now the game would be a vague bobbing of heads near the remote goal of St John's or Christ's, or whatever college we were playing. The far, blurred sounds, a cry, a whistle, the thud of a kick, all that was perfectly unimportant and had no connection with me. I was less the keeper of a soccer goal than the keeper of a secret. As with folded arms I leant my back against the left goalpost, I enjoyed the luxury of closing my eyes, and thus I would listen to my heart knocking and feel the blind drizzle on my face and hear, in the distance, the broken sounds of the game, and think of myself as of a fabulous exotic being in an English footballer's disguise, composing verse in a tongue nobody understood about a remote country nobody knew. Small wonder I was not very popular with my teammates.

from SPEAK, MEMORY *1967*

Judgement and the Art of Goalkeeping

H. D. DAVIES

It used to be accepted as axiomatic that goalkeepers, like wicket-keepers, were 'a slate loose'. That opinion probably originated in the good old days, say the Gay Nineties or the early years of the Edwardian period, when 'rushing the goalkeeper' was a legitimate tactic during the taking of a corner-kick and when goalkeepers often went into the net faster than the ball that followed.

Goalkeepers, of course, though they often had to take things lying down, were not without resources of their own. A stinging right hook at a ball floating into goal, coupled with a firm left jab at a protruding head trying to help it in, used to be the solution to many a goalkeeping problem; and many an inside-forward of those early days needed no other proof of the intensity of goalmouth exchanges than to point ruefully to the number of teeth missing.

Yet the basic qualities required for good goalkeeping vary little, if at all, from age to age. They are keen vision, prompt reflexes, adequate physical endowments covering height, reach, and muscular agility, courage, and daring, and judgement – yes, judgement, that master quality which brings all the others into play at the right spot and at the right time. In this quality of judgement are included so many important things, such as divination of an attacking forward's intentions, a correct sense of positioning, and a knowledge of when to sally forth from goal and when to stay put.

It was the possession of this quality in such marked degree that made Sam Hardy, of Liverpool and Aston Villa, automatic first choice for England for thirteen years and still wins him the vote as probably the surest, if also the least spectacular, goalkeeper so far known. It was such judgement, too, which in the recent match between Manchester City and Manchester United enabled City's experienced Trautmann to outshine United's relatively immature Gregg at the other end.

Splendid as was his performance, to describe Trautmann as the best goalkeeper known to English football would be to fly in the face of known facts and common experience. The pageant of our winter game has been graced by a succession of superb goalkeepers who obligingly fall into clearly marked categories. The quietists, like Hardy or Hibbs, were able to make goalkeeping look easy by the speed and stealth of their preparatory moves (often unmarked by the crowd), and by their uncanny reading of a forward's intentions. The acrobats, Swift, evoking delight and laughter with his gorilla-like reach, his bucket-like hands, and thrilling swoops; the other, Trautmann, as outstanding among goalkeepers for his diving grace as is the swallow among the birds.

In the dare-devil class we may put 'John Willy' Sutcliffe and Dai Davies, both of Bolton Wanderers, types we are not likely to see again. In their intrepidity and indifference to bruises they were characteristic of their age. Both started as Rugby League players for Swinton, and both gained international caps – Sutcliffe for England and Davies for Wales. Both, in turn, were persuaded by the Wanderers to change to Association football and both again won international honours. As might be expected both excelled in the dangerous and difficult task of diving headlong at an oncoming forward's feet and whisking the ball away as they curled up and rolled to safety, a feat performed by Swift as well as any of the moderns in his younger, more carefree days. 'John Willy' could enliven the dullest game by the air of aristocratic disdain with which he would lift the ball over an opponent's head and at the same time allow him to hurl himself into space. Both Sutcliffe and Davies played in FA Cup finals for the Wanderers but neither gained a winner's medal.

And yet, even if the dare-devils of olden time must disappear, may the characters reappear from time to time; men like L. R. Roose of the Sunderland, Everton, and Stoke clubs, an amateur player, wit, and practical joker; Iremonger, of Notts County, humorist, and penalty king; or Foulke, of Sheffield United, an extraordinary barrel-shaped goalkeeper who carried twenty-one stones of too, too solid flesh around.

Though huge and apparently top-heavy, Foulke was amazingly

nimble on his peg-top legs, could stoop easily to ground shots, could catch or pick up a ball one-handed, and could hoist it on a still day three parts the length of the field from a goal-kick. With a following wind of any strength he could even bombard the opposite goal. The sight of Foulke's stomach in goal was said to have been the one thing which would persuade Bloomer to abandon his golden rule when shooting – namely, never to let the ball rise above knee high. The story goes that in one match Bloomer twice knocked Foulke insensible with violent shots in the stomach, and sought to do it a third time. But this time Foulke incontinently fled and let the ball through.

In recent times Bartram, late of Charlton Athletic, has made his mark as a colourful character. His idolators claim him as the finest English goalkeeper who never gained a cap. His alleged fault was a craze for rushing out of goal and making spectacular forays far beyond the penalty-area. His other virtue of ensuring that there was rarely a dull moment when he was playing is one that rarely appeals to international selectors. Gregg of Manchester United has the same mania for leaving his goal and has already been dubbed 'Bartram the second'; with what justification will emerge as time goes on.

Stories based on the idiosyncrasies of goalkeepers, like the best wines, improve with age. And the farther they recede from the date of their origin the more devoutly they are believed. One such story concerns Doig of Sunderland, at Burnden Park. This famous Scottish goalkeeper had a habit, apparently, of leaning negligently against a post with arms folded when play was at the other end, of turning his back on the game, and of exchanging repartee with any obliging customer in the crowd.

One one occasion, it is said, Shepherd, a famous centre-forward in his day and a terrific shot, suddenly let fly from the centre circle in a bold attempt to catch Doig napping. From this point the versions vary. One – the favourite of those who revere Shepherd's shooting powers – holds that the ball flashed through the posts before Doig was aware of the danger. Another states that the ball just missed the posts and knocked Doig's cap off. A third – probably a truer version – states that Doig, warned by shouts of 'Look out!' was just in time to turn and shamefacedly scramble the ball over the bar. Whatever the truth of the matter, this story does at least conjure up two pictures that go far to carry conviction to those who knew Doig and Shepherd – that characteristic posture of Doig, leaning on a post, and the tremendous force which Shepherd could put into his shots.

Another story tells how George, of Aston Villa, once pranced up and down his goal-line like a dancing dervish, beating his knees with his gloved hands and shrieking, 'He's coming again! He's coming again!' when he saw Shepherd bearing down on him at top speed for the second time in the match. George's concern, if true, was not surprising, for broken fingers, sprained wrists, and damaged ribs were often the portion of those goalkeepers who had to face the Bolton terror. Shepherd had just about the most powerful thighs one has seen on any footballer, and that includes Joe Smith, and by assiduous practice he mastered Bloomer's secret of keeping his shots low.

This recalls at least one true incident. On one occasion Shepherd raced through in his usual headlong fashion towards one of the coolest and neatest of all goalkeepers – Elisha Scott – an adept at gathering the ball cleanly and going down on one knee to get his body well behind low shots. The Burnden ground was like a quagmire, the ball 'a ton weight' as we say. Shepherd let fly, straight at Scott, as it happened, and Scott, without flinching, stooped and hugged the ball to his bosom and, still hugging it, felt himself slip back helplessly over his own goal-line. Catching that ball must have felt like trying to catch one of those old iron cannonballs as used in the Napoleonic wars.

Everyone of course has some favourite goalkeeper's yarn. One of the most popular concerns that elongated humorist Iremonger, whose spidery frame – the whole 6ft. 4in. of it – crowned by an enormous cap, used to provoke such mirth in the act of guarding the Notts County goal. The story goes that in one match Iremonger ran the full length of the field to take a penalty-kick, hit the crossbar, wheeled, joined in the mad scramble to get to the other end, and, in a wild attempt to kick clear his opponent's final shot at goal, scored disastrously against his own side! All who remember Iremonger will have no difficulty in filling in the details.

The only reason one has to doubt the authenticity of this story is that, like so many of the W. G. Grace collection, the incident referred to is now claimed to have taken place on so many different grounds. But the general shape of the story does corroborate one indisputable fact, namely that Iremonger, like Shackleton, enjoyed his football so much that he sought to get fun out of it and to make fun for others. And after all what is the basic idea of football but fun?

from THE BEDSIDE GUARDIAN 7 1958

The Goalkeeper

R. C. ROBERTSON-GLASGOW

In big-time Soccer the goalkeeper is the dickens of a fellow. Photographs in the newspapers show him to be perpetually in flight. Excelsior. He is a trapeze-artist without the trapeze. Compared with him the star of Ballet is a rheumatic elephant. None but the cynic would conjecture that this airborne hero, if only he had stayed where he was on the ground, might have saved the goal quite comfortably and altered the result of the Pools.

It is reassuring, therefore, to record that in Junior School football these things are still managed very differently. Here the goalkeeper, so far from being heroic or starlike, is an outcast on the face of the earth; literally so, for most of the time. He rolls in the mud and waits to be sworn at. Every goal that he lets past is no one else's fault. Like Punch in the old show he's a villain by right; and he's beyond care or cure.

And there he stood; as small as life, between the towering uprights. He seemed to have borrowed for the occasion his uncle's boots and his youngest brother's shorts. It was a match. For there was a referee. There were also spectators of a kind. Of these, a few loudly urged the home players on to unlikely feats of skill; two were playing 'conkers'; and one, with his back to the game, had his cap over the right eye while the left eye waited for aeroplanes.

There is a sort of fellow-feeling between us goalkeepers. I too have done my share of retrieving the ball from the net amid rhetorical questions. So I walked round towards the home goal. As I neared it, the visiting inside-right broke away, and, from five yards, shot hard and straight at the goalkeeper. The ball rebounded up the field. I praised the hero of this encounter. 'Oompha loocha,' he said, doubled up into Esperanto. Recovering his wind he winked at me and said, 'Cor'.

Then, while a corner-kick was being taken with uncommon care at the far end, he revealed how he had started as a centre-forward in early September. By Michaelmas he had worked outwards to the left wing and backwards to right-half. He had by-passed full-back, a position which anyhow he rated low; and Guy Fawkes Day had seen him settled in goal; for life, he reckoned.

At this point in his narrative he was summoned to action. In a scrummage to the left of his goal he and the ball were sat on for some fifteen seconds. Recovering, but disorientated, he threw the ball ten yards into the centre, whence it was crashed into the net. Some time after the restart of play, his captain, the left-back, who seemed to devote more time to administration than execution, was still cursing him. Then the ball hit the talkative captain on the back of the neck and passed into the top right-hand corner of the net. 'Getting good with your head, aren't you?' said the goalkeeper. 2–0 against, and mutiny spreading.

from ALL IN THE GAME *1943*

What I Owe to Football

ALBERT CAMUS

Yes, I played for several years at the University of Algiers. It seems to me like yesterday. But when, in 1940, I put on my boots again, I realised that it was not yesterday. Before the end of the first half, my tongue was hanging out like those *kabyles* dogs that one comes across at two o'clock in the afternoon, at Tizi-Ouzou. It was a long while ago, then, from 1928 onwards, I believe. I made my début with Montpensier sports club. God knows why, since I lived at Belcourt, and the Belcourt-Mustapha team is Gallia-Sports. But I had a friend, a shaggy fellow, who swam in the port with me and played water polo for Montpensier. That's how one's life is determined. Montpensier often played at the Manoeuvre Grounds, for no apparent reason. The ground was bumpier than the shin of a visiting centre-forward at the Alenda Stadium, Oran. I quickly learned that the ball never came to you where you expected it. This helped me in life, above all in the metropolis, where people are not always wholly straightforward. But after a year of bumps and Montpensier, they made me ashamed of myself at the lycée: a 'university man' ought to play for Algiers University, RUA. At this period, the shaggy fellow had gone out of my life. We hadn't quarrelled, it was merely that he now went swimming at Padovani, where the water was not pure. Nor, frankly, were his motives. Personally, I found his motive charming, but she danced badly, which seemed to me insupportable in a woman. It's the man, is it not, who should tread on the toes? The shaggy fellow and I had merely promised to see each other again. But years have gone by. Much later, I frequented the Padovani restaurant (for pure motives)

143

but the shaggy fellow had married his paralytic, who must have forbidden him to bathe, as is the usual practice.

Where was I? Yes, RUA. I was very pleased, the important thing for me being to play. I fretted with impatience from Sunday to Thursday, for training day, and from Thursday to Sunday, match day. So I joined the university men. And there I was, goalkeeper of the junior team. Yes, it all seemed quite easy. But I didn't know that I had just established a bond which would endure for years, embracing every stadium in the Department, and which would never come to an end. I did not know then that twenty years after, in the streets of Paris or even Buenos Aires (yes, it happened to me) the words RUA spoken by a friend I met would make my heart beat again as foolishly as could be. And since I am giving away secrets, I can admit that in Paris, for instance, I go to watch the matches of the Racing Club de Paris, whom I have made my favourites solely because they wear the same jerseys as RUA, blue and white hoops. I must say, too, that Racing has some of the same eccentricities as RUA. It plays 'scientifically', as we say, and scientifically loses matches it should win. It seems that this has changed (so they write to me from Algiers) so far at least as RUA are concerned. It needed to change – but not too much. After all, that was why I loved my team so much, not only for the joy of victory, so wonderful when it is combined with the weariness that follows exertion, but also for the stupid desire to cry on evenings when we had lost.

At full-back I had The Big Fellow – I mean Raymond Couard. He had a tough time of it, if I remember correctly. We used to play hard. Students, their fathers' sons, don't spare themselves. Poor us, in every sense, a good half of us mown down like corn! We had to face up to it. And we had to play 'sportingly', because that was the golden rule of the RUA, and 'strongly', because, when all is said and done, a man is a man. Difficult compromise! This cannot have changed, I am sure. The hardest team was Olympic Hussein Dey. The stadium is beside the cemetery. They made us realise, without mercy, that there was direct access. As for me, poor goalkeeper, they went for my body. Without Roger, I would have suffered. There was Boufarik, too, that great big centre-forward (among ourselves we called him Watermelon) who always came down with all his weight, right on my kidneys, without counting the cost: shin-massage with football boots, shirt pulled back by the hand, knees in the distinguished parts, sandwiches against the post . . . in brief, a scourge. And every time Watermelon apologised with a 'Sorry, son,' and a Franciscan smile.

I shall stop. I have already exceeded the limits set for me. And then, I am softening. There was good even in Watermelon. Besides, let us be frank, we paid him back. But without cheating, as this was the way we were taught. And at this point, I no longer want to go on jesting. For, after many years in which the world has afforded me many experiences, what I most surely know in the long run about morality and the obligations of men, I owe to sport, I learned it with RUA. That, in short, is why the RUA cannot die. Let us preserve it. Let us preserve this great and good image of our youth. It will keep watch over yours, as well.

from FRANCE FOOTBALL *1957*

Moscow v. Chelsea, 1945

ALEXEI ('TIGER') KHOMICH

Only one of the Moscow Dynamo team which came to England in November 1945 had really serious experience of international football. That was our captain, Michael Semichastny. But even he had never seen the English play football, let alone played against them. The only one of the Dynamos who turned out to have previously played against the English before was, somewhat surprisingly, myself – the goalkeeper. True the English players whom I had previously faced in my goal were not the same ones as those whom I was to meet in the Fatherland of Football. But they were, nevertheless, representatives of English football. I met them in the matches for the 'Shah's Cup' at Teheran in 1944.

But two years had passed between the Teheran games and our London match. In the meantime I had managed to play for a season with the team which became champions of the Soviet Union. In my twenty games with the Dynamos I let only twelve goals through, but what goalkeeper worth his salt can remain imperturbable at the thought of even a single goal scored against him? The ideal score of 'nil' against him is always on his mind.

Gradually I had begun to succeed where I previously used to fail. Many things still remained difficult, inaccessible. I always mused: 'If I only had a chest broad enough to cover up the entire goal – if I only had arms long enough to grasp both goal-posts at a time – if I only had legs worked by springs, so that I could jump without effort to the furthest corner!'

But, alas, even the world's best keeper has to do without such supernatural gifts. But the goalkeeper's innate talents, strenuous training and rich experience go a long way to fill the gap. The goalkeeper's gloved fist is like that of a boxer: quickness and accuracy win through. When the goalkeeper throws the ball it is like putting the shot; when he leaps after it, it is like a high jump. On other occasions he has to be an acrobat.

As soon as we reached London I was eager, like the rest of us, to see the English play. What was the quality of their game? How dangerous were their forwards? How could they surprise me when I faced them for the first time? Did they try to score by main force, or did they use subtler tactics? I was interested in the team work of the English forwards, in their individual passes and shots. I wanted to see the famous 'Gunners' having a shot at goal as soon as possible, and to make the acquaintance of English celebrities.

And here we are at the Chelsea–Birmingham game. It is a Saturday afternoon. The stands are crowded. The spectators have various ways of showing their pleasure or dissatisfaction. They shout and whistle. They even sing songs. They repeat phrases in a chorus. They make good use of the rattles sold at the entrance to the stadium.

The Dynamo team, leaving its red bus, makes its way to the stand. Many people recognise us; for the newspapers have, for some days before our first match, printed photos of our team, describing our training games and featuring articles about individual players. After our first training game, they nicknamed me 'Tiger.' 'Well,' I thought, 'if I am called Tiger, I might as well act like one. I will try to find out what it feels like to be in a tiger's skin.'

Meanwhile the game had started. We watched the English players carefully. Each of us tried to see something that would prove useful to him. I specially watched Tommy Lawton. He was much talked of and written about in England. They said there had never been a centre-forward like him since Drake, and they added that Lawton was, if anything, even better. 'Oh, Tommy – he is like a machine gun!' 'Lawton – a great player.' Thus spoke those who told us about English football.

'Tommy will score his goals, don't you worry,' they added. These tales didn't make me feel any better.

Lawton is tall and lean, moves quickly, and is always dangerous as he can shoot hard from almost any angle. He is an excellent header. He is a typical prima donna. The entire team plays for him and creates opportunities for him. Lawton runs fast and leaps like a tiger; he can knock the ball out of the goalkeeper's hands with his head. Woe to the goalkeeper who forgets himself even for a second when facing Lawton! The ball will be knocked out of his hands and kicked into the net. English rules allow tackling the goalkeeper in this way. In our country such tactics would incur a penalty.

Lawton was stretching his legs before the match. His movements were free, if somewhat theatrical. The movie cameras were following him around. I saw Lawton shooting. The ball went like lightning to the top right-hand corner of the goal. No. 9! Then he shot a second ball into the other corner this time. No. 9 again! My face, as my comrades later reminded me, became longer and longer. I realised that I would be facing a dangerous opponent who could surprise me very unpleasantly at any moment. It is no joke to hit No. 9 regularly – on order, as it were.

But to explain this No. 9. During our theoretical training, a picture of the goal was divided into numbered squares: 9 covered the squares which are hardest for the goalkeeper to defend. It was there that Lawton's shots went.

The game started. Lawton did not disappoint the experts: he scored twice. One was a header into the upper right corner of the goal, and the other a low, running shot, into the left corner of the net – two masterpieces of their kind. Yes, indeed, my job was not going to be easy!

The day of our first game came at last. It was our match with Chelsea. We were silent when we drove to the stadium in our familiar red bus. With the rest of my kit I took with me a bottle, which I place at the back corner of the goal if the weather is dry. This bottle attracted the attention of the spectators and was the subject of many arguments and guesses. Fifteen minutes before the game we started 'limbering up'. I wanted to create the atmosphere of an international game on the green grass of an English stadium. And then came the referee's whistle. The game was on!

The game was played in surroundings unfamiliar to me. In our stadiums the spectators sit a considerable distance from the field. And here the spectators were sitting and standing at the very goal. Policemen were pacing up and down quietening the crowds. During the first half I had to make many desperate saves which taxed my strength to the utmost.

The English forwards attacked well. The wings made accurate passes into the penalty area, where Lawton stood invariably in readiness, watched by our captain, Semichastny. Sometimes he manoeuvred or moved backwards, but I could always feel that the other English forwards constantly had their eye on their prima donna.

Several times English forwards charged me while I was holding the ball. They wanted to knock it out of my hands or else to push me into the goal with it. I had to avoid this and often punched the ball back with my fist instead of catching it.

How did we lose the first two goals? The first came this way: Lawton shot hard at the goal. I caught the ball; Lawton literally knocked it out of my hands and Goulden shot it into a corner of the goal where I could not possibly reach it. The second goal came quite unexpectedly during a scramble at the goal; the ball hit some player and ricocheted into the net.

It is difficult for me to forget one incident when the score was 2–0 against us. Lawton for once manages to get the ball past Semichastny and is alone in the penalty area. He moves towards me, with our backs close on his heels. They will never reach him, though. Soon he will shoot. But where? ... Clever Lawton does not reveal his intentions. His movements are deceptive. It seems to me that he would like to frighten me. 'Well, Tiger, look out! See what you can make of this one!' I can see nothing but the quick movements of the ball and of Lawton's feet. Then an imperceptible move, as precise as clockwork. The ball leaves his foot at the very moment when at last Semichastny has reached him. I can see not a football but a cannon-ball whistling on its way towards the far right corner of the goal, half a yard above the ground. I make a desperate dive ... I've got it. I've got the ball. I grasp it and press it to my chest. The game continues. From the stands there is prolonged applause and a deafening noise of the rattles. The score remains 2–0.

Need I tell you our feelings with the 2–0 against us? Nevertheless after half-time the game became quite favourable to us.

Suddenly I heard somebody shouting behind the goal 'Khomich – whisky! Khomich – whisky!' At first I could not make out what it was about, but then it became clear to me. Somebody had walked from the stand to see what I was doing with the bottle which I had placed behind the goal. It appears they had made up their minds in the stands that both the bottle and myself were filled with whisky, and that I took a sip from time to time to make me play in true tiger style. They would be very much surprised if they knew that the bottle contained nothing but plain water. I pour it on my gloves because when they are wet they grip the ball easier. If there are puddles near the goal, I wet my gloves in them and don't use the bottle.

Shortly before the end, after we had equalised, a third goal was scored against us by Lawton. I dived to get the ball from under his feet, but he was too fast for me. Radikovsky, who stood in the goal-mouth, cleared it, but Lawton reached the ball with his head, and with the grace of a professional acrobat put it lightly into the net.

We were able to draw the game, as you all know. We were quite satisfied with the result, about which so much was written at the time and is still discussed. We all remembered that it was our first game in England and that a draw against a strong opponent was no small success. John Harris, captain of the Chelsea team, summed up my own part in the game: 'Two of Lawton's shots could not have been saved by any other goalkeeper, but Khomich somehow managed to get at them with his tiger's leap.'

from LILLIPUT *1960*

Close Network

FRANK KEATING

Frank Swift was the first goalkeeper to dominate the six-yard box of my consciousness. He had hands as big as Joe Baksi and, on tiptoe, the peak of his cap could touch the crossbar. Raymond Glendenning would always describe him on the wireless as 'the big fellow'. Then came the first colour photographs, and a shot of Bert Williams turning one round for a corner, wings outstretched in flight like a tacking Spitfire, inspired me to ask my mother to knit me a similar polo-neck jumper of canary yellow.

Swift became a journalist and, representing the *News of the World*, died in the Munich air crash in 1958. The last I heard of Williams he was headmaster of a School for Goalkeepers in the Black Country. In the earlyish 1950s Bert vied for the yellow badge of courage with another Midlander, Gil Merrick, who in the space of three hours on either side of Christmas 1952, let in thirteen goals against Hungary. Thereafter, with his sad toothbrush moustache and spaniel eyes, he always looked like the boxer, Jack Gardner, when Bruce Woodcock was hitting him.

Back in the mists they were called 'net-minders'. In an essay on his craft in 1900, the Southampton polo-neck, Jack Robinson, began: 'We do not grow on trees. Many imagine us custodians of the sticks are as plentiful as berries in autumn. I concede there are thousands who consider themselves keepers of the goal, but you must remember there are thousands upon thousands of men who consider themselves poets. And just as there are poets and poets so there are goalkeepeepers and goalkeepers.' Quite.

Far earlier than that, in *Football at Westminster School*, H. G. Benham had defined the very beginnings for every mittened Horatius. 'A goalkeeper is a duffer or funk-stick. If any player who was playing out showed any sign of funk or failed to play up, he was packed off into goal at once, not only for the day, but as a lasting degradation. On the other hand, if any keeper made a good save of a goal, he was called for immediately to play out, and thenceforth he played out always.'

Since when, of course, the Netminders' Union has become a pretty closed shop. It is not in the least bit chauvinist to say the British have been remarkably well blessed. Offhand, since Glendenning's 'big fellow', I can rattle off a litany of last-liners – Hopkinson and Hodgkinson, Swindin and Bartram, Springett and Ditchburn, Kelsey and Sprake, Uprichard and Gregg, Lawrence and Stepney and Brown. Not forgetting Bonetti 'The Cat' . . . nor Montgomery of the Sunderland save . . .

Oddly, Scotland have seldom fielded reliable hundred per centers. Their glorious talents are reserved for those playing 'out'. I suppose the most celebrated tartan goalie remains John Thomson, who was capped at twenty-two in 1930 but a year later died after diving at the feet of a Ranger. At his memorial service, the theme of the requiem was, 'Greater love hath no man than that he lay down his life for his friends.' His ghost is said still to haunt the six-yard box at Celtic. On braw and wintry full-moon nights at Celtic Park you can still, apparently, hear the eerie, desperate, high-pitched shriek of 'Mine!'

My own particular favourite was the Fulham gloveman a quarter of a century past. When Tony Macedo was good he was very, very good – but when . . . But we loved him. He once lost us a semi-final of the Cup. But we knew he'd got us there in the first place. He was a magnificent madcap. The old *Manchester Guardian* football correspondent, H. D. Davies, may well have seen Macedo the week before he wrote that it was 'axiomatic that goalkeepers, like wicketkeepers, were "a slate loose"'. *

Then Gordon Banks rewrote the rules, re-drew the geometry, upped even the courage. I was in Mexico for the 1970 World Cup,

* *See page 138.*

but was covering another match and never saw for real Banks' save against Pelé, of Brazil and the Universe. On television it is all over and done with in a blurr. But the journalist, John Moynihan, was actually behind Banks' net as:

'Pelé hurtled in, leaping over Mullery, and all for one were shouting "Goal!" and rising to acclaim the "King". Then an outrageous flash of movement, a combination of sprawling arms and legs. Banks was suddenly over to the right of goal lying sideways with his left leg thrust out straight, his other bent at right angles and his groping right hand scooping the ball up and over the crossbar. Banks, in this attitude of a praying mantis after spinning to a new twig, had played the ball up and away with an extended palm into oblivion. It tumbled over the bar and rolled slowly onto the other side of the net with the sudden abatement of an ocean wave after breaking on a rock. And one wondered, amid all the shouting and screaming and commotion, whether England's goalkeeper had broken his arm and suffered grievous damage; he lay on his back with his shoulders on the grass, his colleagues standing around too nonplussed to yell their praise. Already the moment had become a legend, a piece of unique folklore, a gymnastic impossibility. "Did you see that!" roared Harry, turning round to me. His nicotined fingers were trembling with tension. "Christ! Did you see that!"'

Clemence and Corrigan were taking turns in Banks' jumper by the time the hero lost an eye in a motor accident. Now England's Peter Shilton, geometry and agility allied to a rousing, bullying, muscular presence is considered one of the best in the world and a formidable successor to Banks.

And yet, there remains a goalkeeper who plays, week in, week out, in the English Football League, who might, when grandchildren come to write history books, figure with far more twirly gold-leaf script. Up among the jerseyed gods will be Pat Jennings, once of Watford and Tottenham Hotspur, now of Arsenal. He recently played his hundredth game in goal for Northern Ireland.

Jennings, still the same soft and gentle fellow who came over from Newry twenty years ago, is thirty-eight now. He cannot have long times left between the sticks. If fathers care about such things they should summon their sons and go to see Jennings keep goal before he picks up the gloves from the back of his net for the last time, shakes hands with his opposite number in the wintry sunset, and clatters down the tunnel forever.

Like Swift and Williams of my boyhood, Jennings keeps guard of his cluttered stage of bodies and boots and braying, brawling, breathlessness, with athleticism, bravery, grace and chivalry. The olde tyme hero. And I always fancy he, too, plays even that teeny bit better in his yellow jersey.

from LONG DAYS, LATE NIGHTS *1984*

Even Goalkeepers don't go on for ever

A *story by* BRIAN GLANVILLE

Now and again, they'd ask you to fill these questionnaires, magazines, programmes and that. Under Biggest Influence on My Career, I used to put, Mike Paxton, and I could imagine people saying, Mike *who*? though I knew that *he'd* be chuffed. And that he'd believe it.

That day the Borough scout came up to me on Wormwood Scrubs, when I was playing in a schools match, and asked me would I come for a trial, I went up the playground, and I looked for Mike. He was there. He nearly always was, especially this time of year, with the evenings getting lighter.

It was a place we used for soccer, just under the motorway, round the back of Ladbroke Grove, council property, just an open space with an asphalt surface and wire netting all around it, with a couple of slides, and swings.

Mike would turn up there with his bicycle, pushing it, you hardly ever saw him riding it. It was one of them big, black, heavy iron old things, none of your old drop handlebars and plastic mudguards like some of the lads had. He was someone that we all looked up to. He had black hair, a lot of it, with a lot of cream on it, always very neatly combed back in a square sort of style, a pale face; and bicycle clips. I don't think I ever see him without the bicycle clips, whether he was playing football or he'd just got off the old bike.

He lived for football, football was his religion, and he really knew the game. He'd been a bit of a player himself, a good amateur, I think, he'd drop the odd name now and then, Walthamstow Avenue and Enfield and he said he'd once had a trial for the Wolves, but he'd turned them down, because in them days there was a maximum wage and it was very low.

There was a bit of a mystery about him. He lived somewhere about the neighbourhood, nobody quite knew where, and probably on his own. Now and again one of the lads would say he'd seen him, round the back of the Harrow Road, apparently on his way home – cycling, of course – but at those times, Mike never said much. Just waved, and went on his way. Nobody knew what job he did, either, that was something else he'd never talk about, but whatever it was, it seemed to give him plenty of time during the day.

He'd join in quite a few of our games in the playground, he was slow but a very neat ball player, you could see he must have been useful, once. But if you ever come in on him with a hard tackle, he'd say, 'Oh, me leg, me leg,' which was the one that was meant to have finished his career.

Quite often he'd come along and watch us play matches, too, over the Scrubs. He'd lean on his bicycle up near the goalpost, and chat with me. I was doing this wrong. I was doing the other wrong, he was a great one for that, old Mike. Then just now and again he'd give you a big smile and say, like, 'I was really proud of you Saturday, Ronnie, I thought you'd really come on,' and that would make you feel tremendous.

When I first started keeping goal, Mike was a bit discouraging. 'Ronnie,' he'd say, 'your only hope is if you grow. You've got a lot of promise. A lot of ability. But those high crosses, Ronnie. Those are the things that matter. Those are what separate the men from the boys. You've got to have height to deal with those,' which didn't do much for my confidence.

Still, he gave me a lot of tips on things like angles, when to come out and when to stay on me line. Now and again he'd be there when I let in a goal on the Scrubs and he'd tell me what I done wrong, or he'd be there behind the posts and yell out, 'Now!' when a forward was coming through on his own. The only thing was, Mike was always right, there was never any other opinion, which may be why he liked to stick with boys, because boys don't give you many arguments.

Anyway, there he was that evening, right enough, in the playground, doing some fancy traps and flicks, nodding the ball about a bit. He was good in the air, though of course he couldn't jump. He called, 'Let's have you in goal, Ronnie,' and I went in what we called the goal, which was the space between two of the posts that held up the railings, more or less the proper width apart.

I couldn't talk to him at first, he was too busy heading crosses at me, backheeling volleys, telling me, 'Don't catch those, push 'em over, Ron,' and that. Then when a few more of the lads showed up and we was picking up for a game, I told him, 'Borough want me for a trial, Mike.'

Well, that really stopped him in his tracks. 'Borough?' he said.

'Want you for a trial? Straight up, Ronnie? Who'd you hear from? Charlie Macintosh,' which was the manager.

'No,' I said, and give him the old geezer's card, the scout. Mike looked at it, he turned it upside down, he run his thumb across it and at last he said, 'I've *heard* of him, Joe Benning,' like if he'd heard of him, he must be the real thing. 'I'm very, very pleased for you,' he said, 'I'm delighted. Even if it ain't Chelsea.' Which I supported.

'Yes,' I said, 'I'd rather it was Chelsea.'

He looked at me again and said, 'You're a funny bloke, aren't you, Ronnie? Not excited at all. If it had been me, I'd have been doing handstands. The first time I got asked for a trial, it was only Brentford, but I didn't sleep all night.'

I said, 'Yeah, but it ain't Chelsea.'

He looked me up and down, and said, 'You *are* odd. A big club comes along, and you start picking and choosing. What if everybody thought like you? Only wanted to play for the club they supported. Every kid in Glasgow would join Rangers or Celtic. Every Geordie would play for Newcastle. Anyway, you might get *sold* to Chelsea, one day.' And he talked me round.

I played a trial, and it went terrible. Very first minute, I give away a goal, a deflection, it wasn't my fault, but that was about the last time the ball came near me, because we won, 7–1. I didn't go round the playground, I couldn't face Mike, and all the questions. When I did turn up, he asked, 'Well? How did you go?'

'All right,' I said, and he give me one of those looks and said, 'You're disappointed, aren't you, Ronnie? What happened? Didn't they ask you back?'

'They didn't ask no one back,' I said. 'Just said they'd maybe let them know.'

'I don't like that,' he said. 'I'm not impressed by that. To me, with kids, you let them know one way or the other. You don't keep them hanging around in suspense. But how did *you* play?' and I told him what happened.

'I hope you didn't get on and rollick your defence,' he said; he was smiling. 'Not like you sometimes do at the Scrubs.'

Three days later, the letter come. Would I report to the Borough United ground next Tuesday evening, for training. And I signed schoolboy forms.

When I come nearer my sixteenth birthday, I started worrying, would they offer me apprentice pro? 'There's no hurry, Ron,' Mike said. 'Not for a goalkeeper. A lot of keepers don't come into their own until they're thirty.'

'What do you want me to do, then?' I said. 'Stay at school until I'm thirty?'

'Just don't worry about it, that's all,' he said. 'They'll probably take you, anyway; you're definitely improving.'

The end of it was, they did take me. Mike was well pleased. 'I told you they would, Ronnie,' he said. 'Now it's up to you, son. They'll sign you full pro, too, when you're seventeen or eighteen. No doubt about that. And that's when the temptations start, Ronnie. That's when you've got to decide.'

'Decide what, Mike?' I said.

'Whether you're going to be a serious professional,' he said, and I told him, 'Well, of course I am. That's all I want, ain't it?'

He said, 'Ah, that's what you want *now*, Ronnie. That's how you think *now*, when you're living at home and you've not left school and life's a bowl of cherries. But there's a lot of temptations for a player. Things you don't even know about yet. But you'll be all right as long as you remember one thing. Always put your career first. Always look after yourself; first and foremost. That one drink on a Friday night, Ron; that can cost a goal.'

When I did sign full pro and went up the playground to tell them, Mike knew. He always seemed to know everything. 'Well done,' he said, soon as he saw me – he was juggling with a ball, as usual. 'Told you, didn't I?'

I was right surprised. 'How'd you know?' I asked. 'Who told you?' but all he said was, 'I know, I know,' in this way he had, like he knew everyone and everyone knew him, though come to think of it, he may have seen it in some evening paper. He didn't miss much, old Mike. He asked me what kind of contract I'd got, I told him, and he nodded, like he thought that was okay. 'Should have had a word with me though, Ronnie,' he said. 'I might have been able to help you.'

Sometimes I'd wish he tried to help me a bit less, I even wished I hadn't joined a London club, because he seemed to be everywhere; quite honestly, he used to get on my nerves now and again with his advice, and all. I mean, I was grateful and that for how he'd encouraged me, but I was a professional now, and I knew what I was doing. When I done something wrong, I knew that, too. I didn't need no one to tell me.

Like, the first game I played in the reserves was local, up at Shepherd's Bush, against QPR, and when I caught a corner, I heard this voice behind the goal, 'Very nice, Ron, very nice.' I didn't need to look; it was Mike of course. You could never mistake the tone; like he was patting a dog. I sort of half waved, but it distracted me.

From now on, I could feel his eyes on the back of me neck, watching every move.

I done all right, though Peter Morton, our stopper, he was a big Irish international, put an own goal past me. After the game, Mike was outside the dressing-rooms waiting, with me family, patted me on the back, 'Came back well, there, Ronnie,' he said, 'didn't let it upset you.' Then he smiled at Peter Morton like he'd known him for years and said, 'Made a game of it, anyway, Peter.' Peter looked at him in a puzzled sort of way and nodded back, like he couldn't quite place him but reckoned he ought to.

Of all places to make me League debut it was Liverpool, and I wasn't quite eighteen. The first team keeper got hurt, and Charlie Macintosh told me I was in. Mike sent a telegram, 'Congratulations on the first of many,' very nice, and it went all right. I got a couple of knocks, but we pinched a goal on the break and we won 1–0.

Mike come round the next morning, wheeling his old bike, cycle clips on, as usual. He shook me by the hand and said, 'Ronnie, I'm very, very proud of you,' smiling all over his face. 'Mind you, I told you, didn't I? Remember when you were so small? Remember when you were afraid you'd never make it? Well, now it's happened. You're there to stay, Ronnie. There for years. What did Charlie say?'

'Charlie?' I said, forgetting Mike and his names. 'Oh, the Boss. He was very pleased.'

'He's entitled to be,' said Mike.

I'd still see him around. Very occasionally up the playground, when I went there. There wasn't too much time in the season, and in the summer I'd watch but I wouldn't play. They'd say, 'Go on, Ron, go in goal,' especially the younger kids that had come up since my day, and Mike would say, 'Come on, Ronnie, let's see if you've improved, son,' and now and again I'd go in for a few minutes. Not often, though. I wasn't big headed or anything; only that when you're full professional, your attitude changes. You don't want to take risks, especially when you're a goalkeeper, because you know on a Saturday you've *got* to take them. It wasn't easy to explain to them, but I knew Mike saw it a bit, though he'd say something like, 'Got his new gear on today, haven't you, Ronnie? Mustn't spoil *that.*'

About a couple of weeks into the new season, we had a derby game, home to Arsenal. One evening the doorbell went, and it was Mike, looking a bit embarrassed, staring at the ground and that, but in the end he said, 'I don't like asking you, Ron, but if you *have* got a couple of tickets. Complimentaries. I mean, I'll pay; I'll *pay.* They don't have to be comps. Just that the last Borough–Arsenal, they closed the gates, I was locked out. Otherwise I'd go on the terraces, like always. Behind your goal, Ronnie.'

He'd never asked me a favour before. I felt more embarrassed than what he did. I said, 'Yes, Mike, okay, Mike,' though in fact I only got three comps a week, and those always went to the family, but I couldn't take his money. 'All right, Ron,' he said, looking away from me, 'thanks,' and he went off right away, he never stayed for a chat, walking the old bicycle, of course; not riding.

I bought a sports car, a lovely little green Triumph. About a week after I'd got it, I was stopped at the lights in the Portobello Road when a cyclist rode up beside me, stuck his head in through the window, and said, 'Want to mind how you go on that, Ronnie!' I looked round and it was old Mike, he was actually riding his bike for once. I said, 'Oh, hello, Mike.' In a way, I was a bit relieved, him coming across my car the first time like this, making a joke of it, because now and then I'd wondered how he'd take it, I knew that I was bound to see him. But he seemed to sort of accept it, like it was part of a player's life, the way having a pair of boots was. I did offer him a ride in it now and then, but he'd always just smile and shake his head, he'd say, 'No, thanks, Ronnie; feel safer on the old bike.'

Eventually I moved into digs, over Muswell Hill, with another young player, Bob Cullen. It was great to be able to talk football all the time with someone that really knew. At home, the old man always liked to discuss it, but it couldn't be the same, he was outside it. Same with Mike, when I run into him, or he comes round, now and then.

One day when I was home I come across him in Ladbroke Grove and we went for a drink, I had a lemonade. We'd just drawn at home with Tottenham, a right old London derby, very fast and hard, we'd drawn, which was a bit disappointing.

Mike said, 'That cross, Ronnie, the one they scored from, you should have had it before it ever reached the fellow.' And I got a bit edgy, I said, 'A goalkeeper can't get everything, Mike.' And he put on that smile of his I knew so well, the 'I know better than you do' one; he said, 'But Ron, that ball couldn't have been more than ten yards out.'

'No it wasn't, Mike,' I said. 'It was nearer fifteen, and anyway, to me, it was a defender's ball. It should have been Jackie Noakes'.'

'Ronnie,' he said, in this ever so *reasonable* voice he put on, 'a ball that near to goal can't be Jackie's ball, it can't be *anybody's* ball but yours. The first duty of any goalkeeper is he's got to command his area, and besides, a shortish bloke like Jackie is always going to be in trouble jumping with a tall striker that gets up so well.'

'If what you're saying's true,' I said, 'you wouldn't need any defenders in the box at all; they could just clear out and leave it to the goalkeeper.'

'There's no need to get aggressive, Ron,' he said. 'You know that's not what I meant. Of course you need defenders in the box. What *you're* saying is you don't need a goalkeeper.'

'Okay, Mike,' I said, 'you know best. You always know better than anyone.'

'Ronnie,' he said, then, 'I'm disappointed in you. You've changed. You were never like this as a kid. You used to be able to take criticism. What's come over you, Ron? All this big time stuff? You're still only young. You've still got things to learn.'

'I know that,' I said, 'and I know who I can learn them from.' As soon as I said it, I felt sorry that I had, because he didn't mean no harm, old Mike, I realised that afterwards. It was simply his way.

He nodded, then. He said, 'All right. All right, Ron. If that's the way you feel,' and he got up. I asked him did he want another beer, but he said no, he said, 'Just think about what I told you,' then he went out. I waited till he must be gone, then I went, too. It was a shame, but everything was still happening so fast that I hadn't much time to think about it.

Because we had this run in the Cup, we got all the way through to the Final, and when that happened, I knew Mike would be round, wanting tickets, even if I hadn't seen him for so long. I told my parents to say, if he showed up, that I'd look after him and one Sunday, I was there for lunch, he come round to collect the tickets.

He wouldn't come in the house, just stood at the door, holding his cycle.

'Good luck then, Ron,' he said. 'It's all going to happen. I knew it would. I always told you so. I like to think I had a little bit to do with it.'

'You did, Mike,' I said.

'I'm glad,' he said. 'I'm glad that you remember. And later on, Ron, if things ever go wrong. If you need any help, any advice, you know where you can find me.' And he looked me in the eye. 'Even goalkeepers,' he said, 'they don't go on forever.'

Then he went off. Wheeling the bike, not riding it.

originally entitled 'Mike and Me',
from GOALKEEPERS ARE DIFFERENT *1971*

Part Five

PEAKS AND VALLEYS

Pre-Season

EAMON DUNPHY

25 July
The first day. An interesting day. You leave in April tired, cynical, a bit disillusioned. Now you are really happy when you come back. People are always happy to come back. On the first day, you have the photo call, and everyone compares sun tans, and tells lies about the girls they've had. You don't really talk about the season today. It's a day for acclimatisation: getting used to seeing everyone again, and looking at the new faces.

One of the funny things is when you first go into the ground, and you see the pitch with no posts and no lines drawn.

You are very conscious, though, underneath all the clowning, that you have come back to work. People think that the season lasts from the middle of August to the end in April. But it really starts today.

26 July
Today we went to Peek Freans' sports ground on the Sidcup bypass. And it was hard. The first day is always hard. But it is not the hardest. The first day you feel exuberant, you want to run and run, and your legs are tired. But it's the second day. Then you are knackered. You've got a reaction from the first day.

And then you slip into it all so quickly again. You spend the morning working, from half past ten until 12.00, then have some lunch, then work again in the afternoons. You finish about four, and you are really knackered. Yet it is a marvellous spiritual feeling. You have worked hard, and are cleansed. I think that footballers, and all athletic people, when they go away in the summer and eat and drink too much, and stay up too late, have this tremendous guilt. Pre-season training gets rid of that guilt. There is nothing more exhilarating than coming home feeling tired, and sitting down and feeling pure in a way that you never do in the season. The tension of the season is not there yet; the sense of battle has not arisen yet.

There is a great deal of good-natured banter. The atmosphere of a pre-season training camp is idyllic. You are away from the ground, it's secluded, and you feel as if you are in the country. It's sunny, and you're happy. The team has not been picked yet. So there is no competition, and everybody feels they are eligible. The divisions have not been drawn yet. Relationships are very very good. Guys you haven't liked before, and who you will probably hate again later in the season, seem all right in this kind of atmosphere.

The manager is very happy. No problems, no battles yet. All the theories sound great. Benny strolls among us, benign, fond of his players, seeing us in our nicest light.

There is a great feeling of unity at this time. Obviously reserves are worried. Last year I was worried whether I would be in the team; I had finished the season before just in the team. And if you are in that situation of being on the fringe of the team, you are watching everything. You watch the manager's face for expression, for any clue as to how he feels about you. For the first two weeks, it is all work, no mention of teams yet. I waited and waited until he picked the team. I wasn't in it, so I left. I walked out in the middle of pre-season training. I had worried about it all that summer, and when the blow came, I couldn't take it. It was too much; it was unbearable really. It would have been the first time in my career that I did not kick off in the first team. You work so hard in pre-season training; you really kill yourself. And you do it with one thing in mind. The first day of the season. If you are not in the team it has all been a waste. It invalidates the whole thing.

But the worry is for the future. For the moment there's just hard work, and good group feeling.

from ONLY A GAME? *1976*

Peaks and Valleys

Eamon Dunphy

30 September
So I came home last night and had a few drinks. But it doesn't help. When you wake up in the morning, you think 'It didn't happen' or you try to block it out. But it happened. And when you read the Sunday papers you soon learn that it did.

Sunday is very much a down day anyway. You build up all week emotionally and physically to Saturday. You get really wound up, then bang! Saturday afternoon it all comes out. Even the games that look diabolical to people watching, games where nothing has been achieved, nothing creative anyway, you come off the park thinking 'Gotta get in that bath, Jesus!' You have put everything into it physically and emotionally, oblivious of the fact that it is drivel. And by Sunday you are no good for anything.

When you've won, it isn't so bad. Alan and I both have this routine of getting the Sunday papers, looking at the League table, working out who is playing who next week, where it will leave us – 'five points behind, but if they lose it'll only be three', all that sort of thing. But when you've lost like we did yesterday, when even you are conscious you've been in a load of rubbish, the Sunday papers you do not need.

1 October

This morning everyone seemed to have forgotten last Saturday. We are at Sheffield on Wednesday, Forest on Saturday, and the feeling is 'Well, we'll try and nick something there'.

The lads are sick, I suppose, in their own way. But footballers are resilient. They bounce back quickly as a group. Jokes, birds, you talk about anything. Even football. Some of the lads do anyway. When you get older you start talking about the game a bit, seeing things you never saw before, feeling responsible for things you never felt responsible for before. It becomes more difficult to shrug things off.

So we started training. A bit of running to get warmed up, then we were going to have this practice match. Lawrie was handing the bibs out. And he walked past me. 'That is very odd of him.' I thought nothing of it; just a little bit perturbed. I looked after him, and he was giving out first-team shirts. And he was giving one to Robin Wainwright . . . and he gave one to Dennis . . . and I looked around . . . 'I'm dropped! No! But I am!'

I could not believe it. I could not think for a minute. And Benny was standing there as if nothing had happened. No one said anything to me.

He had given me a reserve shirt. 'Play in midfield,' he said. How do you react? It was like somebody had plunged a dagger in my back. I was so hurt. Not so much because I was dropped, but because they had done it like that.

And they could not do it to me! I was choked. I had been playing reasonably well; certainly better than a lot of other people. And I cared! I was part of it. This was me, this was the lads. And then BANG! I'm out of it.

So he said 'Let's have the first-team lads over here. You lot go and have a kick about at the far end'. So they had all gone away, the lads, for a team talk. And I went up the other end with the youngsters. I could not believe it.

I could feel tears welling up in my eyes, but I thought 'Nah, that's no good'. So I just stood there for about five or ten minutes. I don't know how long it was. I can't remember how long the talk went on. The young lads were knocking it about, and I looked round, and there was this little group, and Benny was talking to them. And you feel so left out.

And there's the hurt. It just happens. A snap of the fingers, and you are gone. Out. All the commitment, all the emotion, all the hard work, all the belief. Everything gone. Because some idiot fooled around at the back in the last eight minutes on Saturday.

And my first reaction then was to walk out. There and then. But I thought 'No, anybody can be dropped. Now you have got to show you are a man. Now you have got to show you are big.'

So I made a few jokes with the young lads, picked my chin up, and started playing this practice game. I did my best, I worked hard, and funnily enough I started playing really well. Because again there was this strange feeling of relief. 'Sod it. I'm out of it.' So I just enjoyed myself for half an hour. And all the time, at the back of my mind, I was wondering 'What am I going to do? How am I going to react? What do I do now?'

Seven games of the season had gone. And after all the struggle, all the worry, all the dreams, you are on the scrapheap. That is what the reserves is, when you are twenty-eight. No one had said a word to me. It was the same as if I had never given a damn. They had treated me as if I had never tried.

And I *had* tried. In the games where Dennis had been out, and there was no one there to take responsibility, I had taken it. I had covered for people, I had worked, I had shouted, I had bawled, I had grafted, I had tackled – which I cannot do very well – I had done all of that. And I was missing Dennis being alongside me doing things, because he takes a lot of that responsibility. I took all that on my own shoulders, tried to do the right thing, tried to do more than my whack, to make up for the fact that he was not there. All the time waiting for him to get back into the side so we could get it organised again. Like we had done in the latter part of last season. It never entered my mind that I might be dropped.

It had, funnily enough, when Franky had been playing so well. I

164

thought 'Well, Dennis is going to come back in, and he just might drop me.' But then I had played well in a couple of games, I had made the goal against Wednesday, and I had played well in the first half at Swindon when things were rocky. I had pulled the side together, and I thought I had done very well. So I said to myself 'Now it's OK. You won't be dropped.' I thought he would drop Gordon Hill. I wanted Dennis back in the side.

But he had dropped Gordon Hill and me. And he brought this lad Robin Wainwright in. He has done well in the reserves, and should be given a chance. But he is not a midfield player, he is a winger or a striker.

So I reacted by playing as best I could for the reserves in that practice match. Trying to be manly, trying not to be small-minded. And when we finished I went to see Benny. When I walked through the door he said 'What do you want?'

'You know what I want,' I said. 'I want to leave this place. I want to leave within a week. I'm finished here.'

'Out of the question,' he said. 'You're too good a player.'

So I said 'I don't care why you have dropped me, I don't want to discuss it. Team selection is your business. But I'm finished with it. I have put too much work in, too much commitment, too much caring to be messed around like that. You did not even tell me before that I was dropped. I find out when a guy walks past me with a shirt. That's you, that is this club. No more for me. I'm finished. I want to leave. And if you do not let me leave, I'll leave anyway.'

'Out of the question. Calm yourself down.'

I did not talk about why he had dropped me. I do not believe in discussing team selection with managers. They have got a reason, and whatever the reason is, it is good enough. It is their job. You don't have to take it, if you don't believe it is right.

I was in a terrible temper. My hand was shaking, I could not talk properly. I was hurt more than angry.

So I said 'I'll wait ten days. And if you don't let me go, I'll go anyway. Don't put me on the sheet, don't take me with you.'

'What about the money?'

'You can stuff the money,' I said. 'I don't care about that.'

So I went home. I phoned Sandra first, and told her what had happened. I walked in and just burst out crying. I sat here for quarter of an hour, and I just cried.

I had never cried before about football. Never ever. But this time I did. I don't know why. Maybe it was the hurt, the injustice of it. But that has happened before. Every year, the first sign of the team having problems and it is me he drops. He tells me that he thinks the world of me as a person, but when we lose games the first person he sorts out is me. I do think he likes me. I think the reason he does drop me every time is because of a weakness in him. He is the kind of person who would sooner hurt his friends than his enemies. But I did not think it would happen to me again.

The other lads were surprised. Alan said 'It's scandalous'.

I had not looked for sympathy. When you get dropped, players come up to you and say 'Diabolical.' They always say it whether they mean it or not. But when it happens to me, I try and avoid them. I don't want them to say it, because it does not mean anything. It is not real. What is real is what goes on the teamsheet. The rest is rubbish.

2 October
Being dropped is something everyone in the game has to face. Manchester United dropped Bobby Charlton once. How do you face it? Yesterday I came home and I just cried! We went into Bromley in the afternoon shopping. But it's eating into you the whole time. You can't think about anything else for one minute. You go home and you are restless, edgy. The whole time you are thinking 'What am I going to do?' I was in great doubt whether I should go to the ground today, or stay away. I didn't know what to do. Whether to jack it all in again, or go. Maybe go in for the money, sit on the bench as twelfth man, which means a lot extra on your wages. Or say 'Stuff the money' and keep out of it altogether.

But I went in this morning, and had a long chat with Benny. He called me into his office. He was hovering around me all morning, which is what he does when he knows you have got the needle with him. He called me into his room and said 'Have you changed your mind about going on the teamsheet? Do you still not want to be in it?'

So I said 'Leave me out. See how you do.' I said I wanted no part of it. I'm not going to sit on the bench or in the stand, tearing my guts out every week, wanting them to win in one sense, but basically wanting them to lose, because I cannot get back into the side until they lose. But he said 'Come as thirteenth man; and get your money. Don't be a fool to yourself.' So in the end I agreed.

4 October
Sheffield Wednesday 3   Millwall 2
So we went up to Sheffield. I wasn't on the bench, I went as thirteenth man. You go into the dressing-room before the game, and you smile and say 'All the best, lads.' What does that mean? If they

do well you stay out. And when they get beaten, as we did last night, what do you do? You act. Because you can't come in with a big smile all over your face saying 'Great. Now you've been beaten I can get back in.' Everybody else is sick. But you aren't. You are pleased. So you come in and make faces; pretend that you are sick like the rest of them. But everyone knows that you are acting.

I sat in the stand with John Sissons, who is injured. I was sitting among some Millwall supporters too. They were all saying 'Cor, you not in, Eamon? What a liberty! He should have dropped someone else.' You can't say anything. And they say the same to everyone when they are dropped. Some of them mean it, some don't.

The game was a shambles. Terrible. First half was diabolical. Kingy kept like a clown, gave away two goals. And he was being watched by Manchester City. Their scout left before the end. But while they are out there what am I doing? I'm sitting in the stand, wanting them to lose, but unable to show it. Because there are people around, I've got to pretend to want them to win. I can't jump up in the air when Sheffield score. Which I want to do. And when Millwall score I'm sick, but I have to jump up in the air. And there is this terrible conflict the whole time. And it is the same for everybody who is dropped.

You are always pleased when they have been beaten, because it means you are a candidate again. You are sick for the lads, of course, but your predominant emotion is delight.

I went into the dressing-room afterwards. People were throwing their boots off disconsolately, swearing a lot. I looked at Dennis. He shrugged his shoulders. He wasn't surprised. He looked as if he was past caring. Another confirmation for him of what he thinks about Millwall. I couldn't look at Alan. He is my closest friend, but I couldn't go to him. Because I was still isolated. I had not been part of the defeat. You aren't just isolated from the good things when you're out of the side, but from the bad things too. The lads who played and Benny are sharing the gloom, just as it would be their joy to share if they had done well. So I kept quiet. I sat down and read the programme for the fiftieth time, and tried to grab half a cup of tea. There was me, Benny and Jack while the lads were having their baths. Benny was walking around shaking his head. There was nothing he wanted to say to me; and nothing I wanted to say to him. He went to the mirror to comb his hair, as he always does before having to go and face the directors' room.

Now that's another tough situation. It's always tough for a manager to face that when his team has lost. It is not so much facing your own directors. That comes later. It is the guests and the opposition directors and other managers saying 'Unlucky' and not meaning it.

For the reserve, after about half an hour, when you've helped Jack Blackman get all the gear together, it isn't so bad. By then the lads have forgotten the game and you are all one again. Particularly for an away game like Sheffield, where you are staying overnight. You go off and have a few beers together. And you can feel part of it.

But Benny put a curfew on. So we didn't go out, just had a drink in the hotel lounge. There was a pretty bad atmosphere really.

What does a manager do? Benny could say 'Go on, have a few beers and please yourself.' But it is difficult.

If I was a manager, I would tend to think there was no use in punishing people if they have done their best. And at Millwall they invariably have done their best. Let them go out and have a few beers, win or lose. But it is early season. We have a game on Saturday, so we have got to keep ourselves reasonably fit. The danger is that the lads could go out and drink a lot, pull a few birds and it ends as a four-in-the-morning job. And then you travel back the next day, so there is only Friday to recover.

But I think that players feel much more responsible nowadays than they did. There are far fewer cheats around. Certainly not at Millwall, which is one of the greatest things about the place. Over the years I've played there, one of the greatest joys has been that they have had no bad people. The one or two that came Benny got out quickly. We've always had good lads.

I've seen a few bad ones elsewhere. Going away with the Irish team there have been lads over the years who don't care whether they win or lose. They are looking for something else out of it: the 'big time'.

There is an element of that left in the game, but it is going very quickly. One thing I've always hated is the image of the hard-drinking, hard-living professional sportsman who goes out and stomps all over the world. That was part of the game when I first came into it in Manchester. I remember going out with a couple of the other players one Friday night to the dogs, then on to a nightclub. We were playing the next day, and I was really worried, guilty. And they said 'Nothing to worry about. This is what it is all about.' And to a large extent at that time it was. Particularly in Manchester, there were a lot of playboys around and a lot of places to go. But there is not a lot of that left in football now.

And that has been one of the joys at Millwall. Players are honest. And Benny is normally good. He lets the players go out more often than not. And I think that is right. If a player goes out on a Wednesday night and even if he gets drunk out of his mind, if he is a good pro he will know what he has done. He will make up for it on the Saturday. He will give you that much more because he had that licence on Wednesday.

Last season we played Everton in the Cup. We went to Torquay for four days beforehand. It is a fantastic place down there for nightlife. It was in January. London was terrible. But down there it was really nice. A warm atmosphere and a carefree air about the place. It was quiet, because it was out of season, but there was still a fairly hectic social life. The first couple of days we were down there we went out. Benny was really good and took the leash off. We found a club and had a few drinks. We did not really look after ourselves for those four days. We took liberties. On the Thursday we went back to London to go up to Everton.

I think Benny knew we had stayed up late and drunk more than we should have done. And I think he had done it to relax us. We went out and played like fury. We fought and we battled. It was a hell of a game, and we got a hell of a result.

So we asked if we could go to Torquay before the next round. Benny said yes, so before we played Wolves we went down there again and had a ball. We played really well again at Wolves, even though we lost.

These were isolated instances of us taking liberties. You could not do it every week and get away with it. But if you have got good lads it proves you can let them off the leash, and they will still produce the goods. Especially if you pick the right time.

from ONLY A GAME? *1976*

Closet Wingers

MICHAEL PARKINSON

It is an axiom of the modern game of football that wingmen, like people who thatch roofs and make clogs, are a dying breed. It is remarkable that a country whose one certain contribution to the international history of football is Stanley Matthews should now seem intent on pretending that he never existed.

Once upon a time in the days when footballers wore shorts to their knees and were shod in boots with bulging toe-caps the sight of the wingman improvising his talents down the touchline, delighting and disappointing in turn, was a commonplace on the football fields of Britain. Wingmen were the temperamental artists whose performance was controlled by the state of the moon, or the horoscope in that morning's *Daily Mirror* or more simply by the fact of whether or not they felt like playing well. They were the only members of a side who were allowed the luxury of personal eccentricity by the fans. I once played with a winger who wore a flat cap and woollen mittens on days when the weather was bad. Neither his team-mates, opponents nor spectators ever remarked upon his curious attire because he was a wingman. Had he been a centre-half or a full-back he would immediately have been marked down as a weirdo of some sort and asked to mend his ways or retire from the game.

In those dear departed days the best wingmen were always referred to as closet wingers. It grew out of the days when we had the best team in the Barnsley and District Backyard League. Our success depended mainly on an unbeaten home record which was achieved by the efforts of our right-winger, Albert, and a long row of outside toilets or closets as they were commonly known.

Albert was an absolute master at charging down the wing and, when challenged by the opposing defenders, flicking the ball against the toilet door and collecting the rebound. The only time he was known to fail was on the occasion when the occupant of the toilet opened the door in time to take one of Albert's passes in the midriff.

Albert became well known locally as Geronimo, the closet winger. The Geronimo tag had nothing to do with his footballing ability but derived from his hatred of water and hair-cuts which created an appearance to remind us all of the Indians we saw on the screen at the local flea-pit. In those days our tactics were simple and effective. At every conceivable opportunity we would feed the ball to Geronimo, who was invariably lurking by his beloved closets, and away he would go, flicking the ball against the toilet doors, racing on to the rebound and repeating the act until he had cleared the whole defence.

For a couple of seasons we were unbeatable and Albert the closet winger became a local personality. Inevitably it couldn't last for ever and the slide downhill for both Albert and the team came on the day when we met the Klondyke. The team was so named because the part of the village it represented put one in mind of a frontier town during the gold rush. To describe them as hard opponents would be doing them an injustice. Ferocious is a more accurate description. They had at least two players who would have made Norman Hunter and Peter Storey look like a pair of cream puffs.

It must also be remembered that in the Backyard League there was no referee to penalise dirty play. The simple ethic therefore was: 'If kicked say nothing, but wait and kick back.' Also in these games we did nothing without the normal post-match formalities like shaking hands and congratulating the other chap. Any team which beat the fearsome Klondyke realised that when the game ended the sensible tactic was to race home immediately because any attempt at the normal courtesies would undoubtedly mean a free ride to the local out-patient department.

It was in this frame of mind we began our epic encounter. All went reasonably well until Albert began his first run down the wing. In and out of the defence he went, flicking the ball on to the toilet doors, the rebound magically dropping at his twinkling feet. With the Klondyke defence nonplussed he shot home the first goal.

The Klondyke team, for all the fact that it included many players with surprisingly narrow foreheads and close-set eyes, were not on short swift answers when faced with a problem like this. The next time that Albert set off on one of his runs we were made aware of the Klondyke genius for tactical improvisation. As Albert twinkle-toed along the toilets, the Klondyke full-back, build like a brick brewery, began a diagonal run towards him. As he reached Albert he didn't stop to challenge, he didn't hesitate to decide which way the winger was going, he just kept running as if his target was somewhere on the horizon beyond Albert's right shoulder. The noise of impact, of bone on bone, was terrible, and followed immediately by the sound of splintering wood as Albert, the full-back and the ball smashed through one of the green toilet doors. We peered inside and the wreckage was awful.

Albert and the full-back lay at peace on the floor, surrounded by the fragments of wood and jagged pieces of what is politely termed sanitary ware. We picked them up and revived them and then had to abandon the match because the owner of the toilets turned up on his daily visit and when he saw the damage went to fetch the police. We never played there again because the law warned us off and some time later the council pulled the toilets down along with the houses they belonged to. The inhabitants were shipped off to a new estate with inside toilets and a better view of the pit. Albert went with his parents to the new estate, but he was never the same winger without a row of closets. After a couple of months in his new environment, Albert went into premature retirement in a remand home for stealing lead. But he had made his mark. Whenever we saw a good winger he was always a 'closet winger'.

It is easy to scoff at closet wingers, but in fact they have made a colourful contribution to our game. What is more significant, it was a closet winger who unwittingly decided the future of English football. As is generally known, it was Sir Alf Ramsey who killed off the old romantic notion of wingmen. In Ramsey's team of workers there was no place for the eccentric or the whimsical. It was a beautiful machine and it didn't need adorning with frills. Now contrary to general opinion Sir Alf's plan for wingmen did not occur because he simply happened to think of it one day while taking a bath. It is my theory that his scheme for the liquidation of wingmen had lurked in his mind for some considerable time and had its roots in some kind of deep emotional upset. Which is where a closet winger called Johnny Kelly comes in.

He was a left-winger of genius who played for Barnsley in the early fifties. A shy, square sturdy man with the slightly bandy legs that are the hallmark of all great wingers.

I don't know if you've ever considered the remarkable fact that bandy legs are an asset to most sportsmen. That they helped people who ride horses is a thought too obvious to need explanation. But it is not generally known that they greatly assist cricketers also. I once played in a cricket team with a man who possessed the most splendid pair of hooped legs I have yet seen.

As a batsman he was particularly skilled in the art of back play. Now this technique was generally suicidal in the league in which we played where the umpires worked strictly to licensing hours and granted leg-before-wicket appeals with increasing regularity as opening time approached. In this situation my bandy-legged friend was the only batsman in the league to play back and prosper. Whenever struck on his superbly bowed legs and appealed against he would simply point to the gap between his limbs, through which all three stumps were clearly visible, and say to the umpire in his most pained voice: 'Leg before wicket with a pair of bloody legs like mine?' No umpire, no matter how thirsty, dare give him out!

I digress only in the interests of science and humanity. It is time somebody pointed out the virtues of playing sport on a pair of bandy legs. No one who has them should feel unhappy so long as they always remember to play back.

Which returns us to Alf Ramsey, because those of you with long memories will doubtless recall that he also used to play back — full-back, that is — and very good he was too. But he was no good against bandy-legged wingers, as Johnny Kelly proved. Kelly was the kind of winger you don't see around nowadays. A player of skill and original wit. The sort of wingman who exploded theories, not expounded them. He played only once for Scotland, which was an act of criminal neglect on a player who must have been the best Scottish winger of his day. That he was ignored has obviously to do with the fact that he played for Barnsley. The selectors in Barsnsley obviously thought they played in the Isthmian League. A great pity, because he had the kind of unique skill that should have been spread before multitudes and not just the faithful 15,000 who used to watch Barnsley in his day.

Still, it does mean that there were 14,999 other people who will swear to what I am going to tell you now. They and I were present that important day, many years ago, when Alf Ramsey suffered the trauma that changed his life and put skids under wingers. He was playing right back for Southampton at the time, an urbane, immaculate footballer who seemed as out of place at Barnsley as a bowler hat in a pawn shop.

In this particular game Johnny Kelly had one of those days when all his genius flowed into his feet. If you have ever seen Matthews or Finney or Georgie Best at their finest then you'll know what I mean. He flicked his hips and Ramsey sat down in wonderment. He waved his foot over the ball like a wand, daring Ramsey to guess what might happen next, and as the full-back anticipated a move outside, Kelly came inside and left him for dead. At one stage he demonstrated his complete mastery by beating Ramsey, waiting for him to recover and then beating him again. Had Kelly been on the Southampton side and doing this to certain of the Barnsley defenders he would have had his impudence rewarded with a bed in the nearest emergency ward. But Ramsey played it clean and endeavoured to look as dignified as any man can when he is having his nose rubbed in the dirt.

The crowd didn't help. They relished the sight of Kelly shredding Ramsey's reputation. This, remember, was in the days when footballers were the victims of individual abuse and not the collective sort they get from today's rehearsed choirs. Thus the comments, though not so loud, were more personal and biting. As Ramsey sat down before Kelly's skill a man near me bellowed:

'Tha' wants to learn how to stand up before tha' plays this game, Ramsey.' And again, as Kelly left Ramsey immobile and helpless as a statue, the same man bawled: 'Ramsey, tha' art about as much use as a chocolate teapot.'

This is as much as any man can be expected to take without consulting the Director of Public Prosecutions. My theory is that as

Alf Ramsey sat in the dressing room in Barnsley, scraping the mud from his boots and his reputation, he first thought of his revenge on wingers. He didn't want just Kelly's scalp, but the destruction of the whole tricky race.

It's not a bad theory, particularly when you consider that Alf Ramsey is where he is today, and Johnny Kelly was last heard of manufacturing a liquid bleach. It's an even stronger theory when you realise that wingers like Kelly are now more rare than five-legged giraffes.

But I have cornered whatever consolation there is left to people who love the game in the dear, daft days before Mr Ramsey got his paws on it. When I read of the experts trying to explain to themselves just what he is up to, and why, I sit there giggling gently to myself, nursing my memories, thinking fondly of a grey afternoon many seasons ago when a closet winger with bandy legs and baggy shorts made a monkey of a master mind.

from THE FOOTBALL MAN *1968*

Ireland play England, 1960

DANNY BLANCHFLOWER

Last Saturday I trooped victoriously off the field at Wolverhampton, had a quick bath, made a fond farewell to my Tottenham colleagues, and dashed to catch the boat train to Belfast.

It seemed unbelievable to have beaten the Wolves so convincingly on their own ground. On the boat that night I read some of the English papers, and swayed with the glowing tributes: 'Stupendous Spurs' . . . 'Sensational Spurs'. I got carried away to thinking that the least I could expect on arrival at Belfast next morning was a ticker-tape welcome.

It wasn't quite like that. A constant sheet of rain started falling as the boat docked. A little boat steward sprinted up to and past me, stuck his head out of a door, had a squint at the weather and said out loud, addressing nobody in particular, 'Well that's the end of summer.' I looked at the watch on which I had just put back the hour, and marvelled at the precision of his observation.

I went out to the little town of Larne to see my folks; thinking that at least they would have something to say about my soccer feats. But they were full of admiration for some local hero and his devious ways of outwitting the hire purchase companies and local electricity board. . . .

A man of obscure means, he had gone off to Ballymena with his family in his brand new car to see some relatives. There the hire purchase agent had caught up with him, and left the family stranded in the street of Ballymena without the car.

Regardless of his luck, he had charmed some unsuspecting dealer in Ballymena – a notoriously hard place to do business – and had arrived home in Larne that same evening with a different new car. Only to find his electricity had been cut off. A man of undoubted talents, he had immediately gone to the damned box and, undaunted, connected back the supply.

I began to feel inferior, and got to thinking that perhaps Wolverhampton were nothing and that Tottenham's record-breaking stuff wasn't really so stupendous. Next morning, Monday, I bought all the daily papers to reassure myself. There wasn't a mention of Tottenham. The sports pages were regionalised and full of local stuff. Glenavon had been fined £50 for something and one of their officials had resigned. There was little news about the N. Ireland team meeting next day to prepare for England.

That afternoon I met a man in Belfast who recognised me. He approached with an aggressive glint in his eye, and I was sure he was going to say something bitter about Spurs. He stuck out his hand. 'Come over to get ready for them?' he said, and marched away like he had put me in my proper place.

I mustered with the rest of the Irish team early on Tuesday morning. That little oak of a man, Wilbur Cush, was missing, so were Alfie McMichael and Willie Cunningham. Some of the others had new suits, new styles and stories. They seemed like different people from the ones I had shared glory with over the recent years. But after a few days going through old routines, suffering their partnership at golf, and talking over old times, I began to believe in them once more.

Our training headquarters is at Port Stewart, a north Irish coast resort with golden sands and a timeless air. You can hear the sad, sweet melody of Irish harps in the air and, in the twilight, you can see the 'littlefolk' running about their mischievous business. A few days up here and you can believe anything. The locals charm you with their conviction, the magnitude they can give to things that before have seemed to trivial.

The football talk is about Ireland . . . those gods who have carried the reputation of Ireland to the very pinnacle of the soccer world, those very fellows I met on Tuesday morning and, in a moment's ignorance, probably brought about by the shallow success of eleven wins in a row for Tottenham, somehow doubted.

Right now London doesn't exist for me, and I have not heard of Tottenham.

It is common knowledge that Brazil won the 1958 World Cup. Here you would think that nobody else had played in it but Ireland. In the lasty thirty years of competition, Ireland have beaten England once, in 1957, at Wembley. The rest of the matches have been *moral* defeats for England. Games in which England have scored as many as ten goals were quickly dismissed by our selectors picking an entirely new team next time out – and somehow proving that England had really scored ten goals against somebody else.

It's been wonderful listening to it all. I feel really confident now about playing England. The rest of the Irish boys feel the same. England haven't got a chance.

As you read this you should know the score. If England have managed to score more goals than us again, take no notice. They have just suffered another moral defeat.* And the boys over here will be talking all the more about that game at Wembley in 1957.

from THE OBSERVER 9/10/60

The Hangers-On

Hunter Davies

There are three sorts of fanatical fans, fans fanatical enough to follow their team anywhere. There's the Kids who move in gangs and strut and prance and look for action. There's the Supporters, the honest working men who form the backbone of the supporters' club. Then there's the Hangers-on.

The Hangers-on hate being called hangers-on. They're the ones in the expensive leather coats who look as if they've just had their hair done. They have money to burn and their ambition in life is to burn it on the players.

The nearest a Kid gets to his hero is an autograph on the platform.

---

* *England suffered another moral defeat: by five goals to two.*

The nearest a Supporter gets is when his hero condescends to present the prizes at the supporters' ball. But the Hanger-on, if he plays his cards properly, he can have his hero home for dinner.

Morris Keston has hung on so successfully over the years, despite endless discouragement from the club, that he is now about the closest to the players of all the outside fans. He spends about £3,000 every year in following Spurs. Wherever the team stays, no matter where it is in the world, Morris Keston stays, usually in a bigger and better suite.

He's forty, married with two children and lives in a very posh block of flats at Marble Arch. He has a firm in the East End of London, in Bethnal Green Road, which sells ladies' dresses and coats. He employs a staff of fourteen people and has a turnover of about £800,000 a year. They must be very keen, loyal workers. Morris never seems to be there.

In his office he has large photographs of himself. There are many with Bobby Moore, at balls and dinners, beaming in a splendid dinner suit. There's a photograph of Morris shaking hands with Prince Philip. Morris helped to organise a do which raised money for the British Olympic team to go to Mexico. And there's Morris shaking hands with Lord Mountbatten – thanks to Morris helping to raise money for the Commonwealth Games team.

Morris is a great fund raiser, a form of expression beloved by many self-made, affluent East Enders. He's helped many charities, but mostly those concerned with sport, either for sporting charities or benefits for individual sportsmen.

'My life really revolves round Spurs. I probably only know about twenty people in the rag trade, but thousands know me through football. Everywhere I go, people say there's Morris Keston of Spurs.'

That's the sort of boast which could give a Spurs director apoplexy, but all fans are possessive about their club and talk about our team and our lads and our club. Every big club has a fan like Morris Keston, but few have them as big as Morris.

Fred Rhye, the elderly bookie, is an equally ardent Spurs fan, but he seems almost in a trance as he moves round the world, following Spurs. In many ways Spurs is all he's got. But Morris has a young family, an expanding business, his non-stop social life, his charity stuff. Why waste so much time and energy with Spurs?

'I don't understand it myself. I've had ups and downs in business, lots of them, but I just seem to accept them. But Spurs worry me all the time. I don't actually enjoy watching them. I'm too worried. I must be a masochist. There's a magnetism that draws me to them, yet honestly I'd rather pick up the paper and read the result than go and see them. But I've got to go. I can't keep away.

'I chain smoke all the way through a match and get all worked up. These days I often leave about fifteen minutes before the end because I can't stand it any more.

'Even if they're winning 1–0, there's no point in suffering any longer. I can't stand the agony of watching them perhaps lose their lead.'

If Spurs have a good win, then it's champagne all round at his works on Monday morning. If they lose, then he's miserable and irritable, bad tempered with his family all weekend and refuses to take his wife out.

'My wife's given me up for lost as far as football's concerned. There's nothing she can do about it. Now and again she comes with me, for the ride. She picks her trips, like New York or Greece. She wouldn't come to Iceland or Carlisle.'

When Spurs have a really big win, like the FA Cup in 1967 or the League Cup in 1971, then Morris throws a big party at the Hilton for several hundred people which costs him at least £1,000. It was this 1967 party which led to the open rift between him and the club.

The club had their official celebration party at the Savoy. All clubs who get to Wembley celebrate at a big London hotel, treating the wives and officials as well as players, whether they win or not.

The Spurs Savoy party was a very nice affair, from most accounts, but long before it was over the players, so they say, got bored with the speeches and decided to leave and get taxis across London to Morris's party at the Hilton. The directors have never forgiven him for it. They were left with a celebration party which didn't contain the reasons for the celebration. 'Morris had better groups at his party,' says one player. 'Our party was deadly.'

'I didn't make them come,' says Morris. 'They came of their own accord. I was having a celebration party for the Spurs win, whether the Spurs players came or not. I had over two hundred guests. It would still have gone on and been a success, though of course it was great to have the players there.'

Since then, no official at the club has spoken to him. They're always seeing him of course, but they avoid him and he goes out of his way to avoid them. Things weren't helped a couple of years ago in a train coming back from a match when one of his mates, a ticket tout, physically assaulted one director, incensed by the way he thought Morris was being treated.

From Spurs' point of view, you wouldn't expect them to actively encourage the Morris Kestons of this world. The players are supposed to be superfit athletes. How could they possibly ever approve of someone who wanted to take them out to clubs and hotels?

'I can hold my head high,' says Morris. 'They're surrounded by lots of people and get offers all the time from all over. They come to my parties because I'm genuine. I live for Spurs. I don't want them to do badly.

'Fans never get any credit, not of any sort. I feel sorry for those kids who travel up and down screaming their heads off for Spurs. Their hardships are never recognised. But if gates were to fall, you'd soon hear the club complaining.

'A few years ago I found someone willing to sell me five Spurs shares. I paid him £10 each, which he agreed. I wanted them for sentimental value. The club refused to register the sale. I wrote to them and asked for a reason but they never give me any. They're quite entitled to of course, under their regulations, but I was very upset.

'I'd give anything to be a director of Tottenham, any money. I'd enjoy the fame. It's a human reaction.'

Morris doesn't know why so many of the Hangers-on seem to be from the rag trade. 'There's always been a big following amongst Jewish people in the East End for clubs like Tottenham and Arsenal. Chelsea's a bit different. They get the show business crowd.' I asked if it was because as émigrés, once they get any success they want to identify with something very English like a local football team, but he didn't think so. 'It's probably just that Jewish fans draw attention to themselves so much. There always *looks* a lot of them around.'

One of the many social functions which Morris helped to orga-nise during the season took place on the Sunday after one of Spurs' best wins of the season, their 1–0 defeat of Leeds United. Morris couldn't have chosen a better time. There's nothing that footballers like better than being seen after a good victory. The do was actually in honour of Colin Milburn, a cricketer who had lost an eye, but it was the famous footballers everyone wanted to see and be seen with.

The invitations were very posh. First of all it said 'Ball', nothing so common or garden as a dinner-dance. Dress was black tie and 'Carriages', so the invitation said, were for two a.m. Cabaret was to be by 'the sensational Lovelace Watkins'.

The women were in beautiful ornate dresses, dripping with jewels, their hair high and immaculate and their faces tanned and expensive. And as for the men's evening suits, I couldn't get over the variety of designs – brocade lapels, satin collars, embroidered jackets and shirts in every colour and material. And, like the women, the men were dripping with rings and jewellery and expensive tans.

Morris Keston, in a green creation, seemed to be known by everyone as he glided round saying hello Denis (who turned out to be Denis Howell, the MP and former Minister of Sport) and kissing Liz (who turned out to be the actress, Liz Fraser).

The tickets were £10 each. Drinks were extra. Most of the footballers I talked to had been given their ticket free, by Morris. Not only had he organised it all, he'd paid for many of the tickets. It would have been simpler to have handed over a large cheque, but of course there would have been no fun, no glamour, no rubbing shoulders with the famous.

A lot of guests seemed to be connected with sport in some way: TV sports people like Jimmy Hill and Peter Lorenzo, sports agents like Bagenal Harvey. There was also a sprinkling of film and TV people, like Richard Baker, who reads the news on BBC TV, Mike Aspel, and Moira Lister the actress.

I sat down very quickly at my table, table 40, trying to keep my old fashioned evening suit hidden. I sat alone for some time till luckily Martin Chivers and his wife Carol arrived. He was with Stephen Rutland, a business parter and friend. Also at the table was Billy Walker, the boxer, and his wife, plus two partners of Bobby Moore's. The place seemed to be full of Bobby Moore's business partners. The girl next to me said she worked in his Mayfair shirt shop.

The menu was good but safe, just the job for footballers, smart without being in any way worrying. It was melon, followed by soup, followed by steak and two veg followed by a meringue.

Martin Chivers and his friend Stephen had just come up from Brighton where Stephen has a night-club. He has another one opening soon in London which he talked a lot about. The main reason for going to Brighton was a toy fair. Martin had been making personal appearances, endorsing goods with his name.

Stephen talked over dinner about an idea he'd just had for Martin – a gramophone record of Martin Chivers telling people how to score goals. It would be part of a package deal, with a big photograph of Martin scoring one of his famous goals, plus a booklet about his technique. 'It's what every parent and uncle wants. It solves their problems at Christmas. Every kid wants to be able to score goals like Martin. At fifty pence, it could make a packet. Don't you think so? I'm going to organise a demo.'

I said I thought there would be people to buy it, but what could

Martin actually *say* on the record? Scoring goals is a physical not a verbal activity. How can it be explained in words?

Stephen said the record would perhaps be a come-on to a certain extent. No one could really expect to be *taught* to score goals like Martin. 'It's just part of packaging Martin. The whole of commercialisation of footballers is still in infancy. Nobody yet realises the millions of people out there, all fanatics, all untapped, all interested in *anything* to do with a famous footballer.' Everybody nodded their heads and agreed, especially Martin.

The first speaker after the meal was Morris Keston, who briefly thanked everyone for coming, and then a much longer speech was made by Denis Compton. This led into an amazing ritual which apparently happens at every sportsmen's evening. Each famous star in turn had to stand up when his name was called. He took a bow while everyone clapped him, then he sat down again. He didn't have to make a speech or say a word, just stand up and be seen by all. There was such a crowd that evening – over five hundred guests in all – that it seemed to go on for hours. The footballers who were clapped, just for existing, included Bobby Moore, Geoff Hurst, Alan Ball, Rodney Marsh, Martin Peters and Phil Beal. Martin Chivers got an extra loud clap for having scored yesterday's goal against Leeds.

Looking round the tables, I watched the expectation on every passing famous face as they wondered if they too would be announced and have to stand up. There were two faces not announced who seemed very familiar but I couldn't place them. I was sure I'd seen both at Tottenham, but in open necked shirts and looking very shifty. Now they were resplendent in brocade evening suits and purple dress shirts. I pointed them out to Martin. He knew them at once. Ticket touts. They came to every big do at the Hilton. The flashiest tout of all won a big prize later in a raffle and got a standing ovation.

Martin Chivers said he'd seen Lovelace Watkins three times in the last few weeks, at one place or another. He discussed with other people at the table whether the acoustics for cabaret was better in their experience, at the Savoy, the Hilton or the Talk of the Town. All of them seemed to have spent half their lives at such places. I thought of Bill Nicholson and Eddie Baily back in their days, celebrating with a pint and pie and a game of darts.

The band struck up, the sensational Joe Loss no less, with songs like 'I Love to Go A-wandering'. Quicksteps seemed to be in order. At last I felt that my 1962 evening suit might not be too old fashioned after all. But I hadn't got the energy. I left around midnight, too tired to continue. Being a footballer is a hard life. Being a successful footballer, lapping up the social life which the hangers-on love to provide, must be absolutely exhausting.

from THE GLORY GAME 1972

All Rovers Fans

A story by BRIAN GLANVILLE

On the dingy station platform, among the clamour and commotion of the fans, the chants and shouts, the sudden, swift incursions of police, the guffaws and the obscenities, the man and the boy formed a small, still island of intensity. Both were Rovers fans; otherwise, there seemed no meeting point. The man, who was talking quickly, eagerly, as the boy listened, his face alive with the passion of his discourse, was squat and rough. There was an aura about him of park benches, doss houses, even prisons. Heavy shouldered, he wore a shiny, cheap blue suit, a white shirt open at the neck, although the day was cold. His hair, thick, black and oiled, hung to well below his collar. In his enthusiasm, he did not seem aware that the boy was regarding him with a certain slight unease.

He was about sixteen, a plump boy with a soft, dark, Jewish face. If the man appeared used to be roughing it, the boy looked manifestly pampered. When the train eventually drew into London, he would surely go back to a warm home with fitted carpets, a mother who sat him down to a substantial dinner, while the man would go God knows where – to some squalid rooming house, to a Salvation Army shelter?

Still, they talked. The thickset man was saying, 'That's him, though, innit? Don't see him half the game, forget he's even there, then wallop, goal! Like he done today.'

'Yeah, he's good like that,' said the boy.

'He's good, yes, he's *good*, but he's entitled to be better. With the talent he got, he should be better.'

Both spoke with London accents, but where the man's was the thick, slurred, glottal Cockney of the East End, the boy's, higher pitched, had the slightly nasal overlay of Stamford Hill, or perhaps, stepping westward, Golders Green.

All about them, as the football excursion train came gliding to the platform, swirled skinheads, with their brutal crops, their braces worn over coloured tee-shirts, their thick, heavy, threatening boots; burly youths in jean jackets, scarves dangling from their wrists, a small, gold earring in their right ears; even punks with jagged hair dyed green and purple. The boy's eyes flickered anxiously about him as the crowd rushed past, charged the carriages, wrenched open doors, fought to get through them.

'Come on!' the man said, *'there's* one!' and went dashing down the platform with the boy behind him, now dodging, now bumping and buffetting, reaching a carriage farther down the train, forcing his way through the scrum of people, up the steps, into the carriage, the boy still following in his wake, till they were sitting opposite each other, panting, smiling, in a long, open, second-class compartment.

'Gotta be quick, haven't you?' the man said. 'Gotta be decisive! Like football. Like in the penalty area, innit?' The boy smiled back and nodded.

They sat in the window seats. Beside them were two other fans, one a middle aged man with bushy grey hair and a woollen cap in the club's blue and white colours, the other a tall, thin, fair-haired boy, the club's scarf around his neck.

'Fucking showed 'em, didn't we?' said the man.

As the passengers settled down, as seats were found, the wandering began. Up and down the train went the young fans, shouting, jostling, drinking beer out of cans, hoarse and raucous, chanting their monotonous dirge of 'Rovers, Rovers!' swopping their tales of violence and conquest.

'Twenty of 'em there when we got to the station. Geezer with a bottle, another with a bleedin' flick knife. Nutted one, put the boot in another.'

'Old Bill came steaming in, sorted a few out. Old Terry, 'e got done again.'

Then another chant:

'We 'ate Arsenal!'

'We 'ate Arsenal!'

From all this frantic, motiveless activity, the man and the boy were detached; the man too old to be a part of it, the boy disinclined by nature.

'Don't come for the game, that lot,' said the man, and they exchanged another smile.

'Follow them everywhere, do you?' asked the man.

'Not everywhere,' the boy said. 'Quite a lot.'

'Up to Middlesbrough, places like that?'

'Well . . . sometimes.'

He was still wary. If the fans were not his kind, then neither was the man, who brought into his warm, protected world a harsh breath of the outside. Now and again, as the fans pushed by in their lemming progress, the man exchanged a joke with them. The boy did not speak to them at all; he seemed to shrink physically away from them into his corner. Their scarves, their crops, their earrings and tattooes, their heavy boots, made his own neat, blue anorak, his polished shoes, seem bourgeois and effete.

'Don't your parents like you going?' the man asked, suddenly. It was the first suggestion that there might be barriers between them, that the boy came from another, gentler scene.

'Not much,' the boy mumbled, eyes upon the grubby floor.

'Live in London, do you?'

'Yes.'

'Whereabouts?'

'Willesden.'

'Nice there, is it?'

'All right. Where do . . . *you* live?'

'Round about,' the man said. 'Here and there. Always supported Rovers. Have you?'

'Yes.'

'Same here.'

'We 'ate Arsenal!' chanted a bunch of fans marching past.

As the journey wore on, as the beer flowed from the cans, the tone became harsher and more menacing. There was an edge of violence to it now, as if the fans were seeking prey.

'We 'ate Villa!'

The team had just beaten Aston Villa.

'Any Villa fans 'ere? Any Villa fans 'iding 'ere?'

'We all agree,

'Aston Villa are wankers!'

The man grinned at this, then smiled across at the boy, whose own smile was a grimace.

'Wouldn't get *this* train, would they?' asked the man. 'Not Villa fans.'

Each fresh wave of supporters was more aggressive than the one before.

'We 'ate niggers!' came the new chant. 'We 'ate niggers!'

'Ain't seen none on *this* train,' said the man. 'Just as well, I reckon.'

'Yes,' said the boy, less and less audible. He seemed to be expecting some catastrophe. The man looked at him with quizzical surprise, then turned to talk to the older fan beside him.

'Marvellous shot he's got on him, that Ronnie.'

From the next carriage, a cry floated back, 'Kill the yids!' and now the boy visibly stiffened, seemed to shrink still further into his seat, looking out with desperate intensity at the smooth, green, sloping pasture land that sped by the window.

'Kill the yids!' came more faintly back down the train. The tone was almost jocular, but the boy now bent his whole body round and away from the carriage behind him, his study of the fields outside now so obsessive that it might have been that of a botanist. It was as if he wanted to convince himself that only the fields, the countryside, were real; that the train and its passengers no longer existed.

Now they were coming again.

'The yids, the yids!'

'We gotta get rid of the yids!'

'*Sieg Heil! Sieg Heil!*'

The boy cowered at the window. The man ceased talking for a moment to glance at him, and grin.

Down the train and back, now the youths were singing, to the tune of a pop song: 'We are *Na*-zis, we are *Na*-zis!'

As they came into the carriage, there were about a dozen of them, most of them skinheads, some in jean jackets, all wearing the inevitable boots. When they and their noise had disappeared again, the boy at last looked timidly round, to find the man smiling at him.

'You one?' he asked.

The boy looked at him, petrified, then, almost imperceptibly, he nodded. The man continued gazing at him, smiling, without speaking. He seemed amused, almost pleased. At last he said, 'I wouldn't worry. Songs, that's all it is.'

The boy swallowed, gave another nod, and followed it with the sickly parody of a smile.

'Just songs and that,' the man said.

The boy turned back to the refuge of the window. The man went on looking at him, smiling for a while, then resumed his conversation with the other fan.

'Mind you,' he said, 'I reckon that he likes a pint, old Ronnie. People I know seen him up the Nag's Head.'

The shouts and chants had ceased now, but the fans would be

back; mindlessly, restlessly, ceaselessly in motion, looking for excitement, violence, victims.

The boy turned from the window again, pulled the programme of the match out of his pocket, and began to read it as though he were committing it to memory.

'Collect 'em, do you?' asked the man.

The boy said, 'Yes,' the merest motion of the lips.

'I collected them, and all, when I was your age,' said the man, the smile still on his face. 'The trouble is, they kept on getting nicked. People would pinch them.'

The boy gave a grimace of response, then resumed his tense study of the programme.

'They're different now, of course,' the man said. 'Bigger, lot more pictures. More expensive.'

'Something to read,' said the older fan. 'Something to do while you're waiting.'

'Ever win the Lucky Programme?' asked the man. 'I had one once. Don't know where it was. Somewhere up north – Huddersfield, or somewhere. Years ago. I got a quid – that's all I got, a quid. The Lucky Programme. Kind of luck I've always had.'

The boy did not look up. Now the voices could be heard again.

''E's only a poor little Scouser,
'Is face is all tattered and torn.
'E made me feel sick,
So I gave 'im a brick,
And now 'e don't sing any more.'

As the sound grew nearer, the boy put down his programme and met the man's smiling face in a fleeting, anguished look of appeal, before turning back to the window.

'Kill the yids!' cried the voices. 'Kill the yids!'

The fans were in the carriage now, they were approaching, they were level, they had stopped.

'Any yids in here?' a voice asked. 'Oo's *'e*? What's 'e doing, looking out like that?'

'Looks like a yid.'

The boy did not move. Rigid, he went on staring out of the window as the fields rushed past, a haze of green.

At last, he heard the man speak: 'He's a Rovers fan, isn't 'e? 'E's Rovers.'

'Thought he was a yid,' a voice said. '*Looks* like one.'

'*Nah*,' said the man, ''e's Rovers,' and the boots moved off.

'We *'ate* Arsenal!'

'We *'ate* Arsenal!'

The boy turned slowly from the window. His body shook, his mouth was trembling.

'All Rovers fans, aren't we?' said the man, and winked at him.

from LOVE IS NOT LOVE *1985*

Football Casualty

ARTHUR HOPCRAFT

In January 1965 three of England's best known footballers were sent to prison for four months after their conviction in what was called The Soccer Conspiracy Case. They were Peter Swan, the Sheffield Wednesday centre-half who had played nineteen times for his country, David Layne, the Sheffield Wednesday centre-forward, and Tony Kay, a wing-half, formerly of Sheffield Wednesday but at the time of the disclosure playing for Everton. The gist of the case was that all three, while playing for Wednesday, had conspired to prevent their own team from winning a match to facilitate a betting coup. A few months after the case the three players were suspended from football for life by the Football Association, which meant that any form of officially recognised football anywhere was barred to them. Kay and Swan had pleaded not guilty in court.

The case made a wretched winter for British football. Seven less well-known players and former players were sentenced at the same time on similar charges to terms of imprisonment ranging from four years to six months. The exposure was the work of *The People*, the Sunday newspaper, whose reporters did their job resourcefully and ruthlessly, and the dirty shrapnel of the explosion nicked and wounded people all round the game. Such a revelation was bound to make the public ask each other, blackly, how much 'fixing' of matches was going on which was never discovered. This fear struck at the very roots and heart of football. The footballers, once found guilty, were bound to suffer the complete punishment.

While the tale was being told little sympathy was invited for the men concerned, although Mr Justice Lawton, passing sentence, said he accepted that the Sheffield Wednesday players were involved 'really by chance' and on one isolated occasion; they presented him, he said, 'with the most unpleasant part of my duty'. Excuse may never be possible, but at least the personal tragedy of the event should be acknowledged. The fallen, ruined hero is no figure for callous scorn. Some respected men in the game have given their names to appeals for the players' re-instatement. There is kindness here but also, I think, a failure on their part to recognise the significance of the case. Perhaps it is a matter of being too close to the game to see the extent of the damage. A court conviction on a charge of 'fixing' football is not just a nasty blotch on the wall, but a jagged hole in the fabric. Two or three more like that and the whole structure falls in rubble.

Of the three men I have named, Kay was the most colourful player, and he was notably articulate. He was 27 at the time of the case, and he had played once for England, against Switzerland. He was an extremely tough, quick, enterprising halfback, of the combative, all-action kind: very much the type of player whom Sir Alf Ramsey developed in Nobby Stiles for England's World Cup victory. Stiles played magnificently for England. It is fair to ask whether he would have been given the chance if Kay had been available. That thought was very sharply in my mind when I went to see Kay in Liverpool in 1967.

He looked haggard, although not in the debilitated sense of a man gone to seed. He looked what he was still: a hard-driven athlete, the flesh tight on the bones. He had red, scrubbing-brush hair, and he work thick-rimmed glasses. He exuded an exaggerated ruefulness, a bitter and aggressive self-mockery. There was a distinct television-age, showbiz edge to the back-street wit. 'The cops have it in for me; must have,' he said. 'Have you ever heard of anyone being booked for parking by a copper on a horse? That's Anthony's luck.'

Kay was brought up in Sheffield, and he learned about life and football, which amounted practically to the same thing for him, in the same atmosphere which Derek Dooley had described. His experience even had some of the identical physical characteristics, but encountered ten years later: the street football, the Sheffield YMCA, even Pop Bennett. He knew working-class austerity as people know sweat, through the pores, not book-learnt or observed in passing. Money was important because there was not much of it about. Everton bought him from Sheffield Wednesday for more than £55,000.

The face has a flare of insolence, and now that he had much to regret he played up this component in his personality, telling stories of the persecution and recurrent disaster in his life with a chirpy, gritty comicality. 'Wasn't I always in trouble?' he said. 'Well, I nearly got killed more than once, didn't I? Look how the crowds used to get at me.'

He launched into a story about a match in London, which ended with a mob of the home crowd's fans yelling for his blood round the exit. He walked out disguised in the home team manager's long overcoat and trilby. He said: 'When I got in the coach I took 'em off and tapped the window at the crowd. You should have seen 'em,' and he bared his teeth wide and crooked his fingers on either side of his face, like talons.

Then he said: 'There was that time in Italy when the crowd was at me. "Kay, Bastardo, Bastardo." They were behind this wire grille (bared teeth and crooked fingers again). I banged the ball at their faces. So what happens when we come off at the end? I'm there, with our team in the dressing-room, and I'm standing at the tunnel thanking everyone, and I go up to this Italian trainer, who's only about 7 feet tall. I hold my hand out, and what does he do? He's only got both me arms pinned behind me back. And all the Italian team's giving me one as they go off the field.'

The resentment poured out of him, as he built up a picture of a victimised upbringing. The voice teetered up into a thin malevolence, the voice of childhood's tormentors: 'Right, you've been very, very naughty, and now we're going to rattle your little arse. Whack. Sort that out.'

Kay, the bolshie; Kay, the whipping-boy; Kay, the misunderstood; Kay, the unlucky; he overstated his battering from life, and his fumbling resistance, with the skill of a natural comedian who is beginning to believe the letter as well as the spirit of his material.

'I've always hated referees,' he said. 'To me they're all no-marks. Otherwise, they wouldn't be there. Who are they? All the week they're sitting there in offices, scribbling away, scribble, scribble, and on Saturday afternoons they're on the field with all the big men, and they're saying, "Right, now you do what I tell you or you're going in my little book."' He did a wickedly observed impersonation of a hunchbacked, myopic referee writing in a notebook, his hands up by his nose. He said: 'I've seen blokes kicking lumps out of each other, and what's the referee doing? He's wagging his finger and making a great production out of moving the ball three foot back for a free kick.'

Kay's sadly funny performance was the more disturbing because in his comment on authority, and its view of him, there was a strong thread of truth. As a player he was undoubtedly one of those eruptive influences which infuriate referees. He was known for his bitter tackling and only tough men were prepared to take the consequences. Kay insisted to me that he was a marked man not only in the opposition's dressing-room but in the referee's as well, and he added that he did not mind telling referees so. One of his troubles was that he was never discreet in what he said or what he did. He said to me: 'I was naïve.' He was right. He knew most of the tricks of the trade, but not the most important trick of all, which is to appear not to.

The more Kay talks the stronger is the conviction borne in on the listener that his misfortunes were impelled from inside him. Like everyone else the influences he assimilated from his environment were an imperfect blend; but is it the mixture or the chemistry which makes a man? Kay was embattled against the world, pretty well all of it, so that ultimately he was working against himself. Even in trivial, everyday matters, such as his relationship with road traffic, his progress was interrupted by violent incidents of bizarre complexity, in which his saving grace was to be found in his comic, fatalistic hindsight. One accident, as he described it, involved the inexorable will of some dauntless old lady, launched come what might for the distant haven of the opposite pavement. There was also snow and a steep hill. Then: 'So all of a sudden I'm waking up in me mini, upside down, and this geezer's shouting all sorts at me out of his bedroom winder.' On another occasion the slap-stick disaster ends: 'So here I am, can't move a limb, being wheeled about the station by a porter on a trolley.'

Kay managed to squeeze a few wicked, retaliatory jokes out of his prison sentence. He said that the prison governor was 'a wild football fan, and he couldn't get enough of the game'. Kay said that he and his friends were given full rein to train the prison football team, and that the governor refereed most of the matches himself. 'We only lost one game out of fourteen,' Kay said, adding with a look of feigned distaste, 'and that was because the other lot brought their own referee; the game was *bent*.' He laughed. He said that the first warder he met in gaol was a little man – most villains in Kay's life are little men – who greeted him with: 'Yes, it's through people like you I never win the pools.' Kay said: 'I thought to myself, "Hullo, Anthony, you've found yourself one here. It's your luck again."' He encountered the warder later when the man was a linesman at one of the matches. The story is a symmetry of irony:

'The governor was sold on us. I gave 'em all hell, you know. He used to say, "Well done, young Kay." Well, this little warder – the bad one – he kept sticking his flag up and shouting at me every time I touched anybody. After a bit I said to him, "Why don't you piss off?" He was furious. He said, "I'll have you yet." So I ran across to the governor – he was refereeing again – and I said, "Excuse me, Sir, can't you do something about this linesman? He keeps on at me. I can't concentrate." So the governor went across to this warder, and he said, "Not so much noise, please, Mr So-and-so."' Kay's eyes glinted at the memory.

To judge from Kay's conversation, his attitude to authority always had that cynicism. He reminds one of the bad lad at the back of the class, or the hard case in the barrack-room, who recognises the sneaking respect, and often fear, that the man in charge has for the ones who won't conform. Such men seldom appeal for help, and when they do it is to exploit the boss's sense of importance. Kay told me this story about a match against Fulham:

'I was up against Jimmy Hill, and he was up there towering above me. Every time I went up for the ball there he was, just leaning over the top of me. I thought, "Right, I'm not having this all the game. Next time we go up I'll have his shorts off him." Well, up he went, and I shoved me hand out and I missed 'em. Instead I caught him right between the legs. He screamed the place down. But he kept with me afterwards, all over the field. I went to the ref. I said, "Hey, ref, look at this maniac with the beard. Look at the way he's after me." It worked.' Kay's relished little triumphs can only be properly understood by someone brought up where people never play cards for matchsticks.

I was warned before I went to see him that Kay might be sad; that if the gloom was on him he might even weep. He anticipated my wariness. He had stopped crying, he said, although when he was first told that he could never play football competitively again, he confessed: 'I never cried so much in all me life.' He said it looking straight at me, using the words like a showbiz catchphrase, but not smiling. He knew he had been overdoing the clowning. 'It just hides the tears,' he said. 'You can't cry all the time. You get a reputation for it. No one wants to know after a bit. They say, "Oh Christ, I've got to put up with this crying gett again." You can't just give up, can you?'

It was plain that he had been deeply hurt by what had happened to him; he was convinced it had been imposed and not brought upon him by himself. Every six months, he said, he wrote to the FA, asking if they would reconsider his registration. He did not really think they ever would. People in Liverpool, he said, were friendly and sympathetic towards him. That salty city would never snub a man like Kay. He was as much one of Liverpool's own, pugnacious and at least pretending cunning, as if he had been born there.

But his life was not pleasing him, to say the least of it. At the time I was talking to him he was a family man living away from his wife, and a bookmaker not sure that there would be another year's wages out of his betting shop. What had he been doing since prison? 'Just going round in circles,' he said. 'Getting nowhere.'

He had been playing football, surreptitiously, in scratch matches, giving another name when he was asked, keeping an eye open for men hanging about with cameras. He was training twice a week, and I could believe it when he said: 'I really push myself.' He did much of his training at a school gymnasium, often giving practical instruction to the boys. He said, the edge going out of the voice for the first time: 'They all want to take me on, you know. They think, "Oh, this old Tony Kay, he's finished." I like to get 'em trying to get past me on the outside, and I'm leaving 'em behind, and I'm shouting, "Come on, what are you waiting for, you lads?"'

There was a lot of heart in Kay as a player. Professional sport made him, tested him and broke him. He is one of football's tragic casualties because he was so strongly equipped in nearly all his aspects. His counsel said in court, after his conviction: 'He has given up for £100 what has in fact been one of the greatest careers of any footballer. He was tempted once, and fell.'

from THE FOOTBALL MAN *1968*

'It's hoff . . .'

JOHN MOYNIHAN

It was a nasty brutal October Sunday. Dramatic black clouds plodded in oily battalions over Chelsea as heavy rain turned streets into mirrors and pedestrians into sea lions.

Shortly before lunch I rang through to the Royal Hospital ground on Chelsea embankment to see if our Chelsea Casuals' strictly unadvertised game against the BBC had been called off. As usual the groundsman did not answer the telephone. He had a reputation for lurking among the trees and leaving the telephone to his wife. But his wife had rebelled. So it was a case of taking matters into one's own hands and going down to the ground to find him.

Our left-half had arrived early for the match, having one of those characteristic insatiable appetites for the game which minor Sunday footballers have. We went out into the rain. 'It can't be on,' I said. 'It's pissing.' 'Keep your fingers crossed,' he said, squeezing a copy of *Ancient Chinese Philosophy* to his chest inside his rain coat. 'I've waited a week for this. It can't be off.' 'There isn't a chance,' I said, always a defeatist.

The suspense was awful. I suppose we knew already that the groundsman was waiting to tell us, rubbing his hand, that 'It's HOFF'. How many times had it happened at Hackney Marshes, Parliament Hill Fields and Hampstead Heath Extension? As our left-back had often said about Chelsea Royal Hospital: 'It only has to have a quick slash and that's it, the bastard.'

The rain had eased quite a bit by the time we reached the Embankment and turned right towards the ground. The Thames flowed in streaks of dingy colour along the Battersea fringes. A youth wearing blue jeans and a cowboy hat with a cigarette hanging out of his mouth trudged past us with liquid streaming from his cast-iron ears. Through the gates of the Royal Hospital we saw the cannon balls piled beside those twin, ancient cannons, while the tall, phallic monument to Crimea dividing the two football pitches had buried itself in a greasy ceiling of low weather.

The pitch we had to play on, the smaller one on the right, was flooded with shallow pools of water, but not as much as the main pitch, where both goalmouths were swimming pools. We trudged, shoulders hunched with grief, along the path to the changing rooms. 'I can't stand it,' said the left-half.

Three figures stood outside the rickety hut which Chelsea Borough Council had the nerve to call a dressing room. They looked like grey herons in the rain, static and bloated with moisture.

I recognised the groundsman, a small, beaky-chinned man wearing a faded pin-striped suit, sodden and clipped at the ankles with bicycle clips. His hair was greased back so that the main movement occurred over the ears, two violent waves which roared back over the lobes leaving a thinning, calmer pool of hair on the top. His brown eyes protruded as if waiting for some signal which would shoot them out onto the path. His mouth was permanently open and as we ambled up he spoke in shrill cockney: 'It's HOFF.'

We back away and then sideways as if to combat his statement and make him feel at ease so that he would change his mind. The two other men regarded him with sheer hate. The older one, just visible below a brown corduroy cap, was about thirty. His cheeks were flushed and chubby and there was hardly any mouth, a pink button through which an orange tongue occasionally flicked irritation. His shoulders were massive, his kneecaps prominent through a diarrhoea-coloured raincoat, his shoes Italian pointed, his eyes pig-like and red, probably from constant pints of bitter. His companion was younger and his corduroy cap, blue, was firmly planted over a greyhound-shaped snout. His body was lithe, his thin legs fixed to a pair of waterlogged brothel creepers.

Both men held onto small, leather suitcases, the older one having tied a football to his. It was the older one who spoke, his eyelashes fluttering like dragonflies. 'Did you hear him, did you hear him,' he said turning to us. 'He's joking. There's only a bit of piss out there and it says it's fucking hoff. Hoff. I'm telling yer we're playing.'

'It's hoff,' said the groundsman not giving way an inch. 'No play on pitch one today and no play on pitch two.'

The older player turned to us again and let his voice rise to a high pipe. 'I tell yer something,' he said. 'He's going to get done for this. Fuckin' well is.'

Our team had been overruled and we looked down mumbling that we might be able to play if the rain stopped. 'I'm telling you it's hoff. And when I say it's hoff, it's hoff. HOFF.'

The younger player eased his way forward so he towered over the groundsman, whose smile hung like a cigarette butt on the edge of his mouth. 'We're playing the Wandsworth Sportsmen,' he said. 'Top of the league struggle. You can't put that fuckin' game off, honest to fuck you can't. I tell you we're going to put you in hospital, so'll the Sportsmen, you'll see. Fucking cheek.'

'It's hoff. Both games hoff. I called them hoff this morning. You should have rung like the other lads. They called and I said it's hoff, both teams, both games, they didn't say anything. Stands to reason, look at it.'

'Fucking cheek,' said the older player.

The groundsman flung his chin at him. 'You've got any complaints speak to Chelsea Borough Council. They'll put you right. Go up and see 'em at the Town Hall tomorrow. Don't tell me what my job is. It's hoff.'

The two aggressors turned towards their pitch which was now deeper under water, small air bubbles sending out tiny jets in the goalmouths. On the centre circle a tired group of pigeons pecked hopefully at a small, dry piece of island. But the sight of the two goals nets arranged in all their majesty, rain drops dripping from the rigging, made them squirm with irritation.

'Piss, it's only piss,' said the older one. 'You could play ten games on that and still have anuvver. I tell you something, Tich, you going to get done. Fuck the Council, we'll do them too.'

'And a Wandsworth Sportsman will do 'em and you,' said the greyhound. 'The lads'll get you. A razor job, or you'll get a good thumping.'

'I know you lot,' said the groundsman. 'Always making trouble, bribing the ref, sorting out other lads. Well I'm telling you it's hoff. You can't threaten me. Nobody threatens me. I've had more war service than you've had hot dinners. The Burma campaign, it was.'

'Fuck Burma,' said the greyhound.

'We don't want nothing to do wiz Burma. We'll do you.'

'Fuck you,' said the older one giving the football attached to his suitcase a savage kick, thereby revealing that he was a thick-skinned full-back. He was still holding the suitcase so the effort took him five yards across the path and it looked most ungainly.

'Fucker,' said the greyhound. 'You wait till the Wandsworth Sportsmen catch you. They'll be here soon.'

'They won't. They telephoned.'

'I couldn't get you,' I added meekly.

'Well, that's your bad luck,' said the groundsman. 'And your game's hoff too.' Thus ended our slim hopes that such aggression from the others would influence him to let us play.

'I've seen some fuckpigs in my life,' said the greyhound. He had pulled his cap down so that it perched on the end of his nose. The older one pulled his shoulders back. 'I wouldn't be in your shoes, honest I wouldn't. You're going to get done.'

'See the Borough Council,' said the groundsman. 'It's hoff and now I'm hoff.' He pointed to a notice outside the dressing room door. 'See that.' It read, 'No Play Today.'

We hung around for another five minutes, but nobody came through the rain and nobody came from the Wandsworth Sportsmen. All there was was the noise of the two players and the groundsman saying alternately: 'We'll have you, you cunt, we'll have you,' and 'It's hoff, hoff.'

The rain began to come down in rasping jets and the left-half said: 'Well, that's it. Let's go back to your place.'

We walked moodily away down the patch and could still hear the three men arguing and swearing. When we reached the gates of the Royal Hospital they were a blob of cantankerous human form far away beyond the drenched pitch number one.

'They'll still be there tomorrow,' said the left-half. We had to laugh.

from THE SOCCER SYNDROME (Chapter IX) *1966*

We'll Never Know

John Moynihan

'Hendon League . . . Rawlplugs 5 Apex Reserves 6: A magnificent fighting rally in the closing stages gave Apex Reserves victory over their closest rivals in the chase for the Div 3 championship. After Rawlplugs had taken an early lead, Tony Shadbolt equalised and John Pamplin put the visitors ahead. In the second half Rawlplugs soon drew level and they regained the lead with a penalty. After Shadbolt had scored Apex's third, Rawlplugs put on the pressure and built up a 5–3 lead. In the closing minutes Clive Boyse and Shadbolt equalised and in the last seconds Colin Preen netted the winner.'

So said the *Finchley Times* one day, but we'll never really know what happened, apart from these bare, informative lines, as clinical as a city at dawn. Who was Shadbolt, the fiendish Shadbolt who turned the game for Apex Reserves with his three goals? Was he thick or thin, did he move like a butterfly or a bull, did he scream with ecstasy when he equalised with that vital goal which made it 5–5?

Shadbolt, a good, solid name for a footballer; thick bulging kneecaps, perhaps, with a jaw which munched gum; cool, blue eyes, dirt on white stockings, mud on the navel, clear headed, a little aggressive, a little garrulous, moody, but on this day, this afternoon, moving with grace and confidence, leaping in the air perhaps when his first equaliser sped in, coaxing the Apex Reserves back into the game. We'll never know.

Who were the crowd, a smattering of faces peeping out of dirty mackintoshes, voyeurs or addicts, odd partisans longing for the local, the sudden thrill that the game was a good one, that Rawlplugs had a chance, that Apex Reserves were coming in to win?

Did the wind howl across North London? Where was the game played (the report didn't say)? Were the conditions intolerable; was the game sporting, or mixed with wild obscenities; did the net hiss when the ball hit the net? Was there a raging fandango of pleasure when Apex Reserves scored their last minute winning goal? All this we do not know. We can only imagine the winning dressing room, a small stifled box full of pegs and one shower hissing in the toilet annexe and the team naked and bellowing with pleasure, the smell of dirty socks, greasy shirts, bandages discarded in reels of tape; boots everywhere, as profuse as seaweedy rocks. Mud, mud, mud, and one player perhaps sunk in glorious hibernation with his head in his hands; a woman waiting outside; a voice in the shower, 'Good old Tony,' a highly strung feeling of victory. 'What a goal, Colin,' 'Good auld Tony.' Noise, noise, noise, noise, and afterwards at a local, brown and light ales and the soft haircuts of the winning players linked round in a circle of fluff. 'Good auld Tony, you took 'em well Tony 'onest you did.' 'Well you set 'em up for me. I just cracked 'em in.' But was it like this? We'll never know, we'll never know beyond the report except that Apex Reserves won by 6–5 in the last seconds.

The losers' dressing room, macabre, yellow-faced players less anxious to strip, leaning on their kneecaps, wanting to pound their flesh in frustration, screaming inwardly, hating their team mates, why, oh, why? The men of Rawlplugs shattered, shattered men of Rawlplugs staring perhaps at the opposite wall with glazed eyes. Or were they cheerful, praising their colleagues' rally, cheerfully accepting their late slide. Do they rub themselves down with the look of languid men, wish they were not footballers at this moment, exposed to ridicule? Do they creep home to their wives and girl friends with dull, beaten faces asking only to sink into a settee and contemplate the tele and mutter, 'It was diabolical.' We'll never know.

The Sunday mornings after absorb these games; North London is silent, rows and rows of silent houses, streets silent, only a milkman buzzing past, seagulls sagging on goalposts of local Co-operative Society grounds. The men of Apex Reserves perhaps slept late and woke with joy in their bellies; well they might bellow, 'Hullo, love', but we'll never know.

And then men of Rawlplugs may have woken up and stared at the ceiling and seen a dirty sky outside and thought: 'If only I had passed the ball to so and so instead of passing it to so and so,' and 'if', and 'if,' and 'if,' and 'hell'; We'll never know.

And we'll never know if Apex Reserves met the next day at a North London local with a pop group going in the background and pints of Guinness and bitter all round to celebrate and Shadbolt in the middle being toasted and Colin Preen who scored the winner. Or maybe they were teetotallers and took their game so seriously they didn't drink anything but orange juice and went out with their girl friends and wives after lunch to the pictures and didn't talk about the game because they believed in being modest.

And the team from Rawlplugs: did they go out and dissect their defeat at the local with the traffic swishing by on ramps out of London towards the North, awful bitchy criticism through to closing time, or did they just forget the whole thing and say: 'Well, it was close. We'll win next week.'

Either way it doesn't matter. Footballers tend to be in a weird psychological state after a game, wildly effusive or moody as hell. We'll never know what really happened. But it is easy to imagine.

from THE SOCCER SYNDROME 1966

Playing for Mevagissey

KENNETH SHEARWOOD
(Oxford University and Pegasus)

Early in October I played my first match for Mevagissey in the Junior Football League of Cornwall. The Mevagissey football ground lay above the village, situated in a very rough and sloping field with magnificent views of the sea and coast to the north. I had been elected captain, which I considered a great honour. How this was decided and who had been responsible for the decision I never found out. No one had seen me play, and though I had played for Shrewsbury School for two seasons, nobody knew of this. Even if they had known this fact, it would have meant nothing to a Cornish fishing village.

My recollections of my days playing for Mevagissey are hazy, but several events and one personality in particular stand out clearly.

Catherine was her name, and she was a great supporter of mine. She would sit at her upstairs window overlooking the corner of the harbour by Williams's engineering shop, and watch the fishermen as they went in and out. She lived for her football and hated to see the Mevagissey side lose, which I'm afraid they did rather too often. Around the touch-line on this appalling yet beautiful football pitch, twenty or thirty fishermen would be grouped. They would stand talking and shouting ribald encouragement. Major Barton, the Chairman, who was as responsible as anyone for keeping the club going, would stand a little apart and periodically shout, 'Well played, Mevagissey.'

But the person who really stole the limelight was Catherine, who would stand in the middle and shout her own form of encouragement on these lines.

'Come on Charlie, me old dear. You'm show 'em. Well played!

Ooh, you dirty bastard! Yes you'm did! I saw you. Referee! Referee!' and here she would advance on to the pitch, egged on by the supporters. 'Why don't you stop him, ref, and blow your bloody whistle?' I have always been amused by the comments of male football supporters, but never particularly by women. Catherine, however, was an exception. Perhaps it was that Junior League football in Cornwall has a quality all of its own, and to me Catherine was part of the setting. Whatever the weather, there she would be, exhorting her side with a running commentary, delivered with such amusing emphasis and conviction that in spite of the ferocity of her criticism, I for one could never feel any annoyance at her antics.

One day, however, she almost went too far. The match had been a particularly tough one and we'd gone down with all colours flying. When the final whistle blew Catherine was ready. With a huge lump of mud, she ran at the referee and I saw it go sailing past his head. Not content at her near-miss, she aimed a kick at his backside. But the referee did not stay for more, and Catherine was left disconsolate and angry in the middle of the muddy field.

'Come on, Catherine,' I said. 'We'll win the next match for you.'

'You'm played a wonderful game, me old beauty,' she said. 'Yes, you'm did. A really wonderful game,' and together we walked off the field.

But the matter did not end there, for the Committee had observed Catherine's attack and felt, I think rightly, that something had to be done to protect referees on the Mevagissey football ground from any further assaults of this kind. However, the action they took was too fierce and poor Catherine was banned from watching any more matches.

The following week we played away, but the week after I found myself once again spinning a coin on that wonderful but impossible football pitch. The game had not been in progress for more than a few minutes when I noticed a commotion going on in the hedge that ran up one side of the pitch. The spectators had turned their heads – indeed, all eyes, including the players', were watching the hedge, which was moving about and from which strange noises were coming.

Suddenly it burst asunder and with a shout of triumph Catherine emerged. There was laughter all round, but Catherine wasted no time: 'Come on, me old dears. You show 'em how to play. Go on, Alf! Oh, you dirty devil! Yes, you did. You did it on purpose. Referee. . . .' And so it went on until the end of the game. On this occasion her cup was full, for it was one of the few games we won that season.

Another time we played somewhere inland with snow lying thick on the ground and an icy east wind blowing the full length of the pitch. We were two goals down at half-time and changed ends to face the biting wind. They were a better side than we were, and I found we were well and truly up against it. Of a sudden I felt there was something wrong, and I was right, for our left back had decided he'd had enough and was already halfway to the small wooden shed where we had changed. I pulled back one of our inside forwards to wing half and sent the wing half to left back. Within minutes the right back had decided he'd had enough and was already running towards the wooden shed. The wind shrieked in mockery and the cold was an agony. Our opponents scored twice quickly, and to my utter amazement I suddenly saw our outside-right sprint rapidly from the pitch and make a bee-line for the shed. There was now a very definite wavering in the ranks, and suddenly we all ran for it, as hard as we could, straight for the wooden shed where some relief from the cruel wind awaited us. I was roaring with laughter by the time I had reached the door. But I didn't laugh for long, for hard on our heels were our opponents, followed by their supporters, a very angry-looking crowd indeed. I nipped inside quickly, and not a moment too soon.

There was a loud banging on the door and a furious voice asked us what the hell we were doing.

'Tell 'em to go to hell,' came the helpful advice from Billy More, who was already changing.

I opened the door and cautiously looked out.

'Are you going to finish the game or are you going to give us the points?' demanded their captain with considerable anger.

'Certainly you may have the points,' I replied, and that was the end of that match.

But they were happy and intensely amusing football matches. Later on when I was captain of the Oxford University football side, I brought the team down to play two matches against Cornwall. We won both our matches, and a good number of the fishermen came to watch us. I took the team over to Mevagissey and introduced them to the fishermen.

'He'm never could do any bloody good for us,' said Edgar when I introduced him to Donald Carr, the Derbyshire cricket captain.

'No, and he's not much good for us,' agreed Donald with a laugh.

In 1951 I was to find myself at Wembley Stadium playing centre-half for Pegasus against Bishop Auckland, before a crowd of 100,000. We won 2–1. Two years later we were at Wembley again before another 100,000 crowd, and this time we beat Harwich and Parkeston 6–0. I now had two gold Cup-winner's medals and many telegrams from well-wishers, two of which I was delighted to see were from Mevagissey Football Club and Gorran Cricket Club.

from WHISTLE THE WIND 1959

The Manchester United Disaster

H. E. BATES

Late on a cold February afternoon of this year I was driving home from London when I suddenly saw, under the first lighted street lamps, one of those blue and yellow news placards that are designed so often to shock you into buying a newspaper you don't particularly want and that, nine times out of ten, you would be just as well off without.

'Manchester United In Air Crash', it said. My immediate reaction was, I confess, a mildly cynical one. The announcement seemed to me to belong to precisely the same category as 'Winston Churchill in Car Crash' – the car crash almost invariably turning out to be nothing more than a tender argument between the starting handle of an ancient Austin Seven and the great man's Rolls-Royce somewhere in the region of Parliament Square. I am getting too old, I thought, to be caught by newspaper screamers.

At six o'clock, out of pure curiosity, I turned on my television set. As the news came on, the screen seemed to go black. The normally urbane voice of the announcer seemed to turn into a sledge-hammer. My eyes went deathly cold and I sat listening with a frozen brain to that cruel and shocking list of casualties that was now to give to the despised word Munich an even sadder meaning than it had acquired on a day before the war when a British Prime Minister had come home to London, waving a pitiful piece of paper, and most of us knew that new calamities of war were inevitable.

Roger Byrne, Bill Whelan, Duncan Edwards, Tommy Taylor, David Pegg, Geoff Bent, Mark Jones, Eddie Colman – of Manchester United's flashing young giants hardly one had been out of the cradle at the time of the first Munich disaster. Probably not one of them had kicked a football in that year on the eve of the war when England had sent to Berlin eleven other giants to thrash the team representing Hitler's master-race by six goals to three.

By the time war was over it was inevitable that the heroes of that resounding Berlin victory – men like Tommy Lawton, Raich Carter, Wilf Copping, and Stan Cullis – were on the verge of slipping from the international football scene. A new race of giants had to be found to represent the country that had taught the rest of the world all that was best in the skill and beauty of soccer. And soon, as men like Carter, Drake, Lawton, and Cullis turned their talents to the tutorship of new teams, we began to hear more and more of a man, up in Manchester, who appeared to be dedicated to the apparently revolutionary notion that you can make mature footballers out of boys in their teens.

To me that idea of Matt Busby's never seemed in the least bit extraordinary. There is nothing more true about football than that it is a young man's game. In youth the eyes have a fantastic swiftness, limbs are marvellously supple, with powers of resilience and recovery unknown later. The clay of young flesh is a beautifully plastic thing that can be trained and shaped under skilled teaching in endless and remarkable ways. Not only in football has the principle of shaping extreme youth proved to be an excellent one. Who, twenty years ago, would have dreamed of swimmers of thirteen and fourteen representing their native countries and breaking world records? Today these things are commonplaces.

Gradually, as the Busby principles of teaching were translated into reality, the names of the top students began to emerge. We began to hear of players representing Manchester United in the First Division at the age of seventeen. Presently we were to see the greatest of all the Busby prodigies, Duncan Edwards, an appealing giant of a boy, representing England at the age of eighteen, striding the Wembley pitch like a mature colossus, gaining the first of his eighteen international caps, under each of which he increased in stature so much that at twenty-one he was not only a veteran but clearly England's future captain.

If I select Duncan Edwards as the most compelling of all the young Manchester men who will now never play football again it is because he always seemed to me the epitome of all that was best in skill and character in the team that became popularly known – and very foolishly I think – as the 'Busby Babes'. I have always intensely disliked that cheap journalistic label and I have a fancy that most of the players may have done so too. There was certainly nothing of a babe about Edwards. A more mature young man, both in physical strength and artistry, never walked on to that treacherous and difficult turf at Wembley to play for his country.

You could say almost the same of that excellent and cultured back Roger Byrne, who gained thirty-three England caps; of the energetic and enthusiastic Tommy Taylor; and of Pegg, Colman, and Jones, all of whom, like Duncan Edwards, had been schoolboy stars; of Whelan, who also appeared for his native Ireland, and Bent who travelled to Belgrade as a reserve. Footballers, George Bernard Shaw once said, have their brains in their feet, but I have always had a sneaking notion that Matt Busby liked to be sure that his young men had a few brains in their heads too.

But what these young prodigies possessed above all, I think, was class. It is an attribute not easy to define, but when Manchester United were beaten in the 1957 Cup Final by an Aston Villa playing very robust but not very good football, it was also pure class that made them, I think, as admirable in defeat as they had so often been in victory. And when they were again and deservedly beaten in the 1958 Cup Final it was not merely because they were lacking in the necessary arts and skills. The class was not there.

And how could it possibly have been? Its ashes lay irreparably scattered across a German airfield after the cruellest day in English sporting history. Whether the same degree of class will ever be seen again in the United colours it is too early to tell; but one thing is certain. If it never returns it will not be the fault of Matt Busby, the tutor, happily still with us; or of the young men to whom, so very early in life, he taught the beauties of our national game, and who, having acquired fame in youth, set such an adult example before they were so prematurely and tragically taken from the field.

from F. A. YEAR BOOK *1958*

Old International

NEVILLE CARDUS

'Old International', H. D. Davies (who died in the Munich air disaster), was the first writer on Soccer to rise above the immediate and quickly perishable levels of this theme and give us something to preserve in terms of character, vivid imagery, and language racy of Lancashire county. He once described a terrific shot at the goal which struck the crossbar so that 'it made a noise like a tuning-fork'. He found Al Read's sarcastic spectator long before Read himself spotted him. Only a few weeks ago 'Old International' told us of this sceptical man in the Maine Road crowd, how he shouted, 'Look at 'im, try'n to dribble. Why doesn't he learn? 'E's nothing else to do.'

'Old International' saw a great game against a living not to say agitated background. And he saw that the players were characters, too. 'Old International' was himself a player, and for that reason knew exactly how much of technique he needed to refer to in an article to make it truly illuminating. There is today a growing school of sports-writing which uses technical terms and descriptions as ends in themselves. Few of these writers have ever been first-class players; therefore they are apt to regard technique with indiscriminate awe, not knowing enough about it to select relevant and revealing expertise.

'Old International' always wrote with his eye on the ball. But, because he was more than one-eyed, he also saw the drama and the scene, the crowd spending its passion, and the players, now masterful and godlike, now impotent, cast down and comic in their sudden exposure of mortal fallibility. The younger school of sports writing is almost insulted if you suggest that now and again they might make literature out of a report. As 'Old International' belonged to the school of yesteryear, his spirit will not chafe if I say that out of Soccer, especially out of Soccer played in the North of England, he produced the best 'literature' the game has so far inspired.

Like every born writer, he understood the uses of digression. Even in a small space he could be free and avoid the tightness, the nose-to-the-grindstone particularly of the second-rate reporter. Once, while creating a scene and paragraph calling up visions of some astounding piece of footwork, he even told us of the man in the crowd at an election meeting in Bolton who challenged the speaker's pretensions to omniscience by asking him, 'Hast ever 'ad DTs?' and, being indignantly assured to the contrary, said, 'Well, then, th'a never seen nowt.'

People who knew nothing at all of Soccer turned every Monday to 'Old International's' piece, knowing they would find observation, read a passage of evocative prose, get the sense of rich North-country life. People who knew the game and all the technical tricks of the trade, the players themselves, also turned avidly to 'Old International', certain to find a description which would give them the clue to the way the game was played, as well as all the crucial action, set before the roaring, humorous Lancashire melting-pot of a crowd. 'Old International' was not only the best of Soccer reporters: he was also something of a poet, and very much of a Lancastrian poet.

from THE BEDSIDE GUARDIAN 7 *1958*

King of Sports, King of Games

JEAN GIRAUDOUX

In our universe, where every nation has become nationalist and looks down from the ramparts of tariffs or hate – as watertight in their way as the walls of China – there are only two organisations international by nature; that of wars, and that of games. They hold sway over the same citizens, over the youth of the world; war, meanwhile, maintaining a preference for males. One of them dresses people up in the least visible of uniforms, the other in blazing colours; one armours them, the other strips them, but – through the workings of a parallel process not to be denied – it happens that each country now possesses an army or a militia whose strength precisely equals that of the army mobilised by the most widely diffused sport of all, football.

There is, in this equivalence, a symbol whose nature should be laid bare at the beginning of a book devoted to the glory of football. The forces of play balance the forces of combat in humanity, and do not become confused with them. They form one of the measures whereby nations are weighed, being judged now by their bodily as well as by their armed strength. A nation today is an organism whose moral health expresses itself, as it used to, through its arts and activities, but whose physical health for the first time expresses itself not through its army, but through its sport. The statesman no longer throws into the balance a sword but a naked man, and the effect is the same. Through their Olympic successes at football, Argentina and Uruguay not long ago showed the vigour of South America better than any other propaganda, and have reaped the benefit of it. This flourishing of sport constitutes no threat to any conquests of the spirit, since in some way, whether one cultivates the body or the spirit, each method brings its corresponding gains. The great abstract terms of the world, which call each other forth just as the blow of a mallet runs the flag up in a fairground kiosk, have the same implications in the stadium as in the academy. From the day when the notion of equality or liberty had to shoot to the top of the pole. For example, this principle of the equality of nations, which benefited enormously, in another era, from the fact that liberty of thought or writing was charged to small nations like Holland or Switzerland, now gains from the fact that speed or strength are encharged to Finland or Austria. Let homage be rendered to the various sports, and in particular to football.

For, still more than the king of sports, football is the king of games. All the great games of man are games with a ball, be they tennis, *chistera*, or billiards. In our life, the ball is that thing which most easily escapes from the laws of life. This is its most useful quality. It has, on earth, the extra-territorial quality of some force which has not been fully tamed. It is in no way related to the concept of the animal being, which is that of constriction, and, like a satellite of the globe whose laws it obeys without zest and with flashing defiance, it has the virtue of being nothing down here but a ball. Football owes its universality to the fact that it can give the ball its maximum effect. The football team is the *chistera* wall, suddenly become intelligent, the billiard cloth suddenly endowed with genius. Beyond its own principle, that of resilience, of independence, the team imparts to the ball the motor of eleven shrewd minds and eleven imaginations. If the hands have been barred from the game, it is because their intrusion would make the ball no longer a ball, the player no longer a player. The hands are cheats, they have been given exclusively to two cheating animals, to man and the monkey. The ball will not permit any cheating, but only effects that are sublime. . . .

from LA GLOIRE DU FOOTBALL *1933*

Part Six

FOOTBALL POETRY

The Game

Follow the crowds to where the turnstiles click.
The terraces fill. *Hoompa*, blares the brassy band.
Saturday afternoon has come to Ninian Park
and, beyond the goalposts, in the Canton Stand
between black spaces, a hundred matches spark.

Waiting, we recall records, legendary scores:
Fred Keenor, Hardy, in a royal blue shirt.
The very names, sad as the old songs, open doors
before our time where someone else was hurt.
Now, like an injured beast, the great crowd roars.

The coin is spun. Here all is simplified
and we are partisan who cheer the Good,
hiss at passing Evil. Was Lucifer offside?
A wing falls down when cherubs howl for blood.
Demons have agents: the Referee is bribed.

The white ball smacks the crossbar. Satan rose
higher than the others in the smoked brown gloom
to sink on grass in a ballet dancer's pose.
Again, it seems, we hear a familiar tune
not quite identifiable. A distant whistle blows.

Memory of faded games, the discarded years;
talk of Aston Villa, Orient, and the Swans.
Half-time, the band played the same military airs
as when the Bluebirds once were champions.
Round touchlines, the same cripples in their chairs.

Mephistopheles had his joke. The honest team
dribbles ineffectually, no one can be blamed.
Infernal backs tackle, inside forwards scheme,
and if they foul us need we be ashamed?
Heads up! Oh for a Ted Drake, a Dixie Dean.

'Saved' or else, discontents, we are transferred
long decades back, like Faust must pay that fee.
The night is early. Great phantoms in us stir
as coloured jerseys hover, move diagonally
on the damp turf, and our eidetic visions blur.

God sign our souls! Because the obscure Staff
of Hell rules this world, jugular fans guessed
the result half way through the second half
and those who know the score just seem depressed.
Small boys swarm the field for an autograph.

Silent the Stadium. The crowds have all filed out.
Only the pigeons beneath the roofs remain.
The clean programmes are trampled underfoot,
and natural the dark, appropriate the rain,
whilst, under lampposts, threatening newsboys shout.

DANNIE ABSE

Sur les Souliers de Foot

Gros souliers, base de la jeune jambe, cuir de vache à peine dégrossi,
Seule epaisseur sur ce corps qui n'a contact que de légèretés,
Je vous tire du sac en pagaïe où vous dormiez sous la culotte salie:
Sifflets d'arbitre dans l'air coupant, terrain qui claque . . . je tire tout
    l'hiver.
Entre mes mains, outils de la victoire, vus de si près, un peu
    diminués,
Inertes, vous qui voliez, frappiez, vivants et sous le ordres de l'esprit,
A la fois durs et enfantins, grands et petits, grands et petits,
Tels lui-même qui sait bien les larmes à ses yeux bridés de petit
    condottiere!

Encore poisseux de bonne huile, encore croutés de paquets de terre,
Force fumante avec votre odeur d'algue, votre élégance faite de
    brutalité,
Avec votre poids, vos écorchures, votre cuivrage, votre mystère,
Vous êtes aussi nobles que cette terre et la vie ne vous a pas quittés.
La cheville vous a fait une rondeur tendue comme l'UMBO du
    bouclier,
Le coup-de-pied vous a infléchis, vous êtes moulés à un unique
    exemplaire.

Il me semble, sans le savoir, je reconnaîtrais à qui vous appartenez.
Ma main sur votre contrefort est pleine de respect et de douceur.
Je suis pénétré d'une telle émotion que je me sens brûlé jusqu'au
   fond du coeur.

HENRI DE MONTHERLANT

Translation

Great boots, tip of the young leg, leather scarcely blemished,
Sole thickening of this body which is all weightlessness,
I pull you out of the untidy bag where you've been sleeping beneath
   muddy shorts:
Referee's whistle in the biting air, pattering soil; I'm pulling out the
   whole of winter.
Tools of victory between my hands, a little smaller, seen so close,
Lifeless, you who were flying, kicking, at the command of the spirit,
At once tough and childlike, big and small, big and small,
Like him who knows so well the tears which fill his little warrior-
   eyes!

Still sticky with good oil, still crusted with chunks of earth,
Strong, smoking smell of seaweed, elegance born of brutality,
With your weight, your scars, your copper hue, the mystery of you,
You're as noble as this earth, and life has not passed you by.
The ankle has shaped you as round as the umbo* of a shield.
Kicks have made you supple, you've been moulded into a unique
   object.
It seems to me that I'd know whom you belonged to, without being
   told.
My hand, resting on your blocked-toe, is full of gentle respect,
I'm so full of emotion I feel moved to the bottom of my heart.

* *Shield-boss.*

The Death of The Referee

A shroud, a shroud for Spring-Heeled Jack,
The only honest referee,
A crowd to keep the devil back
And sing in tune *Abide with Me*.

The pit unlocks its cage of doves
To tumble in the dirty air,
And far below the coffin drives
To meet the council and the mayor.

The barges drag through stiff canals,
Milky with clay and black with coal,
And as the varnished coffin falls
The mayor proclaims the grave no goal.

The colours of the local club
Flower to hide the yellow clay,
And all the foundry hammers throb
Their solace of the working day.

At home the silver trophies burn
About the mourning company,
And wishing she could be alone
The widow pours out cups of tea.

For Jack is dead, the man on springs,
Whose whistle trapped the wildest ball,
Whose portrait done in oils now hangs
For ever in the Civic Hall.

Burly with cataracts, the eyes
Are blind at last to local fame
And friends who fail to recognise
A stranger in the golden frame.

But those who know their loss will make
The winter field his funeral,
And peel their caps to Spring-Heeled Jack
While brass bands play the March in Saul.

PHILIP OAKES

Boyhood

To some, engines, meccano, scientific experiment:
To some, stamps, flowers, the anatomy of insects:
To some, twisting elbows, torturing, sending to
    undeserved Coventry:

To some, soldiers, Waterloo, and miniature Howitzers:
To some, football
In the sadness of an autumn afternoon
Studs and mud, the memorable dribble,
Rhododendrons at the back of the net
And the steamy dark gathering over bonfires,
The weight of water from the loosened skies.
And fingers too numb to undo laces.

ALAN ROSS

Cup-Tie Crowds

Moving with these people, one of thousands,
Expectant and excited, devoted as pilgrims,
I think, as we shuffle, joking for joking's sake,
How we might easily be victims
Hoodwinked into some enormous arena, a quicksand
Bearing for each a named stake;
While, round us, laughing, echoed the empty stands.
And how, with the time's irony, our fate
Would be concealed – until too late.

ALAN ROSS

Football Grounds of the Riviera

Rock-cut, railway flanked, with sea edging its flat
Surface, Monaco hangs top-heavy over dwarfed white posts:
Casinos and aquariums bulge above the crenellated coast,
Arc-lights strung along the Stadium like cloche hats.
Below, the pitch is smooth as green Casino baize
Whose wheels spin over water pink with haze.
Coated in sunset, the harbour's neat, dark palms,
Like roulette players, keep stiff their salt-drenched arms.

Scrambling over bald, dusty, but flower-scented ground,
Cactus gesticulating, olive-edged, make-shift, and public-owned,
Ventimiglia's forwards fan out round Bordighera's goal,
Jerseys striped like fishes in a noisy shoal.
Mountains bisect the sky with rocky signature
And sea-air modifies the players' temperature.

213

Mauve waves grow taut and spray the piazza pines,
As fishing boats trail their lamps in golden lines.

Menton at home to Nice, the French League leaders,
Sun only a rind squeezed dry of its heat,
And below us the voices of bathers scratch
At the cellophane air, airing ignorance of the match.
The tide recedes, drawing yachts in gentle retreat.
Outlined against mackerel sky, rack-bound readers
Golden indulgent flesh, absorbed in their books' spilled flush:
The insentient frontier hardens, the coastline in ambush.

                                                    ALAN ROSS

Saturday Afternoon

At the match. Harry's monologue.
HARRY: Come Saturday,
The whole town comes alive.
People are going one way,
From all the streets,
They are going the one way,
And meeting and joining,
And going on and meeting more and more
Till the trickle becomes a flood.
And men are so packed tight
That the cars have to nose their way through.
And you come to the stadium.
And it's humming,
A hum comes from the bowl.
And the people inside seem to be saying,
Come in, come on in,
And you jostle at the turnstile,
And the turnstile clicks and clicks,
And you push nearer and nearer,
Through the dark gap,
Then you're in.
And the great stand of the City end,
It's like a hall,
A great hall,
And you go on,
Through the arch

And you see the pitch,
Green, new shaven and watered,
And the groundsman's made the white lines,
As straight as a ruler,
And the ash is pressed.
And you find your place among the fans,
The real fans,
The singers and chanters and rattle wavers.
And a sheet of tobacco smoke hangs over the crowd.
And the crowd whistles and hoots,
And the policemen circling the pitch
Look up and know they're in for a rough day of it,
And the stadium fills up,
The Open End first, then the City End,
Then the paddock, then the covered seated stand,
Then last of all, the fat directors
With the Lord Mayor and cigars.
And the reporters are in their little glass box,
And the cameramen position themselves
By the goal,
And there's a looking down the tunnel,
Then a hush.
Then out they come.
The lads.
Like toy footballers on a green billiard table.
And a roar goes up . . .
CHORUS (general roar; all sing):
    City, City, City, City,
    We'll support you evermore,
    We'll support you evermore.
    City, City, City, City,
    We'll support you evermore,
    We'll support you evermore.

PETER TERSON
from ZIGGER ZAGGER

Part Seven

FOOTBALL IN FICTION

Callear's Goal

Arnold Bennett

'I'll tell you,' said Denry Machin, 'I wanted to be the youngest mayor that Bursley's ever had. It was only a kind of notion I had a long time ago. I'd given it up, because I knew there was no chance unless I came before Bloor, which of course I couldn't do. Now he's dead. If I could upset old Barlow's apple-cart I should just be the youngest mayor by the skin of my teeth. Huskinson, the mayor in 1884, was aged thirty-four and six months. I've looked it all up this afternoon.'

'How lovely if you *could* be the youngest mayor!'

'Yes. I'll tell you how I feel. I feel as though I didn't want to be mayor at all if I can't be the youngest mayor . . . you know.'

She knew.

'Oh!' she cried, 'do upset Mr Barlow's apple-cart. He's a horrid old thing. Should I be the youngest mayoress?'

'Not by chalks,' said he. 'Huskinson's sister was only sixteen.'

'But that's only playing at being mayoress!' Nellie protested. 'Anyhow, I do think you might be youngest mayor. Who settles it?'

'The Council, of course.'

'Nobody likes Councillor Barlow.'

'He'll be still less liked when he's wound up the Bursley Football Club.'

'Well, urge him on to wind it up, then. But I don't see what football has got to do with being mayor.'

She endeavoured to look like a serious politician.

'You are nothing but a cuckoo,' Denry pleasantly informed her. 'Football has got to do with everything. And it's been a disastrous mistake in my career that I've never taken any interest in football. Old Barlow wants no urging on to wind up the Football Club. He's absolutely set on it. He's lost too much over it. If I could stop him from winding it up, I might. . . .'

'What?'

'I dunno.'

She perceived that his idea was yet vague.

II

Not very many days afterwards the walls of Bursley called attention, by small blue and red posters (blue and red being the historic colours of the Bursley Football Club), to a public meeting, which was to be held in the Town Hall, under the presidency of the Mayor, to consider what steps could be taken to secure the future of the Bursley Football Club.

There were two 'great' footballs clubs in the Five Towns – Knype, one of the oldest clubs in England, and Bursley. Both were in the League, though Knype was in the first division while Bursley was only in the second. Both were, in fact, limited companies, engaged as much in the pursuit of dividends as in the practice of the one ancient and glorious sport which appeals to the reason and the heart of England. (Neither ever paid a dividend.) Both employed professionals who, by a strange chance, were nearly all born in Scotland; and both also employed trainers who, before an important match, took the teams off to a hydropathic establishment far, far distant from any public house. (This was called 'training'.) Now, whereas the Knype club was struggling along fairly well, the Bursley club had come to the end of its resources. The great football public had practically deserted it. The explanation, of course, was that Bursley had been losing too many matches. The great football public simply sulked. It did not kick a man that was down; it merely ignored him, well knowing that the man could not get up without help. It cared nothing whatever for fidelity, municipal patriotism, fair play, the chances of war, or dividends on capital. If it could see victories it would pay sixpence, but it would not pay sixpence to assist at defeats.

Still, when at a special general meeting of the Bursley Football Club, Limited, held at the registered office, the Coffee House, Bursley, Councillor Barlow, JP, Chairman of the Company since the creation of the League, announced that the Directors had reluctantly come to the conclusion that they could not conscientiously embark on the dangerous risks of the approaching season, and that it was the intention of the Directors to wind up the club, in default of adequate public interest – when Bursley read this in the *Signal*, the town was certainly shocked. Was the famous club, then, to disappear for ever, and the football ground to be sold in plots, and the grand stand for firewood? The shock was so severe that the death of Alderman Bloor (none the less a mighty figure in Bursley) had passed as a minor event.

Hence the advertisement of the meeting in the Town Hall caused joy and hope, and people said to themselves: 'Something's bound to be done; the old club can't go out like that.' And everybody grew quite sentimental. And although nothing is supposed to be capable of filling Bursley Town Hall except a political meeting and an old folk's treat, Bursley Town hall was as near full as made no matter for the football question. Many men had cheerfully sacrificed a game of billiards and a glass of beer in order to attend it.

The Mayor, in the chair, was a mild old gentleman who knew nothing whatever about football and had probably never seen a football match; but it was essential that the meeting should have august patronage, and so the Mayor had been trapped and tamed. On the mere fact that he paid an annual subscription to the golf club, certain parties built up the legend that he was a true sportsman, with the true interests of sport in his soul.

He uttered a few phrases, such as 'the manly game', 'old associations', 'bound up with the history of England', 'splendid fellows', 'indomitable pluck', 'dogged by misfortune' (indeed he produced quite an impression on the rude and grim audience), and then he called upon Councillor Barlow to make a statement.

Councillor Barlow, on the Mayor's right, was a different kind of man from the Mayor. He was fifty and iron-grey, with whiskers, but no moustache; short, stoutish, raspish.

He said nothing about manliness, pluck, history, or Auld Lang Syne.

He said he had given his services as Chairman to the football club for thirteen years; that he had taken up £2,000 worth of shares in the Company; and that as at that moment the Company's liabilities would exactly absorb its assets, his £2,000 was worth exactly nothing. 'You may say,' he said, 'I've lost that £2,000 in thirteen years. That is, it's the same as if I'd been steadily paying three pun' a week out of my own pocket to provide football matches that you chaps wouldn't take the trouble to go and see. That's the straight of it! What have I for for my pains? Nothing but worries and these! (He pointed to his grey hairs.) And I'm not alone; there's others; and now I have to come and defend myself at a public meeting. I'm supposed not to have the best interests of football at heart. Me and my co-Directors,' he proceeded, with even a rougher raspishness, 'have warned the town again and again what would happen if the matches weren't better patronised. And now it's happened, and now it's too late, you want to *do* something! You can't! It's too late! There's only one thing the matter with first-class football in Bursley,' he concluded, 'and it isn't the players. It's the public − it's yourselves. You're the most craven lot of tom-fools that ever a big football club had to do with. When we lose a match, what do you do? Do you come and encourage us next time? No, you stop away, and leave us fifty or sixty pounds out of pocket on a match, just to teach us better! Do you expect us to win every match? Why, Preston North End itself' – here he spoke solemnly, of heroes – 'Preston North End itself in its great days didn't win every match – it lost to Accrington. But did the Preston public desert it? No! *You* – you haven't got the pluck of a louse, nor the faithfulness of a cat. You've starved your football club to death, and now you call a meeting to weep and grumble. And you have the insolence to write letters to the *Signal* about bad management, forsooth! If anybody in the hall thinks he can manage this club better than me and my co-Directors have done, I may say that we hold a majority of the shares, and we'll part with the whole show to any clever person or persons who care to take it off our hands at a bargain price. That's talking.'

He sat down.

Silence fell. Even in the Five Towns a public meeting is seldom bullied as Councillor Barlow had bullied that meeting. It was aghast. Councillor Barlow had never been popular: he had merely been respected; but thenceforward he became even less popular than before.

'I'm sure we shall all find Councillor Barlow's heat quite excusable . . .' the Mayor diplomatically began.

'No heat at all,' the Councillor interrupted. 'Simply cold truth!'

A number of speakers followed, and nearly all of them were against the Directors. Some, with prodigious memories for every combination of players in every match that had ever been played, sought to prove by detailed instances that Councillor Barlow and his co-Directors had persistently and regularly muddled their work during thirteen industrious years. And they defended the insulted public by asserting that no public that respected itself would pay sixpence to watch the wretched football provided by Councillor Barlow. They shouted that the team wanted reconstituting, wanted new blood.

'Yes,' shouted Councillor Barlow in reply, 'and how are you going to get new blood, with transfer fees as high as they are now? You can't get even an average good player for less than £200. Where's the money to come from? Anybody want to lend a thousand or so on second debentures?'

He laughed sneeringly.

No one showed a desire to invest in second debentures of the Bursley FC Ltd.

Still, speakers kept harping on the necessity of new blood in the team, and then others, bolder, harped on the necessity of new blood on the board.

'Shares on sale!' cried the Councillor. 'Any buyers? Or,' he added, 'do you want something for nothing – as usual?'

At length a gentleman rose at the back of the hall.

'I don't pretend to be an expert on football,' said he, 'though I think it's a great game, but I should like to say a few words as to this question of new blood.'

The audience craned its neck.

'Will Mr Councillor Machin kindly step up to the platform?' the Mayor suggested.

And up Denry stepped.

The thought in every mind was: 'What's he going to do? What's he got up his sleeve – this time?'

'Three cheers for Machin!' people chanted gaily.

'Order!' said the Mayor.

Denry faced the audience. He was now accustomed to audiences. He said:

'If I'm not mistaken, one of the greatest modern footballers is a native of this town.'

And scores of voices yelled, 'Ay! Callear! Callear! Greatest centre forward in England!'

'Yes,' said Denry. 'Callear is the man I mean. Callear left the district, unfortunately for the district, at the age of nineteen for Liverpool. And it was not till after he left that his astonishing abilities were perceived. It isn't too much to say that he made the fortune of Liverpool City. And I believe it is the fact that he scored more goals in three seasons than any other player has done in the League. Then, York County, which was in a tight place last year, bought him from Liverpool for a high price, and, as all the world knows, Callear had his leg broken in the first match he played for his new club. That just happened to be the ruin of the York Club, which is now quite suddenly in bankruptcy (which happily we are not), and which is disposing of its players. Gentlemen, I say that Callear ought to come back to his native town. He is fitter than ever he was, and his proper place is in his native town.'

Loud cheers.

'As captain and centre forward of the club of the mother of the Five Towns, he would be an immense acquisition and attraction, and he would lead us to victory.'

Renewed cheers.

'And how,' demanded Councillor Barlow, jumping up angrily, 'are we to get him back to his precious native town? Councillor

Machin admits that he is not an expert on football. It will probably be news to him that Aston Villa have offered £700 to York for the transfer of Callear, and Blackburn Rovers have offered £750, and they're fighting it out between 'em. Any gentleman willing to put down £800 to buy Callear for Bursley?' he sneered. 'I don't mind telling you that steam-engines and the King himself couldn't get Callear into our club.'

'Quite finished?' Denry inquired, still standing.

Laughter, overtopped by Councillor Barlow's snort as he sat down.

Denry lifted his voice.

'Mr Callear, will you be good enough to step forward and let us all have a look at you?'

The effect of these apparently simple words surpassed any effect previously obtained by the most complex flights of oratory in that hall. A young, blushing, clumsy, long-limbed, small-bodied giant stumbled along the central aisle and climbed the steps to the platform, where Denry pointed him to a seat. He was recognized by all the true votaries of the game. And everybody said to everybody: 'By Gosh! It's him, right enough. It's Callear!' And a vast astonishment and expectation of good fortune filled the hall. Applause burst forth, and though no one knew what the appearance of Callear signified, the applause continued and waxed.

'Good old Callear!' the hoarse shouts succeeded each other. 'Good old Machin!'

'Anyhow,' said Denry, when the storm was stilled, 'we've got him here, without either steam-engines or His Majesty. Will the directors of the club accept him?'

'And what about the transfer?' Councillor Barlow demanded.

'Would you accept him and try another season if you could get him free?' Denry retorted.

Councillor Barlow always knew his mind, and was never afraid to let other people share that knowledge.

'Yes,' he said.

'Then I will see that you have the transfer free.'

'But what about York?'

'I have settled with York provisionally,' said Denry. 'That is my affair. I have returned from York today. Leave all that to me. This town has had many benefactors far more important than myself. But I shall be able to claim this originality: I'm the first to make a present of a live man to the town. Gentlemen – Mr Mayor – I venture to call for three cheers for the greatest centre forward in England, our fellow-townsman.'

The scene, as the *Signal* said, was unique.

And at the Sports Club and the other clubs afterwards, men said to each other: 'No one but him would have thought of bringing Callear over specially and showing him on the platform. . . . That's cost him above twopence, that has!'

Two days later a letter appeared in the *Signal* (signed 'Fiat Justitia'), suggesting that Denry, as some reward for his public spirit, ought to be the next mayor Bursley, in place of Alderman Bloor deceased. The letter urged that he would make an admirable mayor, the sort of mayor the old town wanted in order to wake it up. And also it pointed out that Denry would be the youngest mayor that Bursley had ever had, and probably the youngest mayor in England that year. The sentiment in the last idea appealed to the town. The town decided that it would positively *like* to have the youngest mayor it had ever had, and probably the youngest mayor in England that year. The *Signal* printed dozens of letters on the subject. When the Council met, more informally than formally, to choose a chief magistrate in place of the dead alderman, several councillors urged that what Bursley wanted was a young and *popular* mayor. And, in fine, Councillor Barlow was shelved for a year. On the choice being published the entire town said: 'Now we *shall* have a mayoralty – and don't you forget it!'

And Denry said to Nellie: 'You'll be mayoress to the youngest mayor, etc., my child. And it's cost me, including hotel and travelling expenses, eight hundred and eleven pounds six and seven-pence.'

The rightness of the Council in selecting Denry as mayor was confirmed in a singular manner by the behaviour of the football and of Callear at the opening match of the season.

It was a philanthropic match, between Bursley and Axe, for the benefit of a county orphanage, and, according to the custom of such matches, the ball was formally kicked off by a celebrity, a pillar of society. The ceremony of kicking off has no sporting significance; the celebrity merely with gentleness propels the ball out of the white circle and then flies for his life from the *mêlée*; but it is supposed to add to the moral splendour of the game. In the present instance the posters said: 'Kick-off at 3.45 by Councillor E. H. Machin, Mayor-designate'. And, indeed, no other celebrity could have been decently selected. On the fine afternoon of the match Denry therefore discovered himself with a new football at his toes, a silk hat on his head, and twenty-two Herculean players menacing him in attitudes expressive of an intention to murder him. Bursley had lost the toss, and hence Denry had to kick towards the Bursley goal. As the *Signal* said, he 'despatched the sphere' straight into the keeping of Callear, who as centre forward was facing him, and Callear was dodging down the field with it before the Axe players had finished admiring Denry's effrontery. Every reader will remember with a thrill the historic match in which the immortal Jimmy Brown, on the last occasion when he captained Blackburn Rovers, dribbled the ball himself down the length of the field, scored a goal, and went home with the English Cup under his arm. Callear evidently intended to imitate the feat. He was entirely wrong. Dribbling tactics had been killed forever, years before, by Preston North End, who invented the 'passing' game. Yet Callear went on, and good luck seemed to float over him like a cherub. Finally he shot; a wild, high shot; but there was an adverse wind which dragged the ball down, swept it round, and blew it into the net. The first goal had been scored in twenty seconds! (It was also the last in the match.) Callear's reputation was established. Useless for solemn experts to point out that he had simply been larking for the gallery, and that the result was a shocking fluke – Callear's reputation was established. He became at once the idol of the populace. As Denry walked gingerly off the field to the grandstand, he, too, was loudly cheered, and he could not help feeling that, somehow, it was he who had scored that goal. And although nobody uttered the precise thought, most people did secretly think, as they gazed at the triumphant Denry, that a man who triumphed like that, because he triumphed like that, was the right sort of man to be mayor, the kind of man they needed.

from THE CARD *1909*

Knype v. Manchester Rovers

Arnold Bennett

Loring, who works in the British Museum, has gone to stay the weekend in Knype, one of the Five Towns. On the Saturday afternoon he is to be entertained by a friend of his host, Dr Stirling. Stirling suggests they visit the Signal *offices where Buchanan, the editor of the paper, shows them his new 'pigeon post' for obtaining the football results quickly. He then suggests that Stirling and Loring go and see the second half of the local match, the news of which, already received by pigeon, is: 'Record gate. Fifteen thousand spectators. Two goals in twelve minutes. Myatt in form. Special report.'*

We went on the Grand Stand, which was packed with men whose eyes were fixed, with an unconscious but intense effort, on a common object. Among the men were a few women in furs and wraps, equally absorbed. Nobody took any notice of us as we insinuated our way up a rickety flight of wooden stairs, but when by misadventure we grazed a human being the elbow of that being shoved itself automatically and fiercely outwards, to repel. I had an impression of hats, caps, and woolly overcoats stretched in long parallel lines, and of grimy raw planks everywhere presenting possibly dangerous splinters, save where use had worn them into smooth shininess. Then gradually I became aware of the vast field, which was more brown than green. Around the field was a wide border of infinitesimal hats and pale faces, rising in tiers, and beyond this border fences, hoardings, chimneys, furnaces, gas-ometers, telegraph-poles, houses, and dead trees. And here and there, perched in strange perilous places, even high up towards the sombre sky, were more human beings clinging. On the field itself, at one end of it, were a scattered handful of doll-like figures, motionless; some had white bodies, others red; and three were in black; all were so small and so far off that they seemed to be mere unimportant casual incidents in whatever recondite affair it was that was proceeding. Then a whistle shrieked, and all these figures began simultaneously to move, and then I saw a ball in the air. An obscure, uneasy murmuring rose from the immense multitude like an invisible but audible vapour. The next instant the vapour had condensed into a sudden shout. Now I saw the ball rolling solitary in the middle of the field, and a single red doll racing towards it; at one end was a confused group of red and white, and at the other two white dolls, rather lonely in the expanse. The single red doll overtook the ball and scudded along with it at his twinkling toes. A great voice behind me bellowed with an incredible volume of sound:
'Now, Jos!'
And another voice, further away, bellowed:
'Now, Jos!'
And still more distantly the grim warning shot forth from the crowd:
'Now, Jos! Now, Jos!'
The nearer of the white dolls, as the red one approached, sprang forward. I could see a leg. And the ball was flying back in a magnificent curve into the skies; it passed out of my sight, and then I

heard a bump on the slates of the roof of the grand stand, and it fell among the crowd in the stand-enclosure. But almost before the flight of the ball had commenced, a terrific roar of relief had rolled formidably round the field, and out of that roar, like rockets out of thick smoke, burst acutely ecstatic cries of adoration:

'Bravo, Jos!'

'Good old Jos!'

The leg had evidently been Jos's leg. The nearer of these two white dolls must be Jos, darling of fifteen thousand frenzied people.

Stirling punched a neighbour in the side to attract his attention.

'What's the score?' he demanded of the neighbour, who scowled and then grinned.

'Two – one – agen uz!' The other growled. 'It'll take our b——s all their time to draw. They're playing a man short.'

'Accident?'

'No! Referee ordered him off for rough play.'

Several spectators began to explain, passionately, furiously, that the referee's action was utterly bereft of common sense and justice; and I gathered that a less gentlemanly crowd would undoubtedly have lynched the referee. The explanations died down, and everybody except me resumed his fierce watch on the field.

I was recalled from the exercise of a vague curiosity upon the set, anxious faces around me by a crashing, whooping cheer which in volume and sincerity of joy surpassed all noises in my experience. This massive cheer reverberated round the field like the echoes of a battleship's broadside in a fiord. But it was human, and therefore more terrible than guns. I instinctively thought: 'If such are the symptoms of pleasure, what must be the symptoms of pain or disappointment?' Simultaneously with the expulsion of the unique noise the expression of the faces changed. Eyes sparkled; teeth became prominent in enormous, uncontrolled smiles. Ferocious satisfaction had to find vent in ferocious gestures, wreaked either upon dead wood or upon the living tissues of fellow-creatures. The gentle, mannerly sound of hand-clapping was a kind of light froth on the surface of the billowy sea of heartfelt applause. The host of the fifteen thousand might have just had their lives saved, or their children snatched from destruction and their wives from dishonour; they might have been preserved from bankruptcy, starvation, prison, torture; they might have been rewarding with their impassioned worship a band of national heroes. But it was not so. All that had happened was that the ball had rolled into the net of the Manchester Rovers' goal. Knype had drawn level. The reputation of the Five Towns before the jury of expert opinion that could distinguish between first-class football and second-class was maintained intact. I could hear specialists around me proving that though Knype had yet five League matches to play, its situation was safe. They pointed excitedly to a huge hoarding at one end of the ground on which appeared names of other clubs with changing figures. These clubs included the clubs which Knype would have to meet before the end of the season, and the figures indicated their fortunes on various grounds similar to this ground all over the country. If a goal was scored in Newcastle, or in Southampton, the very Peru of first-class football, it was registered on that board and its possible effect on the destinies of Knype was instantly assessed. The calculations made were dizzying.

Then a little flock of pigeons flew up and separated, under the illusion that they were free agents and masters of the air, but really wafted away to fixed destinations on the stupendous atmospheric waves of still-continued cheering.

After a minute or two the ball was restarted, and the greater noise had diminished to the sensitive uneasy murmur which responded like a delicate instrument to the fluctuations of the game. Each feat and manoeuvre of Knype drew generous applause in proportion to its intention or its success, and each sleight of the Manchester Rovers, successful or not, provoked a holy disgust. The attitude of the host had passed beyond morality into religion.

Then, again, while my attention had lapsed from the field, a devilish, a barbaric, and a deafening yell broke from those fifteen thousand passionate hearts. It thrilled me; it genuinely frightened me. I involuntarily made the motion of swallowing. After the thunderous crash of anger from the host came the thin sound of a whistle. The game stopped. I heard the same word repeated again and again, in divers tones of exasperated fury:

'Foul!'

I felt that I was hemmed in by potential homicides, whose arms were lifted in the desire of murder and whose features were changed from the likeness of man into the corporeal form of some pure and terrible instinct.

And I saw a long doll rise from the ground and approach a lesser doll with threatening hands.

'Foul! Foul!'

'Go it, Jos! Knock his neck out! Jos! He tripped thee up!'

There was a prolonged gesticulatory altercation between the three black dolls in leather leggings and several of the white and the red dolls. At last one of the mannikins in leggings shrugged his shoulders, made a definite gesture to the other two, and walked away towards the edge of the field nearest the stand. It was the unprincipled referee; he had disallowed the foul. In the protracted duel between the offending Manchester forward and the great, honest Jos Myatt he had given another point to the enemy. As soon as the host realised the infamy it yelled once more in heightened fury. It seemed to surge in masses against the thick iron railings that alone stood between the referee and death. The discreet referee was approaching the grand stand as the least unsafe place. In a second a handful of executioners had somehow got on to the grass. And in the next second several policemen were in front of them, not striking nor striving to intimidate, but heavily pushing them into bounds.

'Get back there!' cried a few abrupt, commanding voices from the stand.

The referee stood with his hands in his pockets and his whistle in his mouth. I think that in that moment of acutest suspense the whole of his earthly career must have flashed before him in a phantasmagoria. And then the crisis was past. The inherent gentlemanliness of the outraged host had triumphed and the referee was spared.

'Served him right if they'd man-handled him!' said a spectator.

'Ay!' said another, gloomily, 'ay! And th' Football Association 'ud ha' fined us maybe a hundred quid and disqualified th' ground for the rest o' th' season!'

'D—n th' Football Association!'

'Ay! But you canna'!'

'Now, lads! Play up, Knype! Now, lads! Give 'em hot hell!' Different voices heartily encouraged the home team as the ball was thrown into play.

The fouling Manchester forward immediately resumed possession of the ball. Experience could not teach him. He parted with the ball and got it again, twice. The devil was in him and in the ball. The devil was driving him towards Myatt. They met. And then came a sound quite new: a cracking sound, somewhat like the snapping of a bough, but sharper, more decisive.

'By Jove!' exclaimed Stirling. 'That's his bone!'

And instantly he was off down the staircase and I after him. But he was not the first doctor on the field. Nothing had been unforeseen in the wonderful organisation of this enterprise. A pigeon sped away and an official doctor and an official stretcher appeared, miraculously, simultaneously. It was tremendous. It inspired awe in me.

'He asked for it!' I heard a man say as I hesitated on the shore of the ocean of mud.

Then I knew that it was Manchester and not Knype that had suffered. The confusion and hubbub were in a high degree disturbing and puzzling. But one emotion emerged clear: pleasure. I felt it myself. I was aware of joy in that the two sides were now levelled to ten men apiece. I was mystically identified with the Five Towns, absorbed into their life. I could discern on every face the conviction that a divine providence was in this affair, that God could not be mocked. I too had this conviction. I could discern also on every face the fear lest the referee might give a foul against the hero Myatt, or even order him off the field, though of course the fracture was a simple accident. I too had this fear. It was soon dispelled by the news which swept across the entire enclosure like a sweet smell, that the referee had adopted the theory of a simple accident. I saw vaguely policemen, a stretcher, streaming crowds, and my ears heard a monstrous universal babbling. And then the figure of Stirling detached itself from the moving disorder and came to me.

'Well, Myatt's calf was harder than the other chap's, that's all,' he said.

'Which *is* Myatt?' I asked, for the red and the white dolls had all vanished at close quarters, and were replaced by unrecognisably gigantic human animals, still clad, however, in dolls' vests and dolls' knickerbockers.

Stirling warningly jerked his head to indicate a man not ten feet away from me. This was Myatt, the hero of the host and the darling of populations. I gazed up at him. His mouth and his left knee were red with blood, and he was piebald with thick patches of mud from his tousled crown to his enormous boot. His blue eyes had a heavy, stupid, honest glance; and of the three qualities stupidity predominated. He seemed to be all feet, knees, hands and elbows. His head was very small – the sole remainder of the doll in him.

A little man approached him, conscious – somewhat too obviously conscious – of his right to approach. Myatt nodded.

'Ye'n settled *him*, seemingly, Jos!' said the little man.

'Well,' said Myatt, with slow bitterness. 'Hadn't he been blooming well begging and praying for it, aw afternoon? Hadn't he now?'

The little man nodded. Then he said in a lower tone:

'How's missis, like?'

'Her's altogether yet,' said Myatt. 'Or I'd none ha' played!'

'I've bet Watty half-a-dollar as it inna' a lad!' said the little man. Myatt seemed angry.

'Wilt bet me half a *quid* as it inna' a lad?' he demanded, bending down and scowling and sticking out his muddy chin.

'Ay!' said the little man, not blenching.

'Evens?'
'Evens.'
'I'll take thee, Charlie,' said Myatt, resuming his calm.

The whistle sounded. And several orders were given to clear the field. Eight minutes had been lost over a broken leg, but Stirling said that the referee would surely deduct them from the official time, so that after all the game would not be shortened.

'I'll be up yon, to-morra morning,' said the little man.

Myatt nodded and departed. Charlie, the little man, turned on his heel and proudly rejoined the crowd. He had been seen of all in converse with supreme greatness.

Stirling and I also retired; and though Jos Myatt had not even done his doctor the honour of seeing him, neither of us, I think, was quite without a consciousness of glory: I cannot imagine why. The rest of the game was flat and tame.

from THE MATADOR OF THE FIVE TOWNS AND OTHER
STORIES *1912*

Football Lesson in the Park

HENRI DE MONTHERLANT

Jacques Peyrony, fifteen and a half years old, captain of the 'Junior I' football team in a great Paris club.

The 'wing-half' of the third team of the same club, twenty-five years old. (He has been to the war.)

On the outskirts of Paris, is a great public park, a vast field, attached to a stadium. It is April, the end of the day. It has been raining. The expanse is closed on the horizon by a mediterranean of trees, overhung from a hillside by the peaceful houses of a little, suddenly revealed market town, a pleasant thing to come on by surprise. And the wing-forward sometimes bends on it the clear, cold look of a conqueror of towns. Are they Partisans, exponents of the sudden raid, who are camping in the plain? The football games are over. Some players are returning to the stadium, with heavy step, a little wearied. Grouped around the goal-posts, as though in bivouac, indifferent to the rain-nourished soil, others are stretched out or sitting, in every attitude of fatigue and repose. A fickle sun plays on the crowns of their heads, laying on each of them a little tongue of fire. Time is suspended. Life itself marks time.

The wing-forward goes up to Peyrony who is putting on his sweater, the game over. The young captain's face is bathed in sweat, black with the earth which his muddy hands have left on it. His features are wan beneath this trickling patina, and his face is burning so much that he blinks his eyelids. In weariness, his mouth remains half open, his gaze has become dull, and his eyeballs strangely pale.

THE WING-HALF: Hallo, little man. What, beaten 4–1? Hm, hm! Did you know I was watching you for the last twenty minutes?
PEYRONY: I saw you.
THE WING-HALF: Well, I like that! When the play brought you over to the touchline, a yard away from me, you looked at me as if I was a stranger. Fair enough! There's a time for everything. But you looked awful – like Achilles in the *Iliad*, 'bearing in your eyebrows the terrible mark of war'. (PEYRONY *lets himself fall on to a mound of grass planted with trees.*) Put this jacket on your legs, so that the muscles don't catch cold. Put your head back: you're quite black. . . .
   (*He pulls down a low branch, whose raindrops* PEYRONY *receives on his face, grimacing, wiping it afterwards with his sleeve.*)
PEYRONY: I've something for you. (*He gives him a rather muddy piece of lemon.*) I didn't have it at half-time. But I ran over to the forest lodge, and drank half a cup of milk there.
THE WING-HALF: Half a cup! How wise of you!
   (*He bites eagerly into the lemon, chewing it, then swallowing the pulp.*)

The man who is beginning the final season of his youth is sitting beside the boy who is entering the flower of it. In one, strength is hidden in weakness (for after all he is a child); in the other, nonchalance; and it is moving that it should be so invisible both in one and the other, concealed and secret like the fire in the earth or the juice in the fruit. Meanwhile, the knees and the lower thighs of the older man, in this moment of relaxation, are knotted with muscle, bulging to the point of being gross, one would almost say romantic. But with the younger, everything is contained, like perfection in more exquisite arts: the courageous legs which run and kick for six quarters of an hour are smooth as a brown wax candle; there's nothing to blemish their clarity. And, just as in both of them strength lies at the bottom of their languor, so, in the freak countenance of the younger there is a slight, faintly savage note, the eyes veined with blood. And they're stretched under the good shade as though in the trough of a weariness that they've wanted.

PEYRONY: I got the ball full in the face. It's given me a headache.

THE WING-HALF: Take an aspirin when you get home.

PEYRONY: That won't be necessary! It'll pass off after a shower.

THE WING-HALF: I like the way you take care of yourself. A week ago, when you had a cold, you told me, 'Oh, with a good massage . . .'

PEYRONY: Well, what do you think of the team?

THE WING-HALF: Everything's possible: they obey you. All the more meritorious when several of them are better than you.

PEYRONY: I know that quite well.

THE WING-HALF: They've understood, then, that to be a good captain you don't have to be an outstanding player. But even if you make a mistake as captain, they still obey you, without comment. When you persisted in playing over-elaborately in the last quarter hour, against a team which had run out of breath – instead of forcing the play – you can be sure that players like Labbé, or that astonishing little fellow with the English head, realised you were wrong, yet they conformed to your tactics, out of discipline.

PEYRONY: The little fellow *is* English.

THE WING-HALF: Really? Ah, what a shame!

PEYRONY: Why?

THE WING-HALF: Because if I was in your place, I'd never keep him in my team.

PEYRONY: What? Him? He's our best player!

THE WING-HALF: All the more reason. You can't run the risk of a French team winning a championship thanks to a foreigner. And then, how can a foreigner share in all your feelings of team spirit? In the war, I could have led a well paid, comfortable, sheltered life as an interpreter in the English or American army. But I chose to remain a soldier in a French infantry regiment; I waited till the Armistice to join the Americans, because none of my great moments of the war would have been complete if I'd lived them with fellows different from our own. For me, the war would have been ruined. And one more last piece of advice: sack Guilhermet. He's thoroughly mediocre. Every time one looks at him during a game, he's sitting on his backside – like one of those trams that's stationary whenever one sees it.

PEYRONY: He's the only one in the whole team who's really a friend of mine.

THE WING-HALF: Remember there are two parts of your life; the first has nothing to do with your team and includes Guilhermet; spend as much time with him as you please. But second, there is the team, which has only one aim: to do what its motto says, its best. Guilhermet, who plays badly is taking the place of somebody who could play well. Sack him gently, but sack him.

PEYRONY: The team would suffer from his absence, because if he wasn't there I should feel less like playing.

THE WING-HALF: Are you quite sure? You think that Guilhermet, who hasn't any athletic value, has a moral value which makes him more useful to the team than a newcomer playing better?

PEYRONY: Yes, quite seriously.

THE WING-HALF: In that case, keep him. Usefulness is our touchstone, and here, sentiment is useful. Long live sentiment, so long as we remain the masters of it!

LESSONS OF A MATCH

PEYRONY, *with an ironic emphasis*: Tell me the 'lessons of the match', the one that you've just played.

THE WING-HALF: One of their forwards had had a couple of pieces of bad luck, the blunderer. I saw that he was a sensitive boy, that he was susceptible. I wanted to dishearten him, and every time he came in contact with me, I made him look silly with a feint. After two of these, he was reduced to nothing; there were still eleven of them, but we were playing against ten. Well, while I was dealing relentlessly with this fellow, I noticed that I was encouraged, spurred on, excited, by a quite obscure part of myself, that I was playing against him with a sort of angry joy which doubled my skill. And this threw light for me on several other matters. You know that a wild beast will throw itself on its trainer when he accidentally happens to fall. Until then, I used to think it was because it told itself, 'Let's take advantage, here's a chance.' I now believe that it's because he conceives a horror of the man, seeing him cut down in size. Thus, the brute who beats his wife doubles his blows if she covers her face and groans. Thus the god from Olympus loses interest in the warrior he protected when he sees him brought down. In the same way, I have three cats: the grandmother, her daughter, and the daughter's son. When he was a few months old, this son started attacking his mother, scratching her, and she, the imbecile, put up with it, with a piteous air. You know what happened? The grandmother, who'd been living very affectionately for years with her daughter (sleeping in the same basket, and all that), suddenly grew enraged with her and now chases her all day, to attack her. How do you explain that, if not because she was exasperated to see her put up with it so passively? Feebleness gives rise to hate; feebleness is the mother of fighting. There's one of the 'lessons of the game'.

PEYRONY: The orator, returning to his seat, receives his colleagues' congratulations.

THE WING-HALF: The second lesson began from an amusing little incident, and I must tell you about it, as you can profit by it. You know we're always told, 'When you take a throw-in, pretend to throw the ball to one of your team mates, so that the other side concentrates on him, then quickly throw it to another man who is unmarked.' It's a trick as old as the hills. Well, then, I picked up the ball, I stared into Beyssac's eyes and then . . . then threw it to Beyssac. What chaos among the Red Lions! By instinct, seeing me pick out Beyssac, they'd marked every one except him, and there was my Beyssac racing away. Well, this trick reminded me of a saying of Aristotle. . . .

PEYRONY: Ah, Aristotle, no, that's got nothing to do with it Let's get on to the flood.

THE WING-HALF: Don't laugh at a saying of Aristotle. It's when we seem to be innovating something that we need above all to feel ourselves supported by the past. The only reason I've such a perfect passion for what we were doing here is that I know it's justified by the opinions of bygone men. I'm constantly consulting them, and if I find that we're in agreement, I go ahead with my mind at rest. Well, Aristotle asked the gymnast to create 'a mind inventive of stratagem, a spirit hardy and prudent, enterprising yet accepting'. Isn't that what our football gives us?

PEYRONY: What strikes me above all is that Aristotle asks the *gymnast* to create only *moral* qualities.

THE WING-HALF: That's true, I never took account of it. And this saying contains one quite beautiful word; an *accepting* spirit. Through an hour and a half's play, what else have I done if not accept? Accept with a free and masculine heart, that's to say accept with regret and with approval. I resigned myself that the sun should disappear when it would have affected our opponents, and reappear when it affected us. I resigned myself that the wind should blow when it was against us, and drop when it would have been with us. I resigned myself to playing my part in tactics which I thought doomed to frustration, as your Labbé and your Englishman resigned themselves to your tactics while condemning them. I resigned myself to effort and fatigue which I knew to be useless, like chasing a man faster than myself, for the sole moral satisfaction of having tried as hard as I could. I resigned myself to Beyssac scoring a goal, being shaken by the hand, earning the smiles of the ladies and having his name on the stadium score-board, when it was I and I alone whose switch of play let him score. I resigned myself to ten occasions when the referee forgot to use his eyes, or used them wrongly, to our disadvantage, and I said nothing. If I'd once begun to protest, Ramondou would have clapped his hand over my mouth. . . . Ramondou is eighteen years old, I am twenty-five, and I'd have accepted his casual brusqueness because as far as justice is concerned, I'd have been in the right, but as far as play was concerned, I'd have been wrong, and this is the place to repeat after Goethe, 'I prefer injustice to disorder.' I accepted my failings which I studied for half an hour, ah! I promise you, without letting one of them escape me. I know I lack wind, that I allow myself to be tackled, that my kicking isn't accurate. I know that there lies in me a power as mysterious as genius or electricity, my *form*; which comes and goes, returns for no reason, defying every common law; which gives me the capacity of a demi-god for ten hours, then weakens my legs for ten and a half and is suddenly reborn from the depths of a complete ruin; which disappears for days of the most strenuous training, so that it makes one think there's a *spirit of the body* quite independent of the other. And I look inside myself at this living-person, who is at once a stranger yet myself and with whom I can do nothing. I know it, I accept it, and so must we all.

We are in the third team, which plainly means that we play better than the fourth team and worse than the second; we know this about our team, just as each of us knows that so and so is a better player, perhaps because he's younger and fresher to the game. And to know one's worth, to know one's place, helps one to know the worth and place of everything.

We honestly want to climb to a higher level, which is our duty, and to strive – we, too – to do our best, without believing on that account that there's anything serious or dishonourable in it if we don't succeed. For the connecting-rod in a car is the equal in dignity of the piston, and a back in a team is the equal of a forward, and the third team, weakest in the club, has its dignity and its pride like the first. This is what we all know, and we approve of it.

The rain has stopped. There has been a moment's sun, and the grass, the mud, the branches, the bark of the trees, suddenly gives off a stronger scent because of the sun. Water falls from the branches with a rapid rhythm, fuller than the twittering of sparrows. The chestnut trees shed their leaves like great drops against the milky sky.

And little by little, night falls.

I can't tell you how many times, here, the whole war leaped into my mind. Like a unit going through the countryside, the team sets off for unknown lands, cheerfully crossing a whole town to get to the opposing club's 'strongpoint', testing the direction of the wind, as if it were carrying gas. We play – and attack, defence, breakthrough, wing, opening, bombardment of goal . . . you only need to mention the technical terms to smell the smell of war. But what you cannot know is the intensity with which the body remembers, recovers its sensations: for example, when a forward line starts moving and we run a few paces apart from one another, how is it possible not to believe oneself back in a wave of assault? When we come off the field harassed, bathed in sweat, our big boots heavy with mud, and cross with the fresh team coming to replace us, how can we not think of relieving troops? And the friendly commotion in the dressing-room, people who don't put on any pretence because they've taken each other's measure and aren't afraid of reality there. And when night comes, the strolls along the quayside, with the fellow who sits on his knapsack (just as it used to be, just as it used to be!) with the craven civilians whom one scornfully stares down. All that, my little friend, is war, that war from which you've reaped all the horror, but which still has something left that's tough and good. Must I sum up again the – what can I call it? – the philosophy of it, to see what it's all about?

Here, there are no moral victories, which one cannot verify. There is certainty. No appeal by the undeserving. *It is*: adorable words.

Man against man, and not against ideas, not against shadows. You can go and have a look at him at the station, when he arrives. 'His wrists are bigger than mine.' 'When we collide at top speed it's I who'll be bowled over,' and all the rest of it.

No *sins* against the unreal, against laws which one breaks without infringing Nature. But offences against rules conceived with a precise aim in view – your victory – and if you break them, you are beaten. Continual contact with reality. One comes in contact with it and replenishes one's strength. Earth and Antée.

The selection: everyone young and healthy. No illnesses. A wound, and it's a clean one.

No illness, no sadness; those two Gorgons compared with which death is quite beautiful.

To stay silent. The team, too, is one great mute.

Self-sacrifice. I pass him the ball – and my own chance with it.

Confidence. The team which sees its goal in danger, but doesn't drop back, confident that the three men in defence will do what's necessary. One's immobility when one's looking on at the play. And to feel in oneself this immobility, what a moving experience, how well worth having lived it makes one feel!

Where else can one find what one finds here? The comrade suddenly twisted with agony, doubled up on the daisy-strewn grass. You see into those depths of a human being which show only under physical shock. You know whether he is brave or not, and how important that is! You say to yourself: perhaps in five minutes it will be I.

CONCERNING ORDERLY VIOLENCE

Concerning calm and orderly violence, courage, healthiness, simplicity, something virginal and rough which takes no account of itself: that's what I liked in war, yes, liked, despite all the distress and the horror, and that's what I've found here, that's what I get from these three days a week, the only ones which meet my demands in a life that's too small for me. Everything here is tied up with nature; the earth, the wind, the sun are pals who play for us or against us, and you can see that just now we were the brothers of the rain, just as in the last war I was the brother of the roots and of the starry night. There's no doubt that it's from this that this great benefit comes. I'm not talking to you about semi-professional teams, whose ways must be pretty crude, nor of the little local clubs, the kind under someone's patronage. I'm talking to you about an old club which isn't Oxford, but where all in all the members are of good quality: in its 'soul' as in its dressing-rooms, there's an odour of clean skin and rich leather. When we have a frugal meal before giving battle, and I see you refuse wine, refuse coffee, refuse a liqueur, refuse cigarettes, when I see your disgust for our neighbours, the tennis players, rude to the waiter and putting their feet up on the chairs, when I see you so indifferent to the snares of the world, whether they be silk socks, liquorice-water, or sentimental refinements, really pure like bread and salt (and at the same time as full of mischief as young fox let loose in a chicken run), it seems to me that the genius of Nature has entered into you during our hours of fresh air, and that it's he, giving you this horror of deceit, who has also given you this horror of evil, without you knowing it. For it's true! We scarcely bother ourselves with being moral, and yet, when we see the townsfolk again in the evening, pusillanimous and feeble, with their 'discontent', with their 'needs', their 'sins', their imbecile 'problems', people who share with us only these functions we share with the animals, I believe I can really see that this life we lead is the life that was dreamed about by the wise men or by God. Peyrony! Peyrony! We can now imagine the Golden Age. . . . And if all that, as we must believe, is merely an introduction to greater things, the stern reflection of the iron century should be welcome in our Golden Age. Paradise lies in the shadow of the sword.

PEYRONY: I am happy, and you too. But we mustn't think about it.

THE WING-HALF: The night is made for us to say these things. One would never dream of saying them in the morning. (PEYRONY *coughs*.) Be careful not to catch cold. Let's go up.

PEYRONY: Cold? A sportsman? You go up, if you feel cold.

THE WING-HALF: And Fred Borotra, and Loren, who were better athletes than you, and who were carried off in only a few days by colds! Come on, up with you! I beg you! You can have a glass of grog up there.

PEYRONY: Pooh, a glass of grog! That's woman's stuff.

THE WING-HALF: Ah, how irritating you can be at times! Listen, it was enough for me to hear you cough once, one single time . . . and I couldn't maintain what I did a minute ago with the same assurance. If you were tossing on your bed with fever tomorrow, with your mother holding your hand, would we repeat the things we've been declaiming here, in the pride of life? Everything we think out here, we think in a sort of drunkenness. In youth and strength, in the midst of Nature, leaping, conquering the others with one's body, one doesn't see a single day, two days together, without seeing the world in another way from those who haven't tasted such wine. One sees it as if there existed only a super-race of men whom we can treat with the same rough frankness we accept for ourselves. And meanwhile the games come to an end and we must go back among the suffering, who need a bit of gentleness, and perhaps we'll be numbered among them tomorrow, if this be the hour of death.

PEYRONY, *with a suppressed smile*: You're in eloquent vein this evening. Unfortunately, this is quite the opposite to your usual harangues against weakness, maudlin sentimentality, and the rest. You're going over to the enemy.

THE WING-HALF: I know, I know. It's partly my fault if sometimes you're surly, cutting, unfair, cruel, with a deliberate lack of subtlety, possessed by some destructive spirit. I've spoken words that I'll retract only with the silence of the tomb, I've written words that I've washed out with my tears, tears which aren't tears of rage, and which I like you well enough to hope that you will shed one day. Believe me, when it's not a question of charity, but just of avoiding misfortune, follow the old advice of the Greeks; be prudent in triumph and fear excess, even in good times. I've never harmed as many people as when I was bursting with virtue. (*Looking at him.*) No, there's no reason to make a face as if I were fooling you. All I ask you is one thing: have you been listening to what I just said?

PEYRONY: More or less.

THE WING-HALF: Will you remember it?

PEYRONY: I can't promise.

THE WING-HALF: Remember it. If only to remind me of it myself, because after a quarter of an hour's play I shall perhaps have forgotten it.

PEYRONY, *after a while*: What would you say to kicking a ball about a bit, before we go? There's one free down there.

THE WING-HALF: But it's dark!

PEYRONY: One can see well enough. We've got a good five minutes.

THE WING-HALF: And your tiredness? And your headache?

PEYRONY: They were just talk.

THE WING-HALF: What do you mean, talk?

PEYRONY: I mean, it's all gone.

PEYRONY *has risen; the far off ball, lying in the middle of a seated group of boys, fascinates him. His eyes suddenly sparkle with excitement. His whole face quivers like water, showing that, beneath the surface, there is who knows what lively humidity, as if the*

241

night, the trees, the wind, the salt of the air had put it there, like the proboscis in the flowers. But the older man's face is abstracted.
PEYRONY: I can see Labbé. We can attack in threes.
THE WING-HALF: No, no, it's stupid.
PEYRONY: Listen, please! I promise you it's sensible. *(With reproach.)* After all you've just told me!
THE WING-HALF: Let's go!
PEYRONY, *voice transformed with delight, and with the tone of command he has already acquired*: Hey, you lads down there, let's have your ball!
THE BOYS: What for? We're going in. It's night time.
PEYRONY: Let's have your ball, I tell you!

One of the shadows gets up, sends over the ball. PEYRONY *hurls himself forward, the wing-half following. Seeing them, a second shadow gets up and runs towards them. One hears a shout of, 'To me!' 'Right away!' A little farther off, three shadows bound to their feet, as if galvanised by seeing this leather globe return to life.* PEYRONY *takes possession, and passes to the wing-half, who passes to a figure which has come galloping up at his side. They disappear into the thick darkness, followed by anonymous footsteps, taking with them that ball which is taking* them, *their breath streaming before them like men. They're a troop of centaurs, drunk with themselves and with that great Everything which is rising up in them, challenging them. And it's* PEYRONY, *the youngest, who is leading them. And one sees his face, silent beneath the steady gaze of his wingers.*

VOICES, *curt, crisp, true, pass along the ground*: Come on, come on!

from PARADIS À L'OMBRE DES ÉPÉES *1934*

Watching Bruddersford

J. B. PRIESTLEY

Something very queer is happening in that narrow thoroughfare to the west of the town. It is called Manchester Road because it actually leads you to that city, though in order to get there you will have to climb to the windy roof of England and spend an hour or two with the curlews. What is so queer about it now is that the road itself cannot be seen at all. A grey-green tide flows sluggishly down its length. It is a tide of cloth caps.

These caps have just left the ground of the Bruddersford United Association Football Club. Thirty-five thousand men and boys have just seen what most of them call 't'United' play Bolton Wanderers. Many of them should never have been there at all.

It would not be difficult to prove by statistics and those mournful little budgets (How a Man May Live – or rather, avoid death – on 35 Shillings a Week) that seem to attract some minds, that these fellows could not afford the entrance fee. When some mills are only working half the week and others not at all, a shilling is a respectable sum of money. It would puzzle an economist to discover where all these shillings came from.

But if he lived in Bruddersford, though he might still wonder where they came from, he would certainly understand why they were produced. To say that these men paid their shillings to watch twenty-two hirelings kick a ball is merely to say that a violin is wood and catgut, that *Hamlet* is so much paper and ink.

For a shilling the Bruddersford United AFC offered you Conflict and Art; it turned you into a critic, happy in your judgment of fine points, ready in a second to estimate the worth of a well-judged pass, a run down the touch-line, a lightning shot, a clearance kick by back or goalkeeper; it turned you into a partisan, holding your breath when the ball came sailing into your own goalmouth, ecstatic when your forwards raced away towards the opposite goal, elated, downcast, bitter, triumphant by turns at the fortunes of your side, watching a ball shape *Iliads* and *Odysseys* for you. . . .

And what is more, it turned you into a member of a new community, all brothers together for an hour and a half, for not only had you escaped from the clanking machinery of this lesser life, from work, wages, rent, doles, sick pay, insurance-cards, nagging wives, ailing children, bad bosses, idle workmen, but you had escaped with most of your mates and your neighbours, with half the town, and there you were, cheering together, thumping one another on the shoulders, swopping judgments like lords of the earth, having pushed your way through a turnstile into another and altogether more splendid kind of life, hurtling with Conflict and yet passionate and beautiful in its Art.

Moreover, it offered you more than a shilling's worth of material for talk during the rest of the week. A man who had missed the last home match of 't'United' had to enter social life on tiptoe in Bruddersford.

As he moved slowly down Manchester Road, the press of fellow spectators still thick about him, Mr Oakroyd found himself brooding over the hollow vanities of this life. He felt unusually depressed. His physical condition may have had something to do with it, for he was hot, dusty and tired; there had been a full morning's hard work for him at the mill; he had hurried through his dinner; walked to the ground, and had been on his feet ever since. Manchester Road after a match had never seemed so narrow and airless; a chap could hardly breathe in such a crowd of folk.

And what a match it had been! For once he was sorry he had come. No score at all. Not a single goal on either side. Even a goal against the United would have been something, would have wakened them up a bit.

The first half had been nothing but exasperation, with the United all round the Wanderers' goal but never able to score; centres clean flung away, open goals missed, crazy football. The second half had not been even that, nothing but aimless kicking about on both sides, a kids' game.

During the time that it took him to progress 300 yards down the crowded road, Mr Oakroyd gave himself up to these bitter reflections. A little farther along, where there was more room, he was able to give them tongue, for he jostled an acquaintance, who turned round and recognised him.

'Na Jess!' said the acquaintance, taking an imitation calabash pipe out of his mouth and then winking mysteriously.

'Na Jim!' returned Mr Oakroyd. This 'Na,' which must once have been 'Now', is the recognised salutation in Bruddersford, and the fact that it sounds more like a word of caution than a word of greeting is by no means surprising. You have to be careful in Bruddersford.

'Well,' said Jim, falling into step, 'what did you think on 'em?'

'Think on 'em!' Mr Oakroyd made a number of noises with his tongue to show what he thought of them.

'Ah thowt t'United 'a' made rings rahnd'em,' Jim remarked.

'So they owt to 'a' done,' said Mr Oakroyd, with great bitterness. 'And so they would 'a' done if they'd nobbut tried a bit. I've seen 'em better ner this when they've lost. They were better ner this when they lost to Newcastle t'other week, better bi far.'

'Ay, a seet better,' said the other. 'Did you ivver see sick a match! Ah'd as soon go and see 'tschooil lads at it. A shilling fair thrawn away, ah call it.' And for a moment he brooded over his lost shilling. Then, suddenly changing his tone and becoming very aggressive, he went on: 'Yon new centre-forward they've getton – MacDermott, or whativver he calls hissen – he'll nivver be owt, nivver. He were like a great lass on t'job. And what did they pay for him? Wer it two thahsand pahnd?'

'Ay.' Mr Oakroyd made this monosyllable very expressive.

'Two thahsand pahnd. That's abaht a hundred for ivvery goal he missed today. Watson were worth twenty on 'im – ah liked that lad, and if they'd let him alone, he'd 'a' done summat for 'em. And then they go and get this MacDermott and pay two thahsand pahnd for him to kick t'ball ower top!' Jim lit his yellow monster of a pipe and puffed away with an air of great satisfaction. He had obviously found a topic that would carry him comfortably through that evening, in the taproom of *The Hare and Hounds*, the next morning, in the East Bruddersford Working Men's Club and possibly Sunday, Monday and Tuesday nights.

Mr Oakroyd walked on in silence, quickening his pace now that the crowd was not so thick and there was room to move. At the corner of Manchester Road and Shuttle Street, both men halted, for here their paths diverged.

'Ah'll tell tha what it is, Jess,' said his companion, pointing the stem of his pipe and becoming broader in his Yorkshire as he grew more philosophical. 'If t'United has less brass to lake wi', they'd lake better fooitball.' His eyes searched the past for a moment, looking for the team that had less money and had played better football. 'Tha can remember when t'club had nivver set eyes on two thahsand pahnds, when t'job lot wor not worth two thahsand pahnds, pavilion an' all, and what sort o' fooitball did they lake then? We knaw, don't we? They could gi' thee summat worth watching then. Nah, it's all nowt, like t'ale an' baccy they ask so mich for – money fair thrawn away, ah calls it.'

'Well, we mun 'a' wer teas and get ower it. Behave thi-sen, Jess!' And he turned away, for that final word of caution was only one of Bruddersford's familiar good-byes.

'Ay,' replied Mr Oakroyd dispiritedly. 'So long, Jim!'

from THE GOOD COMPANIONS *1928*

245

Playing Away

HAROLD PINTER

GUS: What town are we in? I've forgotten.

BEN: I've told you. Birmingham.

GUS: Go on! *(He looks with interest about the room.)* That's in the Midlands. The second biggest city in Great Britain. I'd never have guessed. *(He snaps his fingers.)* Eh, it's Friday today, isn't it? It'll be Saturday tomorrow.

BEN: What about it?

GUS *(excited)*: We could go and watch the Villa.

BEN: They're playing away.

GUS: No, are they? Caarr! What a pity.

BEN: Anyway, there's no time. We've got to be straight back.

GUS: Well, we have done in the past, haven't we? Stayed over and watched a game, haven't we? For a bit of relaxation.

BEN: Things have tightened up, mate. They've tightened up. *(GUS chuckles to himself.)*

GUS: I saw the Villa get beat in a cup tie once. Who was it against now? White shirts. It was one-all at half-time. I'll never forget it. Their opponents won by a penalty. Talk about drama. Yes, it was a disputed penalty. Disputed. They got beat two-one, anyway, because of it. You were there yourself.

BEN: Not me.

GUS: Yes, you were there. Don't you remember that disputed penalty?

BEN: No.

GUS: He went down just inside the area. Then they said he was just acting. I didn't think the other bloke touched him myself. But the referee had the ball on the spot.

BEN: Didn't touch him! What are you talking about? He laid him out flat!

GUS: Not the Villa. The Villa don't play that sort of game.

BEN: Get out of it.
    (Pause.)

GUS: Eh, that must have been here, in Birmingham.

BEN: What must?

GUS: The Villa. That must have been here.

BEN: They were playing away.

GUS: Because you know who the other team was? It was the Spurs. It was Tottenham Hotspur.

BEN: Well, what about it?

GUS: We've never done a job in Tottenham.

BEN: How do you know?

GUS: I'd remember Tottenham.

(BEN *turns on his bed to look at him.*)

BEN: Don't make me laugh, will you?

(BEN *turns back and reads.* GUS *yawns and speaks through his yawn.*)

GUS: When's he going to get in touch? *(Pause.)* Yes, I'd like to see another football match. I've always been an ardent football fan. Here, what about coming to see the Spurs tomorrow?

BEN *(tonelessly)*: They're playing away.

GUS: Who are?

BEN: The Spurs.

GUS: Then they might be playing here.

BEN: Don't be silly.

GUS: If they're playing away they might be playing here. They might be playing the Villa.

BEN *(tonelessly)*: But the Villa are playing away.

(*Pause. An envelope slides under the door, right.* GUS *sees it. He stands, looking at it.*)

GUS: Ben.

BEN: Away. They're all playing away.

from THE DUMB WAITER *1960*

His Normal Game

Harold Pinter

OLD MAN: Compressed. I thought he was looking compressed, didn't you, Fred?

BARMAN: Depressed. He means depressed.

SEELEY: No wonder. What about that game on Saturday, eh?

KEDGE: You were going to tell me. You haven't told me yet.

BARMAN: What game? Fulham?

SEELEY: No, the firm. Firm's got a team, see? Play on Saturdays.

BARMAN: Who'd you play?

SEELEY: Other firms.

BARMAN: You boys in the team, are you?

KEDGE: Yes. I've been off sick though. I didn't play last week.

BARMAN: Sick, eh? You want to try one of my sausages, don't he, Henry?

OLD MAN: Oh, ay, yes.

KEDGE: What happened with the game, then?

They move to the bench.

SEELEY: Well, when you couldn't play, Gidney moved Albert to left back.

KEDGE: He's a left half.

SEELEY: I know he's a left half. I said to Gidney myself, I said to him, look, why don't you go left back, Gidney? He said, no, I'm too valuable at centre half.

KEDGE: He didn't, did he?

SEELEY: Yes. Well, you know who was on the right wing, don't you? Connor.

KEDGE: Who? Tony Connor?

SEELEY: No. You know Connor. What's the matter with you? You've played against Connor yourself.

KEDGE: Oh – whatsisname – Micky Connor.

SEELEY: Yes.

KEDGE: I thought he'd given up the game.

SEELEY: No, what are you talking about? He plays for the printing works, plays outside right for the printing works.

KEDGE: He's a good ballplayer, that Connor, isn't he?

SEELEY: Look. I said to Albert before the kick off, Connor's on the right wing, I said, play your normal game. I told him six times before the kick off.

KEDGE: What's the good of him playing his normal game? He's a left half, he's not a left back.

SEELEY: Yes, but he's a defensive left half, isn't he? That's why I told him to play his normal game. You don't want to worry about Connor, I said, he's a good ballplayer but he's not all that good.

KEDGE: Oh, he's good, though.

SEELEY: No one's denying, he's good. But he's not all that good. I mean, he's not tip-top. You know what I mean?

KEDGE: He's fast.

SEELEY: He's fast, but he's not all that fast, is he?

KEDGE (*doubtfully*): Well, not all that fast . . .

SEELEY: What about Levy? Was Levy fast?

KEDGE: Well, Levy was a sprinter.

SEELEY: He was a dasher, Levy. All he knew was run.

KEDGE: He could move.

SEELEY: Yes, but look how Albert played him! He cut him off, he played him out the game. And Levy's faster than Connor.

KEDGE: Yes, but he wasn't so clever, though.

SEELEY: Well, what about Foxall?

KEDGE: Who? Lou Foxall?

SEELEY: No, you're talking about Lou Fox, I'm talking about Sandy Foxall.

KEDGE: Oh, the winger.

SEELEY: Sure. He was a very smart ballplayer, Foxall. But what did Albert do? He played his normal game. He let him come. He waited for him. And Connor's not as clever as Foxall.

KEDGE: He's clever though.

SEELEY: Gawd blimey, I know he's clever, but he's not as clever as Foxall, is he?

KEDGE: The trouble is, with Connor, he's fast too, isn't he?

SEELEY: But if Albert would have played his normal game! He played a game foreign to him.

KEDGE: How many'd Connor get?

SEELEY: He made three and scored two.

from A NIGHT OUT *1961*

Footballers don't cry

BRIAN GLANVILLE

The phone went at one in the morning, and I knew who it was. Oh, no I thought, not him, but it had to be him. We'd only got the baby off an hour ago.

'Peter,' he said, 'I've lost me job.' There were tears in his voice. It was pitiful, honestly. Him. The Iron Man. But I couldn't sound surprised. It had been coming for weeks.

'Called me in tonight and sacked me,' he said, 'the bastards.'

This was what shocked me; his tone. The feeling sorry for himself, after all he'd dinned into me over the years, right from the very beginning. Don't squeal. Pick yourself up and get on with it. Footballers don't cry. Football's a game for men, not lasses. If they kick you, you kick 'em back. All that, and so much more. Never give up. Never to feel sorry for yourself. And now here he was, how they'd done this to him, how they'd done that to him, full of self-pity, wanting comfort, till it was almost like I was him now and he was me.

'Peter,' he said, 'Peter. I hope you'll never know what it's like to have this happen to you. To be stabbed in the back by a lot of ungrateful, fat-arsed businessmen that know fuck all about this game. That's what hurts. To take it from them; me, that's given my life to the game.'

I was still half asleep. I said, 'Yes, Dad. I know, Dad.' Marion came out of the bedroom, yawning and rubbing her eyes: 'Who is it?' and I said, 'It's Dad. He's just got the push.'

'Not again,' she said. 'It's the middle of the night. You're going to wake John.'

'Dad,' I said, 'I'll phone you in the morning.' I felt bad: I knew he wanted to go on, pouring it all out, and I felt worse, because I knew I didn't want to listen. 'God bless you, Dad,' I said. 'I'll phone first thing tomorrow.' Then I put down the phone and took it off the hook, else I knew he'd be back. It was a terrible thing, that. Little moments, little movements, yet you're changing a whole life.

I didn't sleep. I lay awake, thinking. What he'd done for me, how much I'd always admired him. Just a little lad, going to watch him play, at Bolton and at Rotherham; then later on, when he dropped out of the League, at Wigan and Boston and Kettering. Get in, Dad! Go on, Dad! A centre half, great big fellow, coming in bang with his thick legs, ploughing through the mud with his sliding tackles, taking the man, the ball, the lot; jumping above the centre forward, thump with his head, always first to the ball, a hard man, very tough, very brave, very strong, a bit dirty; though I never thought that, then.

All those little back gardens. Left foot, right foot, left foot. 'Come on, Peter, come on!' I was frightened of him, me. Him so big and me so little. Like Mother; never really growing.

'You'll be a winger,' he said, when what I wanted was to be a centre half, like him. Big and strong. Coming in like a tank.

Later, there were all the piddling little jobs he had, coach of this, manager of that, of nothing. Clubs in the Midland League, clubs in the Northern Premier, always in debt, playing in front of the few hundred people; him having to do everything, mark out the pitch, mow the grass, treat the injuries.

'Peter,' he'd say, 'you're my answer, son. When you make it, I'll make it. The war did me, Peter, as a player. Took the best years of my career away. Stopped me realising my potential. If I'd played for England like I should, there'd have been no stopping me afterwards. Manager of Arsenal, manager of Everton. Look at Matt Busby.

Captain of Scotland, end of the war – manager of Manchester United. A great team ready waiting for him. Me, I had to start with rubbish. I've done miracles with rubbish. Worked wonders with rubbish. I knew about recycling before it had ever been invented. But you get no medals for that.'

And he hadn't. He'd last three months here, six months there, then something would snap, he'd quarrel with the chairman, blow his top to the Press, even thump one of the players, and out he'd go, off we'd go; another little house, poor Mother packing and unpacking all over again. No wonder she was worn out. No wonder she died.

'But you, Peter,' he'd say, 'you will justify me. By your career. By your skill. By your determination. And then, Peter, they may begin to listen. They will begin to see that I practise what I preach; through my own son, who nobody can say I did not develop.' He'd put his hand on my shoulder, this very emotional look in his eye. 'You'll never disappoint me, Peter: I know that.'

I wouldn't; I knew it too. I'd rather cut my leg off.

I'd never been so chuffed as when he got the job with City. More than when I came to Rovers, and to London. Even more than when I first played for England. And, to be honest, I think I know why. There was relief in it. Not just because he'd be happy now, he'd stop complaining now; but because, in a funny sort of way, things were like they should be again. Me an England player, but him a top manager. With only one thing spoiling it; for him, not me. Knowing people were whispering and hinting. Would he have ever managed City if he hadn't been my father, if I wasn't playing for England?

Ignorance, that was. 'And why did I play for England?' I'd ask, whenever I got wind of it. 'Because of him; Dad and his coaching.' But you could see by their faces that you'd not convinced them. I couldn't even convince Marion. 'He didn't make you,' she said. 'I'm sick of hearing that; from him and you. He was lucky to have you.'

'No, no,' I said, 'you don't know football, Marion.'

'I know him,' she said, 'and I know you.'

The next morning, when we woke, the first thing she said was 'He's not coming to stay, is he?'

'I don't know,' I said. 'I've not thought.'

She'd never forgiven him, though I've always told her it was nothing personal, nothing against her, even if he was wrong; just his feelings for me, and my football.

'You mean him and your football,' she'd said.

He'd always told me, 'Don't get married early.' I'd tried to explain it to Marion. 'It's not you,' I said.

'No,' she'd said, 'and it's not you either; it's him, everything for him. He wants you to be a little puppet, dancing to his strings.'

It was a bad time for me, that, pulled one way and then the other. My form suffered. I loved her, I loved him; and I loved football. That was the time I missed a penalty in the semi-final against Leeds at Villa Park, and we went out of the Cup. I didn't see her for a week and I wouldn't talk to him. Then one day I walked into the hairdresser's where she worked and said, 'Come on, I've got the licence,' because it had to be like that; I either had to marry her or give her up, and if I gave her up it would shatter me.

'My mother,' she said, 'my father'; but I told her, 'Never mind them, and never mind my father. I've got two witnesses; we'll have the church wedding later'; and we did. I'd had to do it like that. For the first time in my life, I'd started hating him.

'My own son,' he's said since, 'and I wasn't invited to his wedding.' When we stepped out of that gloomy little registry office, I went straight into the post office along the road and I sent him a telegram: MARION AND I MARRIED TODAY BIGGEST MATCH OF ALL LOVE PETER. We didn't hear from him for ten days, and then he sent a silver teapot that must have cost him a bomb.

'Marion,' he said, when he came over from Hartlepool, where he was coach then, 'I want you to know I've got nothing against you. I never have had; I've always thought you're a wonderful girl, but Peter and me, we've always lived for football, and I'll admit I've been anxious for his career.'

'No more than what I am, Mr Coleman,' she said.

But things changed; it was inevitable. The moment we walked into that registry office, they'd changed; it was the first big thing in my life I'd ever done without him, the first I'd ever done against him. But when he got the City job, that changed things, too; it helped to change them back again. It wasn't me getting two hundred quid a week while he got forty any more, and much too proud to accept anything. Time and again I'd say, 'Look, Dad, it's yours, you did it; I'd be nothing without you.'

'I'll not take a penny,' he'd say. 'The satisfaction I've had from you, you can't buy it.' He's a wonderful man, if you only but know him.

So after breakfast, while Marion was feeding the baby, I telephoned him. He was still in the same state. 'They're being very vindictive about it,' he said. 'There's still nearly eighteen months of my contract to run. Ten grand they owe me, and they've as good as told me I can sue them for it. And this club house; they're turning me out of that, as well.'

252

'Dad,' I said. What else could I say? 'Come down and stay with us.'

'You're sure?' he said. 'How about Marion? What about the baby?'

'There's tons of room, Dad,' I said. 'Marion won't mind. Just until you get settled. Till you get another job.'

'For a week, then,' he said. 'But only that, mind. Just till I get fixed up.'

She was choked when I told her, Marion. 'Without even asking me,' she said.

'Just for a week,' I told her, 'while he looks around. He's shattered, Marion.'

'He'll shatter us,' she said.

He was in a state when he got to us. All tense and taut, that twitch at the left side of his mouth. 'It'll be down to your knees, soon,' he said, looking at my hair. His was the short-back-and-sides he'd always had. 'Hello, Marion,' he said. He kissed her on the cheek, and she took it like it was a vaccination. Then he kissed John, the baby, and his face relaxed; he liked the baby. He started playing with his fingers, but he burst out crying. 'He's tired,' Marion said, and took him away.

The old man glanced around the place. It was a lovely house; it had cost thirty thousand. Nice, big rooms, big picture windows, looking out on a golf course at the back, colour telly. 'By gum,' he said, like he always did, 'things have changed a bit since I were playing.' I hoped he wasn't going to come out with the usual rigmarole, my hair, my hundred-pound suits, my embroidered shirts, because I knew it by heart: 'What's that? The Playboy Club? In my day it was eight pound a week and a pint at the boozer.'

Now he looked out the front and said, 'That your new car?' It was an XJ Jag. He shook his head; I was used to that as well. 'I don't know,' he said. I hoped he wouldn't go on about buses and bicycles.

He sat down on the leather sofa, he slapped himself on the knees, he gave the laugh he always gives when he's miserable, and he said, 'Well! Now let's wait for the offers to come pouring in!'

'It's early days, Dad,' I said.

'Oh, yes,' he said, 'I don't expect them to come rushing. Not falling over themselves. After all, where did I leave City? Only three places off the bloody bottom. Where will they finish now I've gone? Right at the bottom.'

'Don't feel bitter, Dad,' I told him.

'Bitter?' he said. 'I'm not bitter. I'm resigned to it, me. Directors, bloody amateurs, obstructing a professional.'

'That's the system, Dad,' I said. 'You'll not change it.'

'It's a bloody diabolical system,' he said, and I was afraid he'd be off on another of his favourite moans – directors and how ignorant they were – but instead he went quiet, not even looking at me, sitting there like he was embarrassed, till at last he said, 'You don't think there'd be something for me at Rovers?'

It left me speechless. It was the first time in my life he'd ever asked me for anything. 'Well, Dad,' I said, 'there might be. Not as manager, just now, nor as coach. They go together, do those two; everywhere Geoff Creamer goes, Bobby Birchall goes with him.'

'I know,' he said, 'I didn't mean that,' which made it worse, because what else was there? Scouting? Looking after the Reserves? Those weren't for Dad; they never had been.

'Maybe I could help with the coaching and the scouting,' he said. 'Something like that. Weighing up teams they're going to play.' He looked at me. The look was new as well, almost pleading. What had happened to him?

'I'll try tomorrow,' I said. 'I'll see the boss.' Then I made an excuse and left the room. It was too much for me.

I did talk to the boss, Geoff Creamer, next day. He was uneasy, I could tell he didn't want to upset me. At the same time obviously he knew about Dad, his reputation. 'There's not much for him here, Peter,' he said, 'not for him.'

'Just a bit of scouting and coaching,' I said, 'to be going on with. It's shattered him, this. I think maybe he needs to get his confidence back.'

'I'll talk to the chairman,' he said, and a couple of days later he called me in and told me, 'We've got something for your father, on the lines he asked for. I'm afraid we can't pay him a lot, but if he regards it as a port in a storm . . .'

So he started with them, coaching and scouting like he'd wanted, going to look at teams and players for the boss, taking individual players for special skills, out at Epsom, where we trained, nice and near my home. Of course, I was glad he'd got the job, very glad – for him – but it made things strange. Him being at the club, him living at the house. We'd gone back, and yet, if you see, we hadn't gone back. Dad couldn't change; you couldn't expect him to. He'd still tell me what to do, how to play, when to go to bed, even when to go on the job – 'Never the night before a match; it's like losing two pints of blood' – like I was still a kid. Marion could hardly keep quiet if she was there when he did it; she'd wriggle, she'd make faces; I was afraid any moment she'd say something, and afterwards she would.

'I don't know how you put up with it. Treating you like a baby, and he wouldn't have a job if it wasn't for you.'

'I know,' I said. 'That's why I put up with it. He knows it, too. He's on forty-five a week; our reserves earn more than that, but without him what would I be earning?'

But it wasn't easy to get her to see it like that, especially with the baby, keeping her up and taking all her time. She said, 'I've heard of mothers-in-law . . .'

Once a day he'd say, 'I must move out. I mustn't burden you. I'll find a room in a hotel.'

'If I hear that once more,' Marion told me, 'I'll go straight out and find one for him.'

I took her hand; she looked very tired. 'I know,' I said. 'I know.'

But I couldn't hurt him, even if it sometimes drove me up the wall, the diagrams, the salt and pepper pots on the table, the 'action replays', as I thought of them, going over and over some move I'd made or hadn't made, like after a game we lost at home to Newcastle.

'The one-two,' he said. 'It was on. It was screaming at you. Even with that big camel of a centre forward of yours. Going through alone: that was daft, but then you always were a greedy little bugger.'

Another time I missed a penalty at Birmingham. That was good for a week, that. My run-up. The way I'd struck the ball. Hitting it high instead of keeping it low. The position of my body. The goalkeeper's position. 'Low and angled, low and angled. How many times do I have to tell you that?'

A million.

Mind, it was only a year ago or so I'd stopped the phone calls, or most of them, the post-mortems we'd have after every big game, even in Europe, especially with England; I remember phoning him once from Caracas, when I really felt I'd played bad. It began to fall off after I got married. Marion would say, 'Phoning your father again?' or 'I suppose you'll be on the phone for an hour tonight.' Perhaps I'd outgrown it, I didn't need it so much now, but she could never realise how it had helped me all those years.

Now and again I'd look at his face when he thought I wasn't and I'd see the bitterness, the disappointment. That was the end, with City – I knew it and he knew it – the end as far as managing a big club was concerned. He'd upset too many people. No wonder he was afraid to leave us, no wonder he was for ever lecturing me; I was all he'd got left.

And then it started at the club. I'd been afraid it would. First he didn't reckon the coach, Bobby Birchall, which was par for the course; he never reckoned any coach, especially one that was coaching me. He'd be out on the field there at Epsom when Bobby was working with us, shaking his head, clicking his tongue, making faces, till it was obvious that Bobby noticed and naturally he didn't like it. There was no future in it either. It was like I'd told him; where Geoff Creamer went, Bobby Birchall went. Geoff Creamer sat in the stadium and handled the directors and the Press, Bobby Birchall was out at Epsom looking after the tactics and the training. If you knocked Bobby, you were getting at Geoff.

One day Geoff had me into the office; he said, 'Peter, you'll have to talk to your father.' I'd been expecting this. 'We're glad to have him here,' he said, 'till he gets something else, but he must realise Bobby Birchall is coach; and I'm the manager.'

'I know,' I said, 'but it's difficult for Dad. He's used to helping me.'

'Just a quiet word,' the boss said. 'I shouldn't like anything to go wrong,' and he gave me what we used to call his Man Management smile, the smile on the face of the tiger.

Of course, I didn't talk to Dad; how could I? He'd no time for Bobby, and even less for the boss. 'They'll burn you out, this club,' he'd say, 'using you like they do. This 4-4-2. They want you on both bloody wings; and fetching and carrying in midfield. I'm going to have a word with Geoff Creamer, if it goes on. You'll not last three seasons. I'll tell him, "You're killing the goose that lays the golden eggs."'

'Please don't, Dad,' I said. 'I can tell him myself.'

'Ay,' he said, 'but you haven't, have you? It's just as well I'm here.'

The trouble was there was truth in what he said, like there nearly always was; they had been working me hard, for a couple of seasons now, and I was beginning to feel it, but it wasn't any good telling them; it would just make it worse. I'd wince, sometimes, when the boss and the old man were together.

'Work rate?' the old man would say. 'What's all this bloody work rate? Footballers aren't factory hands. Footballers aren't navvies.' And the boss would cock his little head and stick out his little fat arse in the way he had and smile his smile and say, 'Football's changed a lot, you know, Ted.'

'Maybe,' said Dad, 'but it hasn't changed for the bloody better.'

The big blow-up came when we played Milan in the first leg of the European Cupwinners' Cup quarter-final, at our place. Everything went wrong in the first half. They were playing this packed defence with a sweeper, body-checking a lot, shirt-pulling, and when they broke away and scored we got desperate, just banging long balls into the middle, which their defence were eating.

At half-time, Bobby and the boss came into the dressing-room with the old man, who'd been sitting on the bench with Bobby – they'd sent him out there to watch Milan. As soon as I saw him I could tell we were in for trouble; I knew that look on his face. He was bursting to bollock everybody in sight and, to make matters worse, the boss and Bobby just stood there like a couple of dummies with nothing to offer at all. I was longing for them to say something, anything, just to fill the silence, before the old man leapt in; which he did.

He started, 'Well, if you two haven't got anything to say, I have. I've never seen such a pathetic exhibition. You're playing right into their hands. No skill, no method, no intelligence.' On and on he went, and whether the other two were too surprised to try and stop him or too chicken I don't know. The fact is they didn't. He bollocked us for using long balls into the middle; he bollocked us, especially me, for not going to the line and pulling the ball back – 'You try getting there,' I said, 'with the shirt-pulling and the obstruction' – and he was still at full blast when the buzzer went for the second half. Bobby and the boss hadn't opened their mouths; we left the three of them behind us in the dressing-room, and I wondered what they'd say to one another.

The thing was that his pep talk worked; I think that's what they couldn't forgive him. We did get our tails up; we did start playing better; we did start going round the back of them; we equalised, and very nearly won.

After the match the boss didn't show in the dressing-room at all, just Bobby, looking a bit sheepish, and the old man, who of course was just full of it; he never could read situations outside football. 'That was better, lads, that was better. If you'd played like it the whole of the game, you'd have bloody annihilated them!' But all I kept wondering was where the boss was, and what he was saying to the chairman.

There was a reception afterwards, the usual drag, speeches, a cold buffet, and a couple of beers at most, because you knew the boss was looking. He didn't speak to the old man, nor did any of the directors. There was what you might call an atmosphere.

The word went round that a few of the lads were going on to the Sportsman's Club. I asked Dad if he'd like to come, nearly got my head bit off. 'A club? After a game like this? If you'd been trying, you'd all be too tired to do anything but go to bed, which is what you should do, after a match' – another of his favourite moans. So it was a confrontation, the last thing I wanted; the two of us standing there, glaring at each other, but I couldn't back down, not in front of the lads. 'Well, I'm going, Dad,' I said, 'I'll see you later.'

We went on staring for a while and then he said, 'You little tyke,' and walked away. I felt bad leaving him.

We were there till nearly three in the morning, but when I got home the light was still on in the front room. He was sitting there with his head in his hands. I'd never seen him look that shattered, eyes all red; he looked a hundred years old.

'They've sacked me, Peter,' he said, and he began to cry.

'I'm sorry, Dad,' I said, and he said, 'Sorry? Is that all you can say? You're not going to stay there, are you? You'll ask for a transfer?' But I shook my head.

Get up, I thought, get up; footballers don't cry. The words sprang into my throat and choked me. I knew he'd never get up now.

from LOVE IS NOT LOVE *1985*

The Man Behind the Goal

BRIAN GLANVILLE

He had brought his own football. It lay on the ground beside the bench, where he himself sprawled in clumsy comfort, his head pillowed on his hands, his heavy, muddy boots propped against the wooden arm. The bench stood beside some railings, at the foot of a little slope of leafless trees. The park had gone from autumn into winter; puddles lay, blind and brown, in the declivities of the little football field; raindrops hung from the white crossbars of the goals.

I did not greet the man when I arrived; my first reaction was to resent him. He was filling up the bench where we always changed, his boots had fouled it with pats of mud, and – supine and unembarrassed – he gave no sign of moving.

'It'll rain again,' he announced, in an accent I could not quite place. 'See the clouds up there? Black ones. It'll pour.'

I nodded, and began to take off my track-suit. In a moment, I looked up and saw Don coming down the hill that led from the road, his fair, bushy head bowed; unseeing, or not wanting to see: I was never sure. His leather bag swung from his hand.

The man did not speak to me again; he seemed perfectly relaxed. From a haversack beside him, he took out an apple and raising his head like a fish rising to a bait, began to eat it, in noisy bites.

Don was beside us now. We looked at the man, exchanged shrugs and glances, and hung our clothes over the spiked fence. Don took a football out of his case and rolled it on to the ground.

'Hard, is it?' asked the man, casting a sidelong glance. 'Yes, it looks hard. Mine's soft, soft as bloody putty. Useless. Can't get nobody to blow it up.'

Then, as though his attention could be switched on and off like an electric current, he went back to his apple as though he had never spoken, and finally, with a contemptuous flick of the hand, his eyes still fixed on the sky, he threw the core over the fence.

Don and I moved on to the football pitch, and he went into goal; the goal beneath the great, chimneyed monolith of the power station. I shot, the ball rose high over the crossbar, and Don turned to trot after it, a patient and unhurried sheep dog. Out of the corner of an eye, I saw the little man had got off the bench, and was playing with his own football, a small, stooping, under-nourished figure in a blue boiler suit, gambolling about the ball, half gnome, half puppy, head bent over it, in earnest concentration. In his fantasy, he was clearly a forward, tricking and bewildering a host of defenders, now skipping over the ball, now pulling it to him with the sole of his foot, now feinting to his left, and stroking it to the right. From a distance, the ball invisible, it must have seemed like a grotesque ritual dance, a leprechaun frolicking round his crock of gold.

There was a thump and a splash, as our football landed beside me in a puddle; as I turned to get it, the little man suddenly whirled, to kick his ball under the seat — obviously he'd scored a goal. I shot again, looked round again, and now the little man had recovered his ball and was dribbling it towards us over the bumpy ground, with the same dedication, the same ungainly diligence. I wondered for a moment if he meant to join us, but he made no effort to come on to the pitch, merely dribbling the ball on and on, head bent, until he was behind our goal.

Again I shot. This time the ball sailed between the netless goalposts, high past Don's outstretched right arm; and at this the little man turned from his own soft ball and scampered after ours, catching it, turning on it with a short, self-conscious pirouette, as though he were demonstrating to a class, then, with the same, studied technique, he kicked it back to us.

I shouted thanks, feeling a stab of guilt, sorry I had dealt so brusquely with him. I half hoped that he would go away or, if he stayed, concentrate upon his own strange, intense gyrations. But each time the ball flew behind the goal, he was after it like a faithful bird dog, dribbling it back with his painful, stooping run, until at last, with a kick laboured but accurate, he would send it back on to the pitch. 'Thank you!' we called, 'thank you! thank you!' But we were still uneasy; he had placed us in his debt.

We trained once a week, and we thought we had seen the last of him, but he was there again the following Thursday, boots up on the bench, his half-pumped pudding of a ball beside it. Again, he trotted behind the goal when we began to shoot, again he endlessly chased the ball and sent it back to us, but now he maintained a ceaseless and staccato commentary.

'On the ground . . . keep it on the *ground* . . . if you put it in the air, you've lost it, you're *wasting* it!' A breathless dash to retrieve the ball. 'The Scottish way's the best . . . I don't mean the new way, because that's rubbish; I mean the *old* way, the classical way.' Another dash. 'I told them at Tottenham, I was on the terrace . . . Spurs? I said . . . Great *team*, I said? They're not fit to lace the boots . . . up in the air, the whole time . . . that big Smith; the other big one, Norman . . . Up in the air, biff and bang . . . I *told* them, that's not football. Football is on the *ground*.'

I still could not locate his accent, that now, in its harsh fluency, seemed Welsh, now from the North East. When we left the field, he trotted beside us, still urging and admonishing, while we listened with half an ear, responding now and then in monosyllables. Close at hand, he cut an oddly contradictory figure, half boy, half man: boyish in his slim fragility, the clear, washed grey of his eyes, the straight hair dangling, like a boy's, over his forehead; unboyish in the greyness of that hair, the waxy yellow of his sunken cheeks. At moments, I would look at him and think of an old man; at others, almost of a child; but in his humped, compulsive movements, there was nothing child-like. I thought of him as some poor, harmless paranoid; a garrulous tramp with a strange obsession, who probably slept rough, out in the park; a cliché figure made over-familiar by playwrights of the *avant garde*; life imitating art.

He needed a disciple, that was obvious, and he must have known that we – casual, mediocre Sunday footballers – were too old and frivolous for his purpose. But the next week, when we arrived in the rain, the pupil had been found; a sturdy, stupid boy who stood ox-like under the downpour, woodenly watching, as the little man pirouetted round the soggy ball.

'He'll get pneumonia,' I said, and wondered at his toughness, his fanaticism. He was too frail to spurn the weather.

When Don and I reached the goal behind which he was standing – this time, the upper goal – we could hear him instructing the boy with the same, hortatory voice, as though he were addressing a youth rally. 'If you come *over* the ball like this' – a skip and a hop – 'it is useless. What you *want* to do is approach it like *this*, then you take it away like *that*, thus leaving your opponent in two minds.'

The boy nodded his heavy, pink-cheeked head; he was not invited to try for himself.

'More *haste*, less *speed*; it's the same thing with your kicking. With the *in*-step. The toe of the boot *down* – like this. And *then*, the follow-through – like that!' The ball merely skidded across the muddy ground, but the boy did not laugh; nor did he fetch it. Instead, the little man set off after the ball, with his familiar, crab-like run, caught it, dribbled back, and cried, 'I shall now demonstrate the pass with the inside of the foot!'

It was raining more heavily than ever. The boy's coarse, black hair was soaked; raindrops ran down his plump cheeks, but still he stood, impassive. It was 20 minutes before he left, plodding his stolid, unathletic way across the wet grass, to disappear at last over the hill. The little man resumed his old position behind the goal, and now it was us whom he exhorted.

'Too high, too high! I was telling that boy: *always* along the ground! Keep it down, and you'll go *up*! Keep it up, and you'll go *down*!' The slippery ball made his kicking more feeble and erratic than ever, and he began to complain. 'It's my boots are the trouble! If *I* could get these boots right! I can't kick with these. It's no use trying.'

Back and forth he ran, under the teeming rain, fetching and kicking, fetching and kicking. His hair, plastered damply to his forehead, gave him more than ever the appearance of a tonsured monk; I could see him in a brown cassock, hobbling after the ball as he hobbled now.

'If *I* had my boots right! If *I* could only get some boots!'

The next time we trained, I brought him an old pair of shoes. I put them underneath the bench – clotted with mud, strewn with newspapers and ravaged brown parcels – while he pursued his ball, on the football pitch. I did not mention the shoes – somehow the gesture reeked of charity, a need for gratitude – nor did he himself ever allude to them; but he had them on his feet, the following Thursday.

I came upon him unawares that day, though at first I thought he knew I was there. He was talking in a loud, cheerful voice I had not heard before, smiling; stretched full length, again, on the seat. He was reading the *Daily Express* and I saw, with some surprise, that it was the latest.

'You read these things,' he was saying, 'and what do they expect you to believe? Threequarters of it's lies; lies for gullible people. President Eisenhower accuses Kruschev. If you bought the *Daily Worker*, it would say, President Kruschev accuses Eisenhower. Which of them is true? Probably neither! I don't bloody well believe one nor the other.'

I greeted him: 'Reading the paper?'

He tilted back his head, grinning at me. 'I was engaged in listening to the finest music in the world: the sound of my own voice.'

Suddenly I liked him better. For the first time, the harsh, hectoring tone had gone; the eyes, more palely luminous than ever, seen so close, were full of a humour at once subversive and self-deprecating.

'You're here every day?' I asked.

'Every day, rain or shine, wind or weather, hell or high water.'

'And . . . do you camp here?'

'No,' he said, contemptuously. 'I live down in Westminster, at the Salvation Army hostel – if you can call it living. What they give you to eat, you couldn't feed a sparrow on. One rotten little sausage for breakfast, a few mouldy baked beans at night. If I didn't go out and buy my own bread, I'd starve.' He gestured, and I saw beside him, half hidden by his body, a brown loaf, crudely hacked by the penknife that lay beside it.

'Here every day,' he said. 'I never get bored. I never get bored, listening to myself. Out in the fresh air. Sometimes I have arguments; it's a way to pass the time. Other times I recite poetry.'

'What poetry do you prefer?'

'My own!' he said, and gave the same mischievous smile. 'They talk about great poetry.

"In Xanadu did Kubla Khan
A stately pleasure dome decree.
Dee-dum, dee-dum, dee-dum, dee-dum.
Dee-dum, dee-dum, dee-dum, dee-dee."

Call that poetry? *I* don't call it poetry.'

It was a chance to ask him where he came from.

'Northumberland,' he said – as I had half suspected. 'A little village up there. Don't ask me what it's like now; I haven't been back there for 35 years; I never wanted to. I've been all over the world – India, France, Italy, Spain. Why should I go back to a village in Northumberland? I never liked it there. If I go anywhere, I'll go to France again.'

'What were you doing in France?'

'Learning the language. I was there a year ago, I was in Marseilles. When I think I'll go to a place, nobody stops me; I make up my mind, and then I go.'

'And India?'

'I was in the army, I was there till 1939, when the war came. Then I told them I was ill; my stomach, I said. Fifteen doctors looked at me, they had me in three different hospitals, but they couldn't get to the bottom of it, none of them could. They had to discharge me. Because I hadn't joined the army to fight a war, I'd joined the army in peacetime.'

'Is the boy coming today? Your pupil?'

'Oh, him,' he said, 'he'll be here later. I'll make a footballer out of him. I've told him "I'll make you one, if it kills me. I'll make you one if it kills us both". I've got the perfect system, see. I have devised this system lying here and thinking; it is a triumph of mind over matter.' The hortatory voice was coming back. '*Whereby*, if the material is young enough, *any* player can be turned into a champion. I'm too old, now, or I'd use it on myself.'

I looked round; Don was making his steady, long-legged way down the hill. The little man glanced up suddenly at a tree above him and said, 'That's another thing I've been thinking about; photosynthesis. They say a tree keeps alive by what it draws into itself through its leaves. Well, how can *that* tree possibly be alive, then' – and his voice rose as though it were a personal affront – 'how can it *possibly* be alive when it hasn't *got* a bloody leaf?'

Looking again at the little man and his pupil, I knew that whatever scheme he had devised, the plump boy would never make a footballer. Indeed, it grew clearer and clearer as one watched that the scheme was an end in itself, the boy no more than a lay-figure, scarcely permitted a kick at the ball, while his master pranced and pirouetted like a lame pit pony. Indeed, for the boy to be a pupil at all, it was essential that he *should* be inept; a more proficient boy would never have stood for it.

The following week, I brought the little man a parcel of food; a loaf of bread, a packet of butter, a few tins of soup and spaghetti. From his prone position on the bench, he thanked me seriously.

'I need that, it'll help me, that. The food they give you down there . . .' He was silent awhile, looking gravely into space. 'I have decided,' he said, at last, his tone implying lonely hours of contemplation, 'that soccer is the finest game of all: because there is nothing *evolutionary* about it. Cricket, croquet, hockey, billiards: they are all evolutionary. They are played with a club. A man with a club in his hand is only one stage further than an ape. Football is a game that Plato would have liked, it might have been invented by the Greeks; I can pay no higher compliment. That was the finest flowering of human civilisation.'

Looking at him closely, it seemed to me that his yellow cheeks were hollower than ever. Over his blue dungarees, which conferred on him a spurious dignity of labour, he wore an old khaki greatcoat, but it wasn't enough to sustain his Promethean defiance of the weather.

Again the boy arrived, again the demonstration and the exhortations, though this time, he was allowed to do a little more for himself. He did it clumsily, without confidence or optimism, more, without visible enthusiasm. I wondered if he had simply been accosted while passing by, a wedding guest to the little man's Ancient Mariner, hypnotised first into staying, then into coming back, again and again.

The next week, he was for the first time wearing football shorts, showing his plump, white, heavy thighs, but his movements were as rigid as ever. A fortnight later, when I asked about him, the little man replied, 'I have decided he is ready. I have decided he is ready to take part in a game, using the principles that I have taught him. On Saturday, he's playing in a trial match for his school. I am going there, and I shall advise him from the touchline.'

'Have you seen him play before?'

'Never before; it wasn't necessary. It didn't interest me, because he had not imbibed my principles. But even in these few weeks, he has improved; I can see it for myself, and he's told me that he has: his teachers are amazed. Otherwise he wouldn't have been chosen for this trial.'

Suddenly I felt alarm for him. He was trying to impose his fantasy world upon the real, and the consequence could only be failure, disappointment. I could see him wandering up and down the touchline of the football ground, while loutish, spotted schoolboys giggled at him, and their teachers looked at him with outrage. He'd be disillusioned and humiliated; yet how could he be warned?

'Isn't it a bit early?' I asked. 'You haven't been teaching him long.'

'I have been teaching him three or four times a week, up to two hours, for the last five weeks. That is at least 30 hours. All that is necessary to reach a good standard in boys' football is 30 hours tuition. To reach the international standard, I have estimated it will take three hundred hours.'

For a little while, he kicked our football back for us, from behind the goal; then the boy came lumbering along, for his tuition.

The following week, the little man was not to be seen; indeed, his very bench had gone, and I surmised a conspiracy, a persecution of park-keepers. From time to time, as Don and I trained together, I looked up the hill, or behind me into the green distance of the park, half expecting him to appear; but he did not come. I missed him, wondering if we should ever see him again, whether he'd decamped from the park because the boy had failed, and he could not longer face us, the boy, the workshop of his failure.

A week later, the bench was still not there. We had been running up and down, passing the ball, for several minutes, and were just beginning to take shots at goal, when there was a scampering and a flurry of branches on the hillside beneath which the bench had stood, and the little man emerged, his eyes wide and staring – almost, I thought, like poor, mad Ben Gunn. He was wearing his army greatcoat, which hung nearly to the ground, and I wondered how he would negotiate the railings. But just before he got to them, he pulled himself up, with a quick, monkey-like movement, by the branch of a tree and, from the tree, he dropped over the fence.

He shuffled across the field towards us, and the goal, without taking off the coat. Even before I saw his face, I could tell his dejection by the way he moved. He could never be graceful, but now his old, obsessional vitality had left him, too. He seemed to be carrying out a duty, even – incongruously – a job. He took no notice of our greeting, but went on past us without a word. His face looked sick and ravaged, jaundiced, yellower than ever, crumbling away, like the face of a dying man; the eyes had nothing in them but a blank, possessed determination. He kicked the ball back to us as devotedly as ever, but in silence, without commentary or criticism. The change was such that it depressed us both, so that we finished training early. We thanked the little man, but he turned away without a word, hopelessly, making slowly towards the middle of the park.

I caught up with him. 'How did the game go?' I asked.

'Him?' he said, and stopped. 'Him? He was useless. I miscalculated. I shall have to go back to the beginning. I had decided that, using my system, *any* human material could be turned into a successful footballer. Now I can see that I was wrong; there *must* be basic talent, therefore the system is still not perfect. It may take years to perfect; I don't know if I have enough time left to me.'

'Of course you have,' I said, but the words sounded false, the consolation cheap. He made no answer, turning his back to me, as I felt I deserved, and trudged away again. For a few moments, I was half determined to go after him; then I, too, turned away. He was like a sick dog, wanting to be left alone.

He was not there the next week, or the next, and I began to feel anxious for him; he looked in retrospect too much like a wounded animal, crawling off to die. In the third week, I met the boy; he came slowly across the football pitch, while Don and I were tugging off our boots. About him, too, there seemed to be a sadness, something over and above his usual stolidity.

I called to him and, without increasing pace, he came over.

'Do you know where he is?' I asked. 'The little man.'

'I dunno,' he said, in the incongruous, piping voice of plump adolescence. 'I don't think he's well. He may have gone to hospital.'

'Hospital? When did you see him last?'

'About two weeks ago. I wanted him to teach me again, but he wouldn't. He wouldn't speak to me.' Aggrieved, the voice rose higher still. '*I* can't help it if I didn't play well. *I* couldn't help it if they told him to go away; it wasn't my fault.'

'Was he ill, then?'

'Yeah, he looked terrible. He said he hadn't eaten for three days. I came back the next day, I brought some apples for him, but he wasn't there. I never seen him again.'

That evening, I telephoned the Salvation Army hostel, who identified him without difficulty. Yes, they said, he had gone into hospital; they told me which it was. It was exposure, they thought; they were not quite sure. 'Well, I'm not surprised,' said the voice, as though I had somehow accused it. 'The *weather* he stayed out in.'

The following day, I went to the hospital with a paper carrier bag of fruit. I waited on a bench in the dim, bleak entrance hall, among a murmuring, worried crowd of visitors, dragooned and overawed; the poor at the mercy of the hospital. A bell rang and we filed along a twilit corridor. Here and there, we passed the entrance of a ward, where the patients sat up in their beds with taut expectancy. At each of these a few of us would file away, and there would be small cries of joy, embraces.

At last I reached the ward where he was lying, and looked in through the door. It was very long, a row of beds ran down each side. At first I could not see him, but at last I made him out. He sat, motionless and upright, against the pillows, in a bed halfway down the left-hand wall, his face more wasted than ever. But it was not this which shocked me, so much as the expression of the eyes, void now of humour or defiance, merely staring out across the ward.

A nurse came up to me with her brisk, starched walk, and asked whom I wanted to see. I pushed the bag of fruit into her hands and pointed at him, then turned away, fearful he should recognise me.

Nemesis had caught up with him, society and the weather had beaten him at last. I hurried into the street, escaping with the memory of his courage.

from THE DIRECTOR'S WIFE *1963*

Play up, Play up and Get Tore in

GEORGE MACDONALD FRASER

The native Highlanders, the Englishmen, and the Lowlanders played football on Saturday afternoons and talked about it on Saturday evenings, but the Glaswegians, men apart in this as in most things, played, slept, ate, drank, and lived it seven days a week. Some soldiering they did because even a peace-time battalion in North Africa makes occasional calls on its personnel, but that was incidental; they were just waiting for the five minutes when they could fall out crying: 'Haw, Wully, sees a ba'.'

From the moment when the drums beat *Johnnie Cope* at sunrise until it became too dark to see in the evening, the steady thump-thump of a boot on a ball could be heard somewhere in the barracks. It was tolerated because there was no alternative; even the parade ground was not sacred from the small shuffling figures of the Glasgow men, their bonnets pulled down over their eyes, kicking, trapping, swerving and passing, and occasionally intoning, like ugly little high priests, their ritual cries of 'Way-ull' and 'Aw-haw-hey'. The simile is apt, for it was almost a religious exercise, to be interrupted only if the Colonel happened to stroll by. Then they would wait, relaxed, one of them with the ball underfoot, until the majestic figure had gone past, flicking his brow in acknowledgement, and at the soft signal, 'Right, Wully,' the ball would be off again.

I used to watch them wheeling like gulls, absorbed in their wonderful fitba'. They weren't in Africa or the Army any longer; in imagination they were running on the green turf of Ibrox or Paradise, hearing instead of bugle calls the rumble and roar of a hundred thousand voices; this was their common daydream, to play (according to religion) either for Celtic or Rangers. All except Daft

Bob Brown, the battalion idiot; in his fantasy he was playing for Partick Thistle.

They were frighteningly skilful. As sports officer I was expected actually to play the game, and I have shameful recollections still of a Company practice match in which I was pitted against a tiny, wizened creature who in happier days had played wing-half for Bridgeton Waverley. What a monkey he made out of me. He was quicksilver with a glottal stop, nipping past, round, and away from me, trailing the ball tantalisingly close and magnetising it away again. The only reason he didn't run between my legs was that he didn't think of it. It could have been bad for discipline, but it wasn't. When he was making me look the biggest clown since Grock I wasn't his platoon commander any more; I was just an opponent to beat.

With all this talent to choose from – the battalion was seventy-five per cent Glasgow men – it followed that the regimental team was something special. In later years more than half of them went on to play for professional teams, and one was capped for Scotland, but never in their careers did they have the opportunity for perfecting their skill that they had in that battalion. They were young and as fit as a recent war had made them; they practised together constantly in a Mediterranean climate; they had no worries; they loved their game. At their peak, when they were murdering the opposition from Tobruk to the Algerian border, they were a team that could have given most club sides in the world a little trouble, if nothing more.

The Colonel didn't speak their language, but his attitude to them was more than one of paternal affection for his soldiers. He respected their peculiar talent, and would sit in the stand at games crying 'Play up!' and 'Oh, dear, McIlhatton!' When they won, as they invariably did, he would beam and patronise the other colonels, and when they brought home the Command Cup he was almost as proud as he was of the Battle Honours.

In his pride he became ambitious. 'Look, young Dand,' he said. 'Any reason why they shouldn't go on tour? You know, round the Med, play the garrison teams, eh? I mean, they'd win, wouldn't they?'

I said they ought to be far too strong for most regimental sides.

'Good, good,' he said, full of the spirit that made British sportsmanship what it is. 'Wallop the lot of them, excellent. Right, I'll organise it.'

When the Colonel organised something, it was organised; within a couple of weeks I was on my way to the docks armed with warrants and a suitcase full of cash, and in the back of the truck were the battalion team, plus reserves, all beautiful in their best tartans, sitting with their arms folded and their bonnets, as usual, over their faces.

When I lined them up on the quayside, preparatory to boarding one of HM coastal craft, I was struck again by their lack of size. They were extremely neat men, as Glaswegians usually are, quick, nervous, and deft as monkeys, but they were undoubtedly small. A century of life – of living, at any rate – in the hell's kitchen of industrial Glasgow, has cut the stature and mighty physique of the Scotch-Irish people pitifully; Glasgow is full of little men today, but at least they are stouter and sleeker than my team was. They were the children of the hungry Thirties, hard-eyed and wiry; only one of them was near my size, a fair, dreamy youth called McGlinchy, one of the reserves. He was a useless, beautiful player, a Stanley Matthews for five minutes of each game, and for the rest of the time an indolent passenger who strolled about the left wing, humming to himself. Thus he was normally in the second eleven. ('He's got fitba',' the corporal who captained the first team would say, 'but whit the hell, he's no' a' there; he's wandered.')

The other odd man out in the party was Private McAuslan, the dirtiest soldier in the world, who acted as linesman and baggage-master, God help us. The Colonel had wanted to keep him behind, and send someone more fit for human inspection, but the team had protested violently. They were just men, and McAuslan was their linesman, foul as he was. In fairness I had backed them up, and now I was regretting it, for McAuslan is not the kind of ornament that you want to advertise your team in Mediterranean capitals. He stood there with the baggage, grimy and dishevelled, showing a tasteful strip of grey vest between kilt and tunic, and with his hosetops wrinkling towards his ankles.

'All right, children,' I said, 'get aboard. . .'

It was a pleasant enough voyage, marred only by two fights between McAuslan on the one hand and members of the crew, who had criticised his unsanitary appearance, on the other. I straightened them out, upbraided McAuslan, and instructed him how to behave.

'You're a guest, you horrible article,' I said. 'Be nice to the sailors; they are your friends. Fraternise with them; they were on our side in the war, you know? And for that matter, when we get to the Island, I shall expect a higher standard than ever from all of you. Be a credit to the regiment, and keep moderately sober after the games. Above all, don't fight. Cut out the Garscube Road stuff or I'll blitz you.'

Just how my simple, manly words affected them you could see from the glazed look in their eyes, and I led them down the gangplank at Grand Island feeling just a mite apprehensive. They were good enough boys but as wild as the next, and it was more than usually important that they keep out of trouble because the Military Governor, who had been instrumental in fixing the tour, was formerly of a Highland regiment, and would expect us not only to win our games but to win golden opinions for deportment.

He was there to meet us, with aides and minions, a stately man of much charm who shook hands with the lads and then departed in a Rolls, having assured me that he was going to be at every game. Then the Press descended on us, I was interviewed about our chances, and we were all lined up and photographed. The result, as seen in the evening paper, was mixed. The team were standing there in their kits, frowning suspiciously, with me at one end grinning inanely. At the other end crouched an anthropoid figure, dressed apparently in old sacking; at first I thought an Arab mendicant had strayed into the picture, but closer inspection identified it as McAuslan showing, as one of the team remarked, his good side.

Incidentally, it seemed from the paper's comments that we were not highly rated. The hint seemed to be that we were being given a big build-up simply because we were from the Governor's old brigade, but that when the garrison teams – and I knew they were good teams – got us, we would be pretty easy meat. This suited me, and it obviously didn't worry the team. They were near enough professionals to know that games aren't won in newspaper columns.

We trained for two days and had our first game against the German prisoners-of-war. They were men still waiting to be repatriated, ex-Africa Korps, big and tough, and they had played together since they went into the bag in '42. Some of our team wore the Africa Star, and you could feel the tension higher than usual in the dressing-room beforehand. The corporal, dapper and wiry, stamped his boots on the concrete, bounced the ball, and said, 'Awright fellas, let's get stuck intae these Huns,' and out they trotted.

(I should say at this point that this final exhortation varied only according to our opponents. Years later, when he led a famous league side out to play Celtic, this same corporal, having said his Hail Mary and fingered his crucifix, instructed his team, 'Awright, fellas, let's get stuck intae these Papes.' There is a lesson in team spirit there, if you think about it.)

The Germans were good, but not good enough. They were clever for their size, but our boys kept the ball down and the game close, and ran them into a sweat before half-time. We should have won by about four clear goals, but the breaks didn't come, and we had to be content with 2–0. Personally I was exhausted: I had had to sit beside the Governor, who had played rugby, but if I had tried to explain the finer points he wouldn't have heard them anyway. He worked himself into a state of nervous frenzy, wrenching his handkerchief in his fingers and giving antique yelps of 'Off your side!' and 'We claim foul!' which contrasted oddly with the raucous support of our reserve players, whose repertoire was more varied and included 'Dig a hole for 'im!', 'Sink 'im!' and the inevitable 'Get tore intae these people!' At the end the Germans cried 'Hoch! hoch!' and we gave three cheers, and both sides came off hating each other. . . .

So the tour progressed, and the Island sat up a little straighter with each game. We came away strongly against the Engineers, 6–0, beat the top civilian team 3–0, and on one of those dreadful off-days just scraped home against the Armoured Corps, 1–0. It was scored by McGlinchy, playing his first game and playing abysmally. Then late on he ambled on to a loose ball on the edge of the penalty circle, tossed the hair out of his eyes, flicked the ball from left foot to right to left without letting it touch the ground, and suddenly unleashed the most unholy piledriver you ever saw. It hit the underside of the bar from twenty-five yards out and glanced into the net with the goalkeeper standing still, and you could almost hear McGlinchy sigh as he trotted back absently to his wing, scratching his ear.

'Wandered!' said the corporal bitterly afterwards. 'Away wi' the fairies! He does that, and for the rest o' the game he micht as well be in his bed. He's a genius, sir, but no' near often enough. Ye jist daurnae risk 'im again.'

I agreed with him. So far we hadn't lost a goal, and although I had no illusions about preserving that record, I was beginning to hope that we would get through the tour unbeaten. The Governor, whose excitement was increasing with every game, was heard to express the opinion that we were the sharpest thing in the whole Middle East; either he was getting pot-valiant or hysterical, I wasn't sure which, but he went about bragging at dinners until his commanders got sick of him, and us.

But the public liked us, and so did the Press, and when we took the Artillery to the cleaners, 3–2, in one of the fastest and most frantic games I have ever seen, amateur or pro, they were turning crowds away from the stadium. The Governor was like an antelope full of adrenalin, eating his handkerchief and shivering about in his seat, crying, 'Oh, my goodness gracious me!' and 'Ah, hah, he has, he hasn't, oh my God!' and flopping back, exhausted. I was too busy to steady him; I was watching (it dawned on me) a really fine football team. They moved like a machine out there, my wiry, tireless wee keelies, and it wasn't just their speed, their trickiness, or their accuracy; it was their cool, impregnable assurance. What gets into a man, who is nervous when a sergeant barks at him, but who, when he is put out in front of 20,000 shouting spectators, and asked to juggle an elusive leather ball, reacts with all the poise and certainty of an acrobat on a high wire?

I didn't need to tell them they were good. They knew it, and perhaps some of them knew it too well. Following the Artillery game, two of them got picked up by the MPs, fighting drunk and out of bounds, and I had to pull out all the stops to save their necks. I dropped them from the next game (which we won narrowly, 4–3), and then came our final match, and we won it 4–0, and that was it. I relaxed, the Governor took to his bed for a couple of days, wheezing like a deflating balloon, and my team took it easy at last. That is to say that during the day they punted the ball about on the practice pitch, crying 'Way-ull' and 'Aw-haw-hey,' and at night they sat in the bars, drinking beer and eyeing the talent, and keeping their bonnets over their eyes.

With the pressure off they drank more and ate more, and I was not surprised when, a few days before we were due to leave the Island, two of them came down with one of those bugs which inhabit melons in foreign parts and give you gyppy tummy, or as they call it in India, Delhi Belly. They were packed off to bed and I read the others a lecture on the perils of over-indulgence. . . .

That evening I was called to the phone. It was the Governor, excited but brisk. 'MacNeill,' he said. 'How's your team?'

Wondering, I said they were fine.

'Excellent, capital. I think I can arrange another game for them, farewell appearance, y'know. That all right with you?'

I was about to mention the two men in hospital, and that we wouldn't be at full strength, but after all, we were here to play, not to make excuses. So I said, 'Splendid, any time,' and before I could ask about our opponents and the where and when, he had said he would ring me later and hung up. Evidently he thought victory was a formality.

It seemed to me he was taking a lot for granted; after all, our opponents might be somebody really good. But we'd beaten the best in the Island, so we probably couldn't go wrong.

So I thought, until I heard from the Governor's aide late that night. 'Two-thirty, at the Stadium,' he said. 'Full uniform for you, of course, and *do* see, old man, that your Jocks are respectable. Can't you get them to wear their hats on the *tops* of their heads? They tend rather to look like coalmen.'

'Sure, sure. Who are we playing?'

'Mmh? Oh, the other lot? The Fleet.'

For a moment I didn't follow. He explained.

'The Fleet. The Navy. *You* know, chaps in ships with blue trousers.' He began to sing *Heart of Oak*.

'But . . . but . . . but,' I said. 'That's like playing the Army. I mean, there are thousands of them. They'll be all-professional . . . they'll murder us . . . they . . .'

'That's what the Admiral thought,' said the aide, 'but our Chief wouldn't see it. Got rather excited actually; they're still arguing in there; can't you hear 'em? Amazing,' he went on, 'how the Chief's manner changes when he gets worked up about a thing like this; he sounds positively Scotch. What's a sumph, by the way?'

I wasn't listening any longer. I was sweating. It wasn't panic, or the fear of defeat. After all, we had done well, and no one could expect us to hold the Navy; we would just have to put on a good show. I was just concentrating on details – get the boys to bed quickly, two men in hospital, choose the team, balance it as well as possible. I ran over the reserves: Beattie, Forbes, McGlinchy, myself . . . Lord, the Fleet! And I had fourteen to choose from. Well, barring miracles, we would lose. The Governor would be in mourning; that was his hard luck, if he didn't know better than to pit us against a side that would be half First Division pros, and possibly even an internationalist. Suddenly I felt elated. Suppose . . . oh, well, we'd give them something to remember us by.

I simply told the boys at bedtime who they were playing, and they digested it, and the corporal said:

'Aw-haw-hey. Think they're any good, sir?'

'Not as good as we are.'

'We're the wee boys,' said the corporal, and the wee boys cried 'Way-ull,' mocking themselves. They were pleased at the thought of another game, that was all. I doubt if their reaction would have been different if their opponents had been Moscow Dynamo or the Eye Infirmary.

The corporal and I pored over the team all morning; the one doubtful spot was left-wing, and after much heart-searching we fixed on McGlinchy, but the corporal didn't like it. He at least knew what we were up against 'an' we cannae afford a passenger. If Ah thought he'd wake up mebbe half the match, OK, but no' kiddin', sir, yon yin's no' a' there.'

'He's all we've got,' I said. 'Beattie's a half-back, and I'm just not good enough. It's got to be McGlinchy.'

'Aye, weel,' said the corporal, 'that's so. But by half-time I'll bet we're wishin' we'd picked . . . McAuslan, even.'

In the unlikely event that we had been daft enough to do just that, we would have been disappointed. For when we embussed for the stadium McAuslan was mysteriously absent. We waited and swore, but he didn't appear, so Beattie was detailed to run the touchline, and off we went. With any luck McAuslan had fallen in the harbour.

The dressing-room was hot and sunny under the stand as we sat around waiting. The boys chewed gum and McGlinchy played 'wee heidies' against the wall – nodding a ball against the partition like a boxer hitting a punch-ball. ('Close-mooth, tanner-ba' merchant,' muttered the corporal.) Outside we could hear the growing rumble of the crowd, and then there was the peep of a whistle, and the referee's step in the passage, and the boys shifted and said, 'Way-ull, way-ull,' and boots stamped and shorts were hitched, and outside a brass band was thumping out *Heart of Oak* and a great thunder of voices was rolling up as the Fleet came out, and the corporal sniffed and said:

'Awright, fellas, let's get stuck intae these matlows,' and I was left alone in the dressing-room. . . .

The roar hit me in the face as I came out into the stand. I sat at the back of the main box; down from the Governor was starting work on his first handkerchief of the game, and beside him was a massive, grizzled hero in blue, with gold lace up to his armpits. That would be the Admiral. Their henchmen were about them, full of well-bred enthusiasm; the stadium was jammed, and every second man seemed to be a sailor. Our support was confined to a handful of khaki down below the box: our own reserves and a few associates.

'Flee-eet!' rolled across the brown, iron-hard pitch, and I saw the concentration of yellow shirts down near one goal: the Navy were attacking, powerful dark-blue figures with red stockings. They smacked the ball about with that tough assurance that is the mark of the professional; I saw the corporal slide in to tackle, and red stockings deftly side-stepped and swept the ball past him. The roar mounted, there was a surge in our goalmouth, and then the ball was trickling past into the crowd. I felt slightly sick.

'Get tore intae these people!' came from in front of the box, to be drowned in the Navy roar. Yes, I thought, get tore in. . . .

The hard ground and the light ball were on our side, for we were ball-players first and last; on grass the Navy would have been just too strong. They didn't rush things; they passed with deliberation and looked for their men, unlike our team, who were used to fast, short passing controlled by some sort of telepathy. If we played at their pace we were done for, so we didn't. The doll-like yellow figures moved and ran as though they were at practice, easy and confident.

We scored in the sixth minute, a zig-zag of passes down the middle that left Campbell, the centre, clear of the defence, and he lofted the ball over the Navy's goalkeeper's head as he came out. There was a shocked roar from the crowd, a neigh of triumph from the Governor, a perceptible empurpling of the Admiral's neck, and an exulting 'Aw-haw-hey!' from below the box.

Two minutes later Campbell had the ball in the net again, but was ruled offside. Then he headed against the cross-bar, and we forced three corners in a row. But you could feel it slackening; the Fleet were as steady as ever, and presently they came away, swinging long passes through the open spaces, using their extra length of leg, keeping the ball up where their height counted. They *were* good; in their way. And for a moment, as they broke through on the left and centred and their inside right chose his spot in the net and banged in the equaliser, they were imposing that way.

There was worse to come. The Fleet went ahead with a penalty, when the corporal, in a momentary lapse into close-mouth warfare, obeyed our supporters' behest to 'Ca' the feet fae 'im,' and brought down a Navy forward close to goal. It was a critical point: when we kicked off again the Navy, one goal up, came storming through. Their centre got away and side-footed the ball past the advancing goalkeeper. It was rolling home, but the corporal came from nowhere and stopped it on the line. And then he did the ridiculous, unspeakable thing. I can still see him, the stocky yellow figure with his foot on top of the ball, watching three blue jerseys tearing down on him; alone, in his own goal. Bobby Moore himself would have belted it away for touch and been thankful. But not our boy. He shifted his hips, beat the first Navy forward on a sixpence, showed the ball to the other two, feinted amidst agonised yells of 'Get rid of it!' stepped over a scything foot, looked about him, and patted the ball into the hands of the goalkeeper, who was so stricken with anxiety that he nearly dropped it.

It was perhaps the cheekiest piece of ball-juggling that I've ever seen; it shook the Fleet momentarily for it seemed to indicate a careless contempt. It said, more clearly than words could have done, that there was no sense of panic in this defence. The Admiral roared with laughter, and I hoped again.

We scored again, just before the interval, a goal against the run of play headed in from a long, free kick, and the teams came off and the Marine band marched up and down playing *Iolanthe*. I stayed where I was, listening to the Governor chattering Good game, good game, my goodness, and the Admiral's bass rumble, and staring out at the sunlight on the great crowd lining the saucer of the arena. There was no point in my going down to the dressing-room; we were doing well, and nothing I could say could make it better.

The second half began disastrously. A high ball went into our goalmouth, the centre-half and the Fleet centre went up for it; the sailor came down on his feet and our man on his back. He lay still, and my heart turned over. I watched them lifting him, crowding around, but his head hung forward, and presently they took him behind the goal. 'Dirty! dirty!' came the cry from down front, drowned in the answering roar of 'Wheel 'im off!' from the Navy. The referee bounced the ball to restart the game, and as the injured man was supported towards the dressing-room I was bounding down the stairs.

He was slightly concussed, the doctor said; he wanted to go back on, but the doctor said it was out of the question. I watched while they bandaged his head, and told him – what I honestly felt – that it didn't matter a damn about the game. His face took on that look of whining rage that the Glaswegian wears in times of stress, and he said, 'We had them bate. We'd've sorted them this half.'

Maybe we would, I thought; with ten men it was certain that we wouldn't now. The doctor broke in to say that he ought to go to bed, and as they took him away I went back to the stand. Dimly I had been aware of the distant roar swelling and dying; when I climbed into my seat we were kicking off again. We were down 4–2.

The Fleet were out for blood now. Even the Admiral was joining in the roar, and the Governor was just sitting eating his hankie. Ten men don't look very different on the field from eleven; for a time they may even play above themselves, but they don't win. They never deserve to lose, but they lose.

Oddly enough, we held our own now, and with the tension gone I began to take in details. McClinchy was playing like an elderly horse; he hadn't seen much of the ball in the first half, and now he was using it as if it was a landmine, shying away from it, stumbling, and generally living up to the corporal's expectations. His inside man, little Forbes, was obviously cursing himself hoarse. The crowd enjoyed it.

'Windy!' roared the Fleet.

'Ah, you sharrap! Get back on the front o' the Players packet!'

'Turn blue, pongoes!'

'Play up,' cried the Governor. 'Come along, come along.'

The admiral said something to him, and they both laughed, and I watched the handkerchief being twisted. There were about fifteen minutes left.

Then it happened, and you can read about it in the files of the Island's leading daily paper.

McGlinchy got the ball and lost it; it came back to him and he fell over it and it went into touch. The Navy threw in, the ball ran to McGlinchy again, and for once he beat his man and was moving down the wing when a sailor whipped the heels from him. The crowd roared, McGlinchy got up hopping painfully, the Governor exclaimed, 'Oh, I say,' and little Forbes went scurrying in, fists clenched, to avenge the foul. Oh no, I said, please God, don't let Forbes hit him, not out there with everyone looking. Please don't, Forbes. But the referee was in between, shaking his finger, Forbes was hustled away by his mates, and the referee gave a free kick – against McGlinchy.

It was taken amid much hubbub, and I watched McGlinchy, standing looking puzzled, too surprised to protest, and then his head lifted, and the ball was running towards him. He stopped it, turned, swerved past the half-back, and was away. He could run when he wanted; he swerved infield, then out again towards the flag. The back went sliding in and McGlinchy side-stepped him and came in along the by-line, teasing that he was going to cross the ball, but holding it, like Matthews in his good years.

'Get rid of it!' cried an unhappy voice, but he held it, sand-dancing, looking up, and then he made a dart towards the near post, with the back straining at his heels, and he passed across and back when he couldn't have been more than three yards out, and Forbes had the empty goal in front of him.

The net shook, and the Admiral pounded his fist amidst the uproar, and the Governor made strange sounds, and I could see the corporal slapping McGlinchy's back and upbraiding him for holding on so long, and I thought regretfully that that had been McGlinchy's one brilliant flash. He was trotting back thoughtfully to his wing, with the applause dying down. It was 4–3 for the Navy and perhaps twelve minutes to go.

Then he did it again. Or very nearly. He went down the touch-line and then cut square across the field, beating two men on the way. He had an opening towards goal, with the Fleet defence floundering, but being McGlinchy he back-heeled the ball to nobody and it was cleared. I saw the corporal beating his breast, the Governor tore his handkerchief across, the Admiral bellowed jovially – and McGlinchy got the second chance he didn't deserve. The back's clearance hit a Fleet man and ran loose. McGlinchy, still in midfield, fastened on and this time went straight ahead, turned out to the left as the centre-half closed in, and centred hard and high. Duff, the right-winger, met it at the post with his head, and I realised that I was making ridiculous noises of triumph and delight. It was 4–4, the Fleet defence were gesturing at each other, and the little knot of yellow shirts was hurrying back towards the centre circle, embracing as they ran.

Then the Navy showed how good they were. They attacked, and for the first time in my experience of them I saw my team panicked. They had snatched a possible draw from certain defeat, and they were scared stiff of slipping back. They were wild; they fouled twice, once perilously close to the eighteen-yard line, and I could see, although I couldn't hear, the corporal barking at them, swearing horribly, no doubt, steadying them. He was wise, that corporal; whenever he got the ball he looked for McGlinchy. He sensed, like me, that he was in the presence of a phenomenon; it couldn't last, but he knew to use it while it was there. 'Feed him, feed him, he's bewitched,' I found myself saying, and McGlinchy went off down the wing, fair hair flying – I made a note to make him get it cut – and was tackled and the ball ran out.

He clapped his hands for it, trapped it as it was thrown in, back-heeled it through an opponent's legs, and ran on to it. He stopped, on the edge of the centre circle, foot on the ball, looking round. And for a split second the sound died. Then:

'Coom to 'im, man!' in a great Yorkshire voice.

'Get rid o' it, mac! See the winger.'

The roar swelled up, and he swerved away, dummied past a half-back, reached the penalty circle, slid heaven knows how between two defenders, almost lost the ball, scratched for it, flushed it forward, feinted to shoot, swerved again, and now he was on the penalty spot, with the blue jerseys converging, and little Forbes screaming for the ball, unmarked, and Campbell on the other side of him beating his hands. But he went on, the Admiral covered his face, the Governor rose to his feet cramming his handkerchief into his mouth, McGlinchy had one sailor at his elbow and another lunging desperately in front of him; he checked and side-stepped, looked at Forbes, shoved the ball under the tackler's leg, went after it, and just for a split second was clear, with every sailor except Lord Nelson thundering in on him, the goalkeeper diving at his feet, and then the blue flood swept down on him.

'Get rid o' it!'

'Kill him!' bawled the Admiral, decency forgotten.

'Get tore in!' cried the Governor.

He went down in a heap of navy jerseys, and a sudden bellow went up from behind the goal. I couldn't see why, and then I saw why. The ball was lying, rolling just a little, a foot over the goal-line. It came to rest in the net, just inside the post.

At such times, when all around is bedlam, the man of mark is distinguished by his nonchalance and detachment. Calmly I took out my cigarette case, selected a cigarette, struck a match, set fire to my sporran, roared aloud, dropped cigarettes, case, and matches, and scrambled on my knees along the floor of the box trying to beat the flames out. By the time I had succeeded the box was full of smoke and a most disgusting stench, one of the Admiral's aides was looking round muttering that expressions of triumph were all very well, but the line should be drawn somewhere, and the Fleet were kicking off in a last attempt to retrieve the game.

They didn't make it, but it was a near thing. There was one appeal for a penalty when the corporal seemed to handle – if I'd been the referee I believe I'd have given it – but the claim was disallowed, and then the long whistle blew. We had won, 5–4, and I found myself face to face with a red-faced petty officer who was exclaiming, 'By, you were lucky! I say, you were lucky! By!'

I made deprecating noises and shot downstairs. They were trooping into the dressing-room, chattering indignantly – it was their curious way not to be exultant over what had gone right, but aggrieved over what had gone wrong. I gathered that at least two of the Fleet should have been ordered off, that the referee had been ignorant of the offside law, that we should have had a penalty when . . . and so on. Never mind, I said, we won, it had all come out all right. Oh, aye, but . . .

The Governor looked in, beaming congratulation, and there was a lot of noise and far too many people in the dressing-room. The team were pulling off their jerseys and trying to escape to the showers; clothes were falling on the floor and bare feet were being stepped on; the Governor was saying to Forbes, Well done, well played indeed, and Forbes was saying See yon big, dirty, ignorant full-back, and at last the door was shut and we were alone with the smell of sweat and embrocation and steam and happy weariness.

'Well done, kids,' I said, and the corporal said, 'No' sae bad,' and rumpled McGlinchy's hair, and everyone laughed. Through in the showers someone began to make mouth-music to the tune of *The Black Bear*, and at the appropriate moment the feet stomped in unison and the towel-clad figures shuffled, clapping and humming.

'Not too loud,' I said. 'Don't let the Navy hear.'

I went over to McGlinchy, who was drying his hair and whistling. I wanted to ask: What gets into you? Why don't you play like that all the time? But I didn't. I knew I wouldn't ever find out. . . .

I saw McGlinchy many years after, from the top of a Glasgow bus. Although his fair hair was fading and receding, and his face looked middle-aged and tired, there was no mistaking the loose-jointed, untidy walk. He was carrying a string bag, and he looked of no account at all in his stained raincoat and old shoes. And then the bus took me past. I wondered if he remembered those few minutes out in the sunlight. Perhaps not; he wasn't the kind who would think twice about it. But I remember McGlinchy when . . .

abridged from THE GENERAL DANCED AT DAWN *1970*

Acknowledgments

The editor and the publishers would like to acknowledge the use of copyright material to the following authors and publishers:

To Mr Paul Gardner for two extracts from *The Simplest Game: The Intelligent American's Guide to the World of Soccer* (published by Sports Illustrated/Little, Brown & Co.), and 'Pelé' from *The Complete Handbook of Soccer* (Associated Features Inc.);

To Mr Roy Hattersley and *The Listener* for 'Never Walk Alone';

To Mr John Moynihan for four extracts from *The Soccer Syndrome* (Grafton Books: A division of the Collins Publishing Group);

To Mr John Arlott for 'Reading – A Supporter's Piece' from *Concerning Soccer* (Longmans, Green & Co.), and for 'Portugal v. North Korea' from *World Cup '66* (Eyre & Spottiswoode);

To Mr A. J. Liebling and Russell and Volkening Inc. for 'Yugoslavia v. Russia' (*The New Yorker*);

To Mr Geoffrey Green and Times Newspapers Ltd for 'England v. Hungary, 1953' and 'Sweden v. Brazil, 1958'; also to Mr Green and Allen & Unwin (Publishers) Ltd for two extracts from *Pardon me for Living*;

To Mr Hugh McIlvanney and Eyre & Spottiswoode for one extract each from *World Cup '66* and *World Cup '70*;

To Mr Hunter Davies and Weidenfeld & Nicolson Ltd for two extracts from *The Glory Game*; also to Mr Davies and the *Sunday Times* Magazine for 'Bryan Robson';

To the New York Times for 'Argentina v. Holland, 1978' and 'Italy v. Brazil, 1982' by Rob Hughes (International Herald-Tribune);

To Guardian Newspapers Ltd for 'Brighton v. Manchester United, 1983' by Mr David Lacey; for 'Judgement and the Art of Goalkeeping' by the late H. D. Davies; and for 'Old International' by the late Neville Cardus;

To William Heinemann Ltd for 'G. O. Smith – Corinthian', the Introduction by the late C. B. Fry to *Corinthians and Cricketers* by Mr Edward Grayson (Naldrett Press); also to William Heinemann Ltd for 'Watching Bruddersford' by the late J. B. Priestley for *The Good Companions*;

To Mr Alan Ross and The Observer Ltd for 'Stan Mortensen', and to Mr Ross for three poems;

To Mr Arthur Hopcraft and A. P. Watt Ltd for two extracts from *The Football Man* (Collins);

To Mr Peter Ball and Time Out Ltd for 'Terry Venables';

To Mr Frank Keating, Punch Ltd, and Robson Books Ltd for 'Fast Forwards' from *Long Days, Late Nights*;

To Weidenfeld & Nicolson Ltd, for 'Keeping Goal at Cambridge' from *Speak, Memory* by the late Vladimir Nabokov;

To Alan Ross Ltd for 'The Goalkeeper' from *All in the Game* by the late R. C. Robertson-Glasgow;

To France-Football for 'What I Owe to Football' by the late Albert Camus, and for 'King of Sports, King of Games' by the late Jean Giraudoux;

To the successors and assigns of Lilliput Magazine for 'Moscow v. Chelsea, 1945' by Alexei 'Tiger' Khomich;

Acknowledgments

To Mr Eamon Dunphy and Penguin Books Ltd for two extracts from *Only a Game?* (Kestrel Books);

To Mr Michael Parkinson for 'Closet Wingers';

To Mr Danny Blanchflower and The Observer Ltd for 'Ireland play England, 1960';

To Mr Kenneth Shearwood for 'Playing for Mevagissey' from *Whistle the Wind* (Grafton Books: A division of the Collins Publishing Group);

To the Football Association for 'The Manchester United Disaster' by the late H. E. Bates;

To Dr Dannie Abse for 'The Game';

To Editions Gallimard for 'Sur les Souliers de Foot', and for 'Football Lesson in the Park' from *Paradis à l'ombre des épées*, both by the late Henri de Montherlant;

To Mr Philip Oakes for 'The Death of the Referee';

To Mr Peter Terson for 'Saturday Afternoon' from *Zigger Zagger*;

To Mr Harold Pinter and Methuen London Ltd for one extract from each of *The Dumb Waiter* and *A Night Out*;

To Mr George MacDonald Fraser and John Farquharson Ltd for the abridged version of his story 'Play up, Play up, and Get Tore in' from *The General danced at dawn* (Pan Books Ltd).

Finally, the editor would like to thank his own publishers for permission to reprint stories from *Love is not Love*, *The Things he Loves* and *Goalkeepers are Different*.

Index of Authors